Come By The Hills

Cameron McNeish

Foreword
by
Robert Macfarlane

SANDSTONE PRESS

First published in Great Britain
Sandstone Press Ltd
Suite 1, Willow House
Stoneyfield Business Park
Inverness
IV2 7PA
Scotland

www.sandstonepress.com

ISBN: 978-1-913207-28-1
ISBNe: 978-1-913207-29-8

Jacket design by Raspberry Creative Type, Edinburgh
Typeset by Iolaire Typography, Newtonmore
Printed and bound by CPI Group (UK) Ltd, Croydon, CR0 4YY

CONTENTS

ACKNOWLEDGEMENTS AND DEDICATION

Given that climbing hills and exploring Scotland's wild places are such solitary pastimes, there is a surprisingly large cast to thank for their contributions, intended or otherwise, to the writing of this book.

The title, *Come by the Hills*, was first the title of a song that I and many others, including the celebrated duo that were The Corries, and Finbar and Eddie Furey from Ireland, have been singing for decades. It isn't, as many imagine, a traditional song but the work of the late W. Gordon Smith. It's a song of hope and vision, as I hope this book will be.

A list of all the people who have walked and climbed the Scottish hills with me over the years would fill these pages, so I will just mention a few who have been particularly influential in my thinking about the wild places of this great country of ours. Special thanks go to Roger Smith, Jim Perrin, Chris Townsend, Hamish Brown, Jim Crumley, John Manning, Tom Prentice, John Lyall, Paul Tattersall, Bob Telfer and John Hood. For sharing some great cycling adventures in recent years, many thanks to my lifelong pal Hamish Telfer.

Hearing the stories of fellow adventurers has always been inspirational to me and I wish to thank those who have contributed with their own words of wisdom: Laurence Main, Dennis Gray, Robert Macfarlane, Julie Fowlis, David Craig, Alan Riach, Llinos Proctor, Jimmy Marshall, Ian Mure, the late Dick Balharry, Donald Fisher, John and Marie Christine Ridgway, Duncan Chisholm, John Ure, Iain and Willie Grieve, Dr Margaret Bennet, Lee Craigie and Paul Tattersall.

Television has played a big role in my life in the past quarter century and I want to thank Richard Else, Margaret Wicks, James Else and Kate Hook of the Adventure Show Production Company for their enduring patience and friendship. There can't be many television presenters who have worked with the same production company for their entire career. Many thanks go also to David Harron, our Executive Director at BBC Scotland, for his continued support and personal friendship.

Presenting a television show is only a small part of what is always a team effort and I'd like to give special thanks to the guys who do their best to make me and the Scottish landscape look good, our camera operators: Paul Diffley, Simon Willis, Ben Pritchard, Andy McCandlish, Dominic Scott, Keith Partridge and Chris McHendry. These are the guys who stand around in the wet and cold, or in the snow, while I blether with guests, the guys who follow me up hill and down dale carrying heavy cameras and tripods, never complaining. Well, not very much.

I've also been greatly encouraged by the editors and publishers of the magazines I write for so thanks go to Darren Bruce at Newsquest, Paul and Helen Webster at Walk Highlands, Robert Wight and Garry Fraser at the *Scots Magazine*, Emily Rodway, formerly at the *Great Outdoors* magazine, Joe Pontin at *Countryfile* magazine and Geneve Brand at *Campervan* magazine. A special thank you to those editors who gave me permission to re-use or re-write various pieces that have previously appeared in their titles.

Also, a very special thanks to the team at Sandstone Press. I'm really thrilled to be working with such a top-notch international publishing house that is based here in the Scottish Highlands, and I very much appreciate the help and wise counsel offered by fellow Munroist Robert Davidson. To have a publisher and editor who is also a hillgoer is a huge bonus for anyone writing about Scotland's wild places.

A huge thanks to award-winning author, mountain man and longtime friend Robert Macfarlane for kindly taking time from his busy academic life to write the foreword to this book. I clearly recall Ted Peck, his grandfather, proudly telling me about the young Robert and his love for the Scottish hills. What Ted didn't know was that his grandson was to become one of our most influential and wise environment commentators. I'm proud his name graces the cover of this book along with my own.

Finally, my life as an outdoors writer and television presenter wouldn't have been possible had it not been for the support and encouragement of my two sons, Gordon and Gregor, and their own support teams, Hannah and Sarah. My two granddaughters, Charlotte and Grace, are a constant source of joy. The work I have done and still do, the writing, television appearances and everything else, wouldn't have been possible without the consideration, understanding and endless support of my wife of almost 50 years. This book is dedicated to Gina.

Cameron McNeish
Newtonmore, 2020

LIST OF ILLUSTRATIONS

List of Illustrations

18. Muckle Flugga and Out Stack, Britain's most northerly islands
19. Lifting my beloved campervan onto the pier at North Ronaldsay
20. The tombolo connecting St Ninian's Isle to Shetland mainland
21. Approaching the summit of Ben Gulabin
22. Contemplating the Craigallion Memorial and all it means to me
23. The graveyard at Blackwater Dam
24. Paul Tattersall, first person to take a mountain bike over all the Munros
25. Fun is to be had in the hills, even when the years wear on

FOREWORD

by Robert Macfarlane

One of the first times I heard the name 'Cameron McNeish' was from my grandparents, who lived on and off for thirty years in an old forestry cottage near Tomintoul, perched above the River Avon where it rushed towards its flood-plains from the Cairngorm plateau. My grandparents were mountain-people; they'd spent their lives climbing and exploring from the Alps to Mount Kenya, from the Rwenzori to the Himalayas. The Cairngorms was their heartland, though — and along with Cameron they were part of the early resistance to the ill-conceived construction of the funicular in the Northern Corries.

My grandparents were then, as Cameron is now, into their eighth decade, but age hadn't dimmed the light of their love for the hills. As Cameron shows here, slowing down can also mean sharpening up. So it was with them. Grandad still got out on his old wooden touring skis, as tall as him and about half as heavy (they're now in the National Museum of Scotland), and we still made our multi-generational ascents of Lochnagar and Cairn Gorm, foraged blaeberries and swam in the deep brown river-pools of Glen Feshie. My grandmother was a superb botanist, especially good on Alpine flora, and I remember my childish frustration at her

gradual pace mingling with my surprise at her knowledge
of the plant-life that surrounded us. '*What do you mean,
you can't recognise a gentian!?*' she once reprimanded me,
in genuine (and rightful) horror.

I grew up with Cameron's writing and programme-
making. I watched him cover the miles and the peaks on
television, amazed at the landscapes he was unfolding for me
and millions of others. Grandad would post me clippings of
Cameron's journalism, and on my twentieth birthday I was
given a copy of his *The Munros*. It became, along with the
SMC Hillwalkers' Guide, my companion to the Highlands.
It still is. For the past quarter-century, really, Cameron's
been an ageless and indestructible figure in my imagination:
an unstoppable force, shaking sense into public debates
over land use and mountain culture, climbing top after top,
writing and fighting for the good and the wild.

In one way it's been unsettling to read *Come by the Hills*,
and to learn that this Scottish superhero is somehow human
after all, subject to aches and limps, strapped to the 'dying
animal' (Yeats's phrase) of the mortal body like the rest of us.
There's a painful honesty to the experience of ageing here,
and to the geographical limits that are imposed by becoming
a *bodach nam beinn*, an 'old man of the hills'. But what
rings far louder than regret is his joy – sheer bloody *joy* – in
the mountains and what they give to us. There's a passage
early on where he describes nearly abandoning hill-climbing
because the discomfort of movement is too great. But then
he feels a far greater pain: 'a feeling of loss ... like bereavement', caused by the idea of losing his 'love of mountains
and wild places'. That struck straight to my heart — it is
impossible, really, to imagine living without the hills. So,
what is needed with older age is a moderation of ambition,

a changing of scale. Which is of course, in its own way, a turn back towards the wonder-years of childhood, when the height of a mountain is irrelevant, and when as much amazement can be found on the bank of a burn or a forest floor as up on the ridges and peaks.

Early on, Cameron quotes the great Alastair McIntosh on the 'ecology of the imagination'; a way of thinking of the world that leads both inwards to specific detail and outwards to a webwork of connections. These chapters partake of that imaginative ecology. They blend natural history, folklore, geology, topography, community and literature, understanding that what we call 'landscape' is always a weave of many strands, an irreducibly complex texture of human and more-than-human histories. So it is that these ecumenical essays are open to plurality of several kinds, and celebrate a version of Aldo Leopold's 'land ethic' – which extends the notion of a region's 'community' to include creatures, soil, water, rock and air – without shying away from the hard work involved in improving landscapes for people and for nature. Romanticism and pragmatism for once make good partners here.

Come by the Hills is also a testimony to the many folk who have shaped Cameron's path in life, including the mountaineer-writer W. H. Murray, the climber Syd Scroggie, the folk-singer and story-collector Hamish Henderson, and Cameron's wife Gina. One of the most moving chapters is Cameron's tribute to the inspirational conservation pioneer Dick Balharry, who I remember telling me in my early twenties to hold fast to a definition of 'wild land' in Scotland as that which gives safe home to golden eagles (still a good rule of thumb, I'd say). Cameron writes of how Dick changed minds, won hearts, put backs up, and transformed landscapes: 'Dick articulated his love of the outdoors in such a way that it touched others, enthused them and changed their lives'. Well, Cameron too has unmistakably done this — though he'd never claim as much himself.

Above all, though, this book is a late-life love letter to the hills, sent from the glens. Again and again come moments that will be recognisable to anyone who loves the Scottish mountains: the 'shudder of wonder and awe' that passes through Cameron whenever he enters Glen Coe, the 'gnawing realisation of what is important' when he is in wooded Glen Affric. 'Mountain and wildness settle peace on the soul', he writes late on, 'It's a wonderful phenomenon and doesn't need any help'. Reading this fine book — with its sense of the infinite capacity of mountains to give to those who love them, I was frequently reminded of lines from the end of Nan Shepherd's slender masterpiece about the Cairngorms, *The Living Mountain*.

> However often I walk on them, these hills hold astonishment for me ... There is no getting accustomed to them.

Robert Macfarlane
February 2020

INTRODUCTION

After a lifetime of climbing mountains and exploring wild places, the arrival of my greybeard years meant a change of direction and focus for me. The biblical 'threescore years and ten' meant not only slowing down and a growing creakiness in the joints, but also a new awareness of my own mortality. That awareness fostered an element of resolve, and a determination to focus more sharply on the things that are important to me, the many things I can still do. I'm very reluctant, just yet, to exchange my boots for a pair of slippers.

Although the ageing process has robbed me of the physical fitness I enjoyed in earlier years, I can still creak my way over the hills, and a slower pace brings its own benefits. It allows me to look around and observe the things I missed when hitherto I would impatiently strive for the summit. It's worth remembering the words of the poet William Henry Davies, no matter what age we are.

> *What is this life if, full of care,*
> *We have no time to stand and stare.*
> *No time to stand beneath the boughs*
> *And stare as long as sheep or cows.*
> *No time to see, when woods we pass,*
> *Where squirrels hide their nuts in grass.*

No time to see, in broad daylight,
Streams full of stars, like skies at night.
No time to turn at Beauty's glance,
And watch her feet, how they can dance.
No time to wait till her mouth can
Enrich that smile her eyes began.
A poor life this if, full of care,
We have no time to stand and stare.

A few minutes here and there, sitting on a rock, allows me to ponder the moment and to wonder with renewed astonishment at the beauty around me: the moss campion that clings to life on the bare screes of our highest hills, the joyful sound of a skylark and the often breathtaking drama of a far-flung view.

The 'pull of the hills' has never diminished, and I regard it as a sort of gravity for the soul: my anchor, and the foundation from which I have created a kinship that has stood me in good stead when the world has occasionally appeared a little darker. The exercise, the beauty, the simplicity and drama, all combine for the good of our mental and physical health, and the sounds, the smells, the air like wine, the textures of the trees and rocks serve to increase not only my awareness but also the sheer joy at being in and amongst Scotland's beautiful places.

The song from which this book takes its name includes the line, 'Come by the hills to a land where fancy is free.' That little phrase suggests to me places and landscapes that allow my imagination full expression, to remember times past and hope for a better future. It encourages me to cast aside the prejudices and preconceptions of a working-class Presbyterian upbringing and consider the far-reaching influences of our Celtic past, and how our ancestors' reverence for wild landscapes can influence us in the future.

Unlike my autobiography, *There's Always the Hills*, this new book is not especially about me. *Come by the Hills* is littered with conversations with people who have inspired and encouraged many of us, who bring a new slant of appreciation to those places we all hold dear.

On foot, by bike and in my wee red campervan, *Come by the Hills* is an exploration of Scotland in which reaching mountain summits is still enjoyed, but is no longer a priority. It's an exploration of the wider Scottish landscapes: hills, forests, coastlines and glens, and those ancient tales and legends that extend our knowledge of Scotland's turbulent history. Most of all, I hope *Come by the Hills* will be an inspiration and spur to those outdoor folk who suspect their best years are behind them.

1

THE PULL OF THE HILLS

Ben Starav isn't the tallest mountain in Scotland, but you have to earn every inch of its height. Climbing from the shores of Loch Etive to the mountain's square-cut summit ridge is long and relentless, a brutal ascent by any standard, but that severity is the mountain's saving grace. The steep slog makes you stop at frequent intervals and, when you do, the views simply take your breath away, should you have any to spare. There's little respite as it rises in grassy steps from the headwaters of the sea-loch to the upper reaches of the rocky Coire da Choimhid. Recently, I climbed it on a still autumnal day, with stags roaring from the inner recesses of the corries and other beasts answering across the glen. Water from overnight storms poured from the higher slopes like a thousand wriggling snakes, and curtains of clouds sporadically hid the higher reaches of the mountain.

At the top of the corrie, on my first glimpse of the loch, I recalled the tale of Deirdre of the Sorrows, one of the great legends of grief and loss in Celtic literature. Deirdre was a first century Pictish princess who was betrothed to Conor, the High King of Ulster, before fleeing to Etive-side with her lover, Naoise, one of the three Sons of Uisneach. Celtic tales tell of her delight in these hills, where she lived a content and happy life in the company of her lover and his warrior companions.

After some time, a messenger arrived from Ulster. Conor desired the return of the Sons of Uisneach to help him repel the invading forces of Connaught, promising them a warm welcome and forgiveness. Deirdre was fearful and suspected treachery, but Naoise and his brothers, born to the thrill and excitement of battle, were excited by the prospect of returning to Ulster. In contrast Deirdre was heartbroken at having to leave her beloved Alba, a passion that's easy to understand.

By now the wind had rent great holes in the cloud cover and sunshine illuminated the views. At the top of Glen Etive stood the twin herdsmen of Etive, Buachaille Etive Beag and Buachaille Etive Mor, the Pollux and Castor of Rannoch. To their left the Bidean nam Bian massif appeared as a steep, jagged swell of hills. Across the fjord-like sliver of Loch Etive lay Beinn Trilleachan, with a sweep of granite crags falling from its whaleback ridge, crags that are known to rock climbers as the Etive Stabs. When seen, head on, from Starav these boilerplate slabs seem to hang from the mountain like a grey curtain, and they contain some of the most surreal friction climbs in Scotland.

Even after at least half a dozen ascents of this mountain, I'm always taken aback by how far there is still to go from the top of the corrie. The angle of the slope relents for a short distance, but then the ridge narrows to become a mild scramble along an edge of broken crags until the slope rises in a confusion of boulders. The small summit cairn is reached suddenly and without fanfare, and with some relief it has to be said. Cloud swirled around me, but I could discern the gleaming silver slit of the loch far below. It was easy to imagine the war galleys of the Sons of Uisneach gliding down the loch, sails unfurled, banners flying as they faded into a fret of sea-mists below Beinn Cruachan. Their journey was into an unknown and perilous future, the young woman curled up in the stern of one of the galleys, her emotions conflicted and confused, her love for Naoise tempered by a profound sense of loss for the place she was leaving: Etive and her glens, peaks that pierced the sky and her sunny bower above the rocky crags of Lotha.

Inmain tir in tir ud thoir
Alba cona lingantaibh
Nocha ticfuinn eisdi ille
Mana tisain le Naise.

Beloved is that eastern land,
Alba (Scotland), with its lakes.
Oh that I might not depart from it,
Unless I were to go with Naos!
THE POEMS OF OSSIAN

For many of us the emotional magnetism exerted by the beauty and challenge of mountains is hard to resist. It eats away at us, fills our hopes and dreams, and harbours our ambitions. In meeting the challenge of the hills, we open ourselves to everything associated with such places: flora and fauna, geology, history and legend, song and spirit of place. Too many of us are unaware of how powerful and enduring that pull can be until we are in danger of losing it, an insight that hit me hard as I approached the cliff-edge of my eighth decade. A series of age-related issues had made me seriously consider giving up. Long descents were particularly painful and on more than one occasion I had serious doubts about whether I would make it home. Several times I told myself that the time had come to bid my farewell to the high tops, but after a few days I would again feel that familiar urge, the need to be among them, as powerful and controlling as any addiction. Unable to resist its power, off I would go, shuffling and limping into the blue upland yonder, another *bodach nam beinn*, another old man of the hills, reluctant to submit to the inevitability of age and decline.

This addiction first embraced me as a child. On family holidays on the Firth of Clyde I would often gaze across the sea to the Isle of Arran, and soon became infatuated by the shape of the hills, the distant vision of high corries, silver streams and the changing textures of the slopes. To my young eyes Arran was a world away and not a mere dozen miles. On other family excursions I was only really happy when we were close to hills and mountains. Flat landscapes didn't inspire me, but if there was a rise in the ground, even a dim outline of hills in the distance, I experienced a trembling excitement that made me curiously joyful and upbeat. On one occasion I watched two men descend from a mountain in Glen Coe. Sun-browned and lithe, they wore tartan plaid shirts and breeches and were bronzed by the sun. One of them carried a coiled rope over his shoulders. To my youthful eyes they were like gods come down from Parnassus and, at that precise moment, I knew I wanted to be one of them. Away beyond the path they walked, from the slopes they had descended, the screes and gullies and buttresses that made another world, the domain of ridges, plateaux and summits that belong to the mountain gods. Here was a world as unknown and mysterious as Atlantis and I wanted to discover it.

My first hills were modest: the Campsie Fells, the Luss

hills above Loch Lomond and the tumbled braes of the Trossachs, but even on their humble heights I felt the first creeping tentacles of obsession. I was in my early twenties when I gave in, more or less abandoned all other interests and decided I would commit my life to climbing hills and mountains and exploring the wild places of our wonderful little country. It was a decision never to be regretted because it gave me a wonderful career as a writer, magazine editor and television presenter, and the opportunity to travel the world. That career has spanned almost half a century but I'm still acutely aware of the pull of the hills, even though they have almost been the end of me on several occasions. I've fallen down crags and been avalanched. I've been lost (or at least temporarily misplaced) and suffered hypothermia, so it most certainly is an obsession, but one that is both delectable and fulfilling. I'm still thrilled in the proximity of mountains and still worry myself silly about the day that will inevitably arrive when I can no longer immerse myself in them.

That spectre has hovered over me several times in recent years. Various medical problems, predominantly degenerative issues (medical term for old age) in my feet and legs have threatened to end my hill-climbing days for good. On a number of gloomy occasions, I've taken the decision that enough was enough, I couldn't stand the pain and discomfort any longer, but each time I was hit by such a feeling of loss it was like bereavement. I was terrified at losing the very thing that had driven me for most of my life: my love of mountains and wild places. I can still hobble about the hills, but I am painfully aware that age can rob us of so much and the sense of loss has been profound. Fortunately, medicine and technology have helped to overcome much of the discomfort caused by chronic plantar fasciitis, plantar plate tears, Morton's neuromas and osteoarthritis in the toes. I can, with some adjustments to pace and effort, still get on the hills. More seriously, I was recently sidelined for almost two years by a torn medial knee ligament. Uphill was hard, but descending was tortuous. My doctor kept telling me to be patient, but patience has never been my strong point.

The problem began as a minor irritant at the end of a great day on Bidean nam Bian. It was the beginning of summer, and skylark song filled the air. Glen Coe was looking at its most glorious as I wandered through Coire nan Lochan and became aware of a slight pain on the inside of my knee. Within a couple of days it reduced to a dull ache, and a couple of weeks later I was back filming for the BBC on the Isle of Arran. We had climbed Goat Fell and took our time, stopping every so often to position the camera and video me delivering a piece to camera. Such is the nature of television work. All went well; we all enjoyed the views of A' Chir and Cir Mhor across the glen. Unfortunately, things changed dramatically during the descent. Every downhill step was slow and painful, though the situation wasn't entirely without humour. My producer, Richard Else, who is also qualified to carry a bus pass, was moving equally slowly because of an historic knee injury of his own. Richard's wife Meg carried the heavy tripod and a load of heavy gear, so she too was moving slowly. As the three of us hobbled down the southern ridge like extras from *Last of the Summer Wine* a couple of hillwalkers spotted the gear and asked if we were making a film. We said we were and of course the lads asked what it was for? When we answered *The Adventure Show* it felt hilariously ironic. But age is no respecter of health, and the next morning I found it painful to walk. When sitting down I had to straighten my leg very slowly before it could bear weight; getting in and out of a vehicle was even worse, and my knee was hot and swollen. I've been relatively fortunate during my mountain career in terms of injury. I've survived an avalanche and several falls but, overall, avoided the normal knee and hip problems.

As a young man I was mad keen on track and field athletics and was a reasonably successful long jumper and sprinter. The training for long jump and triple jump put a lot of pressure on the knees and hips and I shudder to recall doing squats with 200 lbs on my shoulders when I was sixteen. My track career came to a premature end after a series of injuries. More pertinently, the mountains were exerting their pull. That was in youth. More recently, after reaching the grand old age of sixty-five, various problems began to manifest. Nothing that I couldn't manage, though, and throughout that summer the knee problem seemed to improve.

With my lifelong pal Hamish Telfer, I cycled the length of Ireland, from Mizen Head to Malin Head, and later in the year we cycled the length of the Outer Isles, from Vatersay to the Butt of Lewis, but climbing hills was a very different matter. Each time I attempted something strenuous the knee would give way and I found myself back at square one. I was too stupid to consider resting for any length of time (when you earn a living from climbing hills you can't afford to be away too long) and the last thing the viewing public want to see is a greybeard presenter as he limps and hirples across the landscape. Eventually the pain became too great and I had to cancel a shoot.

My doctor diagnosed a damaged medial ligament in the right knee, and was backed up by Julie Porteous, my sports physio in Aviemore. The prognosis? It would get better if I rested it for four to six weeks. My doctor suggested that since I had been abusing my body, in the nicest possible way, for over forty years by carrying heavy packs up hills and along trails I should expect a reasonable amount of wear and tear. I responded by reminding him that our forefathers wandered the hills every day of their lives and managed to cope. His answer had a certain inevitability about it: most would have been dead and buried before they reached my age. Touché!

Fortunately, there was some good news amid all this gloom and doom. An X-ray showed no serious problem with the knee joint. No evidence of osteoarthritis and only the usual wear and tear below the kneecap and down the front of the knee. The downside was that a damaged ligament takes a long time to heal, but with proper rest and gentle exercise will get better ... eventually. I was a little shaken when he told me that if a fit young footballer of only twenty-one came to his surgery with a similar injury he would tell him he was out of the game for six months. I decided to rest.

The doc was right. While holidaying in the Alps my knee suddenly felt better and by the end of the holiday it was only slightly sore at the end of a hill day. Nine months later it had completely recovered. I wished I'd taken my doctor's advice earlier when, instead of resting the injury, I simply kept the problem recurring. The moral of the story is very simple. Don't try and live with pain or injury. Don't try and work through it, pretending it isn't there, particularly if you are approaching, or actually living in, the autumn of your years. Do something to prevent it getting worse, or you could end up like me with a whole summer wasted.

It took me some time to come to terms with the fact that age has robbed me of the physical fitness I have enjoyed throughout life. It has taken me a long time to get it into my thick brain that I'm no longer capable of multi-day expeditions over the hills and mountains, or complete long days in the hills, and I certainly can't travel very far with a heavy pack on my back. However, I can still creak my way over smaller hills, and still enjoy shorter days. I've become more familiar and appreciative of forest, woodland and coastal walks and now enjoy other aspects of the hill game, like photography and birdwatching. I also cycle a lot. Indeed, I did have thoughts of calling this book 'There's Always the Bike'.

Gina and I travel around the Highlands and Islands of Scotland in our campervan, discovering places that we ignored during our mountain days. We visit castles and keeps, explore glens and coastlines, learn of ancient tales and legends and extend our knowledge of Scotland's turbulent history. We still climb hills when aching limbs and joints allow. This gradual metamorphosis from fit mountaineer to *bodach nam beinn*, old man of the hills, has paralleled my professional life. I stopped editing *The Great Outdoors* magazine when I was sixty. Around the same time, my long, televised backpacking trips were replaced by even longer journeys along *Roads Less Travelled* in a campervan: television shows that saw me walk, cycle and packraft in various out-of-the-way places. I began writing a monthly column for the *Scots Magazine*, the oldest consumer magazine in the world, which is a milestone in my career. My old friend and mentor Tom Weir wrote his first article for the *Scots Magazine* in the year before I was born and I now follow in his footsteps.

The magazine's editor, Robert Wight, asked me recently to read through Tommy's very first article, published exactly seventy years earlier, and produce a column reflecting on both his skills and how our landscapes have changed. Reading through that very first feature, I found myself taken back decades to when I was possibly the only teenager in the land to possess a *Scots Magazine* subscription, an unexpected birthday gift. While my peers were buying the *New Musical Express* and *Melody Maker*, I was more interested in the monthly stravaigings of a tweed-clad character who magically opened the curtains of my urban upbringing on landscapes undreamt of: hills and mountains, exotic-sounding birds and animals and a hardy population of fascinating people.

Tom's 'My Month' began in 1956 when the editor, Arthur Daw, asked if he'd like to try it for a year. In fact, the monthly column lasted almost fifty years. Arthur's advice to Tom was simple: get as much variety as you can into the articles. This new commitment came about at an interesting time in Tom's life, when he was spending much of his time abroad. In 1945 he had become a member of the Scottish Mountaineering Club, of which he later became President. Although he had climbed previously it appears that his performances improved dramatically in the latter years of the forties and throughout the fifties, particularly with partners like Archie MacPherson and Douglas Scott. Inspired by the writings of mountaineer Frank Smythe, he travelled to the Alps where he climbed the Dent Blanche and enjoyed a ski-mountaineering ascent of the Finsteraarhorn in the Bernese Oberland. His Alpine exploits led to inclusion in a Scottish expedition to the Indian Garhwal region along with Scott and two notable mountaineers of the time, Tom MacKinnon and Bill Murray. All three became firm friends for the rest of their lives.

That initial expedition saw success on the 20,000-foot/6,200-metre peak of Uja Tirche. Writing later, Tom remarked, 'Looking back on it I remember no other mountain day so full of surprises and sustained interest. Weariness fades before the enduring values, the joy of a hard-won summit, and the contentment of spirit in a new appreciation of being alive.'

Attempts were made on several other peaks, but their most notable success was the discovery by westerners of a huge area of the Indian Himalaya, a genuine journey of exploration. Other expeditions followed throughout the fifties: to Arctic Norway with Scott and Adam Watson from Aberdeen; to the Rolwaling area of Nepal (the account of that expedition became a book in 1955, *East of Kathmandu*); to the High Atlas mountains of Morocco and an area that he later described as his favourite, the Sat Dagh and Cilo Dagh regions of Kurdistan. His final major expedition was with Sir John Hunt (who had led the successful Everest expedition in May 1953) to Scoresbysund in Greenland in 1960. Tom assisted fellow SMC member Iain Smart in collecting and collating data on Arctic Tern populations.

Following that concentrated bout of exploratory expeditions in the fifties, marriage to Rhona and a move to the Dunbartonshire village of Gartocharn saw Tom Weir settle to the life of a freelance writer, informing and entertaining his growing band of *Scots Magazine* readers while occasionally dabbling in other forms of media like radio and television. He made a series of television 'shorts' with producer Russell Galbraith at Scottish Television which were later compiled into longer television features before *Weir's Way* was eventually launched, the television series that was to raise Tom to national stardom. No scriptwriters were employed on *Weir's*

Way or the follow-up series, *Weir's Aweigh*, or the series that followed that, tracing the post-Culloden journey of Prince Charles Edward Stuart.

Tom wrote the storylines himself: tales of Rannoch Moor and Glen Coe, historical events and the opening of the West Highland Way amongst others. For me one of the highlights was when he interviewed two of his long-time pals in the glow of a crackling little campfire on the banks of Loch Lomond. Jock Nimlin was a Clydeside crane operator and one of Scotland's finest climbers, and Professor Sir Robert (Bob) Grieve was, at the time, inaugural chair of the Highlands and Islands Development Board. The three men sat in the glow of the fire and simply chatted about their love of wild places, outdoor politics and their own very different careers. It was a mirror of the Craigallian Fire of the thirties, at which both Nimlin and Grieve had toasted themselves, as had Tom's other great friend, Matt Forrester. Tom's first feature, 'Remotest North,' was a seven-page description of a convoluted and diverse expedition to the far north-western quarter between Cape Wrath and Ben Klibreck, an on-foot exploration of the mountains beyond Loch Shin. Remarkably, considering the ease with which we can now reach these once-remote places, he makes it sound like an epic trip to Arctic Norway. In those days, seven decades ago, it probably took as much planning.

'A walking-cum-climbing holiday in north-west Sutherland is not planned overnight – at least not by those who wish to eat at fairly regular intervals,' he wrote, before embarking on a description of what he called 'the staff work': the logistics, necessary permissions and the booking of the train journey from Glasgow to Crask, just north of Lairg.

Tom and his companions (he never mentioned their names

or how many there were) travelled to Inverness and onwards by train, eventually to Lairg, 'with long halts at each stop,' before a local bus to Tongue dropped them off at the old inn at Crask. The weather was foul, but it didn't deter them. They tackled Ben Klibreck 'at a furious pace.'

Despite careful planning there is a gloriously haphazard feel to this early expedition, and much speculation about the possibilities of future trips, but no reference to guidebooks or ticking off Munros (Scottish mountains over 3,000 feet) or Corbetts (Scottish hills between 2,500 feet and 2,999 feet). This was unadulterated exploration: peeping around corners, gazing at far horizons, discovering raw adventure in an area of Scotland that, at the time, attracted few visitors. Tom once told me that he believed his generation 'had the best of it'. It was an era when people still lived in remote glens, when exploration and discovery were genuine and not something you just googled on a computer.

'I treasure memories of spending time with families like the Macraes of Carnmore in Letterewe or the Scotts at Luibeg in the Cairngorms. The glens are emptier now that they have gone. The hills weren't so busy then and people weren't rushing to climb Munros and Corbetts.'

It's difficult to assess Tom Weir's contribution to Scottish life and culture, simply because he was such a 'lad o'many pairts': writer, photographer, climber, explorer, ornithologist and television presenter. His influence on others was immense and he was always keen to share his vast knowledge of Scotland and of ornithology through his writings, his television programmes and innumerable slide shows. I'm certain his association with the *Scots Magazine* partly assured the title's great longevity and popularity, and he outlasted several editors. Indeed, I'm told the online collection of his 'My Month' columns is still extremely popular, just as his television programmes, which for many years were broadcast during the wee, sma' hours, eventually found new audiences among Scotland's insomniac community. That would have made him smile.

Perhaps it's best to leave the last word about Tommy to his great friend and colleague, W. H. Murray. Before submitting the manuscript of his autobiography *Weir's World* to the publisher, Tom asked Bill Murray to read it and offer a criticism. This is what he said:

> The general impression I have is one of amazement at all you have managed to pack into your life. In a book of life one can turn the pages, back as well as forward; the ingredients are so many, not set down in chronological order, that it's like a well-stirred brew. I wish you all good fortune and sales.

The autobiography was published in 1994.

Tom passed away in a care home in Balloch on 6th July 2006. We'll never see his likes again.

The pull of the mountains, and its rewards, is not something you can buy online or in a shop. You can't ask someone to manufacture it for you. Mountains and wildness settle peace on the soul. It's a wonderful phenomenon, and it doesn't need any help. The sheer beauty of it, and our appreciation of that beauty, is partly because, as the Harvard author and naturalist Edward O. Wilson once said, 'it's beyond human contrivance.'

I consider myself very fortunate to live in Scotland. Here, lying on the edge of Europe, I'm proud to live in what is recognised as one of the most beautiful countries in the world. Small but perfectly formed, we can boast some of the finest, and most diverse, wild landscapes. Add to that the best access legislation in Europe and what you get is a paradise for hillwalkers and mountaineers. The weather isn't perfect, I'll give you that, and we often curse the Highland climate that sometimes feels like five months of winter and seven months' bad weather, but that's rarely the truth of it. The weather can be fickle but it's those very meteorological complexities that create the moods and impressions – the atmospheres – that make hillwalking in Scotland so unique. Our mountains may not be high, but they are diverse, and there is fascination and wonder in that diversity. Try comparing the Cairngorms with the Cuillin, or the ancient rocks of Torridon with the rounded hills of the Borders, or the hills of the Trossachs with the individualistic monoliths of the far North-West Highlands.

There is a diversity in our culture too, and in our language and music, a richness that creates continued interest. Folklore and heritage are amongst my own passions and the hills and wild areas of Scotland have enriched that. These are not 'empty lands' as some proclaim or, as I saw it described recently on social media, a 'blank canvas', but areas that still exhibit the hand of man almost everywhere: traces of the ancient runrig systems of agriculture, the faint lines of the lazybeds on a hillside, historic stalkers' paths and military roads, gables and drystone walls of old homes, and unin-habited villages still alive with whispers and memories.

I cycle most days, and climb hills as often as the body allows. I spend a lot of time exploring out-of-the-way corners of the Highlands and Islands, researching articles for the *Scots Magazine* and other titles. I still edit the quarterly magazines *Scottish Walks* and *Scottish Cycling* and take a lot of pleasure in producing a little series of videos that are broadcast on YouTube. Gina and I still chill out at folk festivals and the annual Celtic Connections festival in Glasgow. All these things and the elements that link them provide a fascinating and satisfying lifestyle, an existence that provides an outlet for that continual pull of the hills.

2

ECOLOGY OF THE IMAGINATION

Few countries in the world can boast the amazing diversity of landscape found in Scotland. Compare the windswept, rolling landscapes of Aberdeenshire, or Banff and Buchan, with the jagged upthrusts of Wester Ross. Or contrast the physical attributes of the mastiff-like Cairngorms with the serrated skyline of the Skye Cuillin, to appreciate that diversity. Running parallel is a multiplicity of culture. The good folk of Harris enjoy a culture, and a language, very different from the Doric of Banff and Buchan and I suspect such contrasts are why I love to visit the polar opposite of my own home area of the Cairngorms.

The Scottish Borders is as different as rugby is from shinty, but I feel comfortable there, a contentment largely due to a long-standing passion for traditional ballads, the reivers and the folklore and legends to be found amongst the cleughs and rolling hills. I've always felt very much at ease there, particularly in springtime.

When Gina and I ran the youth hostel in Aviemore in the late seventies, we always greeted the arrival of winter with a genuine welcome. Days of skiing and winter climbing lay ahead, and we embraced the cold and icy forecasts with the enthusiasm of innocent bairns, but by March that childlike enthusiasm had waned. We were tired of trudging through slushy snow and digging out the driveway every couple of days. By then winter had lost its appeal. Those were the days when the Scottish Highlands were almost guaranteed white winters, when the village of Aviemore thrived as a ski resort and it wasn't unusual to have snow on the ground from November to March.

At that time I taught cross-country skiing and winter hill-craft courses in the Cairngorms and was climbing, hiking or skiing on snow most days, so by the end of February I was snow-stir-crazy and desperate to walk on green grass again, eager to smell the earth. To escape the monochrome landscapes we used to drive over to Skye where my pal Willie Wallace ran the Broadford Youth Hostel. Being close to the sea it was rare for Broadford to get any snow at all, so not only did we enjoy the social aspect of visiting Willie and his wife Judith but we also relished the milder temperatures, and seeing the land shake off the winter doldrums with signs of new life.

When Willie died and Judith moved away, we changed our late-winter holiday destination and drove to the Borders instead. With the Highland hills still streaked with snow it was a real joy to head south to where springtime was more advanced, daffodils swayed in yellow dance and newborn lambs gambolled on a green sheen of new growth. It was another world, and only a few hours from home, but there was another aspect of Border life that always attracted me. This is a land where an aura of mysticism pervades local culture, a land rich in legend and folklore. The author H. V. Morton described it well:

> How can I describe the strange knowingness of the Border? Its uncanny watchfulness. Its queer trick of seeming still to listen and wait. I feel that invisible

things are watching me. Out of the fern silently might ride the Queen of Elfland, just as she came to Thomas of Ercildoune in this very country with 'fifty silver bells and nine' hanging from her horse's mane.

I believe these ancient and long-loved tales are more than faery stories, more than magical fables. They are what author and environmentalist Alastair McIntosh would call part of the 'ecology of the imagination': 'Ecology emanates from the cosmic imagination. Imagination leads back to ecology.'

Could imagination be part of a greater realm that contains the wilder reaches of ecology and of poetry, or is it a quality that we only possess privately? I believe it may be both, and folklore may help us reconcile those things that live in our mind's eye as well as events that may, or may not, have shaped history. There is nowhere else in Scotland that I sense this 'uncanny watchfulness' as intensely as I do here. It lurks on every hilltop, in every cleuch, and in every castle ruin.

For a few precious days each year we would head south to climb the snowless hills, ride our bikes and spend the nights in our campervan in some out-of-the-way places. On one occasion Gina adopted a donkey at the Scottish Borders Donkey Sanctuary so we took the opportunity to visit him with a gift of carrots. He returned the favour by biting her on the arm, giving some credence to Robert Louis Stevenson's assertion that donkeys were pretty untrustworthy creatures. We often stay near Peebles, 'the comfortable, sonsy and still good-looking matron of the Borderland,' to quote novelist and historian Nigel Tranter, and cycle some of the easier routes at Glentress Mountain Bike Centre, a place buzzing with technicolour lycra and expensive-looking bikes. If

Peebles is the sonsy matron of the Borders then Melrose surely has to be the posh, well-to-do aunt.

Melrose has been described as 'the only upper-middle-class town in the Scottish Borders.' It certainly has a Cotswold middle-class feel to it but at the same time is undeniably Scottish. Despite its county-town feel, the appeal is enduring. The Romans settled here, establishing the supply camp of Trimontium, and one of sports longest-lasting events was devised here in 1877. The Melrose Sevens, one of rugby's most popular events, attracts the television cameras and about 16,000 visitors every year, filling the pubs and hotels to bursting; but Melrose's most popular attraction is undoubtedly the Abbey.

Founded in 1136 by Cistercian monks from Rievaulx in Yorkshire, Melrose Abbey is today the starting point of the popular sixty-four-mile St Cuthbert's Way, which crosses the Borderlands on its way to Holy Island. St Cuthbert was part of the abbey community before he moved to the island of Lindisfarne, just off the Northumberland coast, and to eternal glory at Durham, as one of the north's best-loved saints. The abbey is also the resting place of Robert the Bruce's heart after it had been taken as a talisman by Scots crusaders, and author Dan Brown may have found some interesting material here for his novels on religious cults and Freemasonry. The masons who worked on the abbey have been linked to the Freemasons' Lodge of Melrose – St John No 1. Here you'll find a plaque bearing the masons' coat of arms. The date on it is 1156.

It's said that Michael Scott the Wizard (what kind of name is that for a wizard? Merlin or Gandalf or even Lord Voldemort, but Michael Scott?) is also buried in the grounds of the Abbey, along with his magic books. He is said to have predicted his own death by a small stone falling on his head. Despite his un-wizardlike name, Michael Scott became a legend and there is little doubt that he did exist. According to many written accounts he was a thirteenth-century philosopher who studied at Oxford, Paris and Toledo universities, and became known as Michael Mathematicus.

It's believed he was court astrologer and physician to Frederick the Second, the Holy Roman Emperor known as Frederick the Great. Sir Walter Scott mentioned him in his *Lay of the Last Minstrel* and James Hogg, the Ettrick Shepherd, wrote about him in his book, *The Three Perils of Man*. The Scottish novelist John Buchan also referred to him in his 1924 book *The Three Hostages*, but Michael Scott the Wizard may have another claim to fame, one more important than philosophy, mathematics or magic. It has been suggested that he is the father of Scotch whisky.

Surviving copies of manuscripts attributed to Scott refer to distillation of aqua vitae (water of life), sometimes known as aqua ardens (burning water), the earliest name for distilled alcohol. In the Middle Ages people distilled spirits and used them to cure their ills, much as we do today, but I really like the reference to whisky by another Borderer, James Hogg. The Ettrick Shepherd wrote, 'If a body can just find oot the exac' proper proportion and quantity that ought to be drunk every day and keep to that, I verily throw that he might leeve forever without dying at all, and that doctors and kirkyards would go oot o' fashion'. I can certainly drink to that.

Towns are certainly nice for a quick dram or two, a meal or a good cup of coffee, but before arriving in Melrose we often enjoyed the view from lowly Bemersyde Hill. Like Sir Walter Scott, we would gaze across the winding River Tweed to admire one of the great landmarks of the Borders:

the Eildons. A round of those landmark hills would once again be one of our weekend walks. I'm not sure how many times I've climbed the Eildons but I never tire of them. I've written about them, made television programmes on them, I included them in my long walk between Kirk Yetholm and Cape Wrath, the Scottish National Trail, and I'm always keen to climb them again.

When Sir Walter Scott saw the Eildons across the Tweed from Bemersyde Hill he claimed it as one of the best views in the Borders. Little did he know that he was gazing at the remnants of a volcanic lava flow that time, wind, rain and ice had weathered into a distinct triumvirate of dumpy hills. They were known to the Romans as Trimontium.

I suspect there is one thing that Sir Walter Scott and I have in common. We are both romantics and, like the famed novelist, I prefer the less prosaic and infinitely more romantic reasoning for the creation of the lovely Eildons. The local tradition casts aside geological hypotheses and meteorological theories to make a simple claim. Michael Scott the Wizard was ordered by the devil to split a single Eildon into three separate humps.

If you find that difficult to swallow then consider the fate of another local hero, the songster called Thomas the Rhymer. Thomas was a thirteenth-century bard and seer who claimed to have been spirited away by the Queen of the Faeries to spend seven years in Elfland, below the Eildon Hills. As if that's not enough, Borders lore has it that Merlin, the great wizard at the court of King Arthur, was stoned to death and buried at nearby Drumelzier on the banks of the Tweed. This area of the Borders wears its history like an ornate ball gown. It dazzles and intrigues you.

I admit I'm a sucker for tales like these, especially when

wrapped in the verses of a Border ballad. Arriving in Melrose we noticed an advert for an evening of traditional songs in one of the hotels, so once we had eaten we spent the rest of the evening with pints of beer, guitars, fiddles and small pipes and some great singing. It was magic, but not as magical as climbing the Eildons' North Hill next morning: the site of an ancient city, the home of the ancient Selgovae tribe. Archaeologists suggest there could have been over 300 hut circles here around 2,000 years ago. Later, the Romans used the site as a fort and signal station.

It didn't take us long to reach the foot of the hills from the Abbey, from where we could see the low col between the two main summits, North and Mid Hills. Beyond the col the track becomes a bit steeper and we found ourselves working a tad harder than we had anticipated for a 1385-feet/422-metre hill! But it was well worth it, for Mid Hill has a prehistoric burial cairn and a view indicator that emphasises just how unusual these hills are. Rising from a comparatively flat landscape they most certainly dominate the surroundings. Delighted by the views and the clear, dry weather, we dropped back to the col and followed the obvious footpath that runs through the remains of the Iron Age hillfort to the summit of Eildon Hill North, 1,325-feet/404-metres, and its Roman signal station. Most folk simply return to the col from here and wander back to Melrose, but we wanted to complete the Eildon trio and climb the lower Eildon Wester Hill too. This was straightforward enough, and gave us views of the two bigger Eildons. From the col between Mid and North Hills we walked south towards the edge of a forestry plantation and across the heather moorland between Mid and Wester Hill, and here discovered another Eildon curiosity. We couldn't work out why the third top is called Wester Hill?

Surely, if anything, it should be called Eildon Southern Hill? If nothing else it gave us a good discussion point as we made our way back, amongst the yellow gorse bushes, to Melrose and a rather genteel afternoon tea and scones.

From Melrose we drove to Yarrowford, on the A708 west of Selkirk, from where we intended walking a circular route that would visit the Three Brethren before returning us to Yarrowford by the Minchmoor Road. There's a small parking area near the telephone box and from there we headed back beside the Yarrow Water towards Selkirk. Ballads from the previous evening still swirled through my mind:

> *There lived a lady in the West,*
> *I neer could find her marrow;*
> *She was courted by nine gentlemen*
> *And a ploughboy-lad in Yarrow.*
> *These nine sat drinking at the wine,*
> *Sat drinking wine in Yarrow;*
> *They made a vow among themselves*
> *To fight for her in Yarrow.*

Some folk believe the hero of the ballad was John Scott, the sixth son of the Laird of Harden. Local legend reckons he met a treacherous and untimely death in nearby Ettrick Forest at the hands of his own cousins, the Scotts of Gilmanscleugh, in the seventeenth century.

We climbed to the Three Brethren cairns from the old Yair bridge that spans the Tweed. Built in 1762 to replace the old ford at Caddon Water its triple span structure has changed little since the eighteenth century. The previous evening we had used it as a grandstand to watch dozens of youngsters in a whitewater canoe slalom. As they hurled themselves and their stumpy kayaks down the rapids we delighted in their skills and youthful enthusiasm and fearlessness. Some of them weren't even in their teens.

Leaving the river behind, forest tracks led us through the mixed woodland of Yair Hill itself, climbing gently through sun-dappled woods to pick up the line of the Southern Upland Way, one of Scotland's official long distance trails. We had walked this section between Moffat and Galashiels years before and I'd wandered along the ancient route of the nearby Minchmoor road several times without accessing it from this point. I looked forward to visiting it from a different route and perspective. The Minchmoor itself is of considerable antiquity. Edward I came this way to conquer Scotland in 1296 and, after the nearby Battle of Philiphaugh, James Graham, the Marquis of Montrose, crossed the route to Traquair where he hoped to find hospitality and shelter at Traquair House. In 1931, a party of Scottish Youth Hostel Association officials crossed the Minchmoor to officially open Broadmeadows Youth Hostel, SYHA's very first hostel. They were followed fifty years later by another party, this time celebrating the Association's Golden Jubilee. I remember, as I was working as a youth hostel warden at the time and am still encouraged by the idealism of the movement. Sadly, Broadmeadows Youth Hostel, the association's oldest hostel, was sold in 2013, but I'm heartened that hostels like Loch Ossian, Carn Dearg and Glen Affric remain to carry the flag for those who like the idea of 'cheap, simple accommodation in remote areas'.

The Three Brethren dominate the skyline as three tall, slender cairns, each three metres high. Built in the sixteenth century they mark the meeting of estate lands belonging to the lairds of Selkirk, Philiphaugh and Yair. Unfortunately, forestry plantations now threaten to swamp the Three Brethren but, climbing just beyond the top of the hill, you leave the conifers behind for open views across the Tweed towards the gentle side of the Borders: the small, rolling hills that eventually ease into the Berwickshire Borderlands and the east coast. I always think of the Borders as a region of contrasts, between the wilder aspects of Tweeddale and Ettrick and the softer, gentler landscapes of Berwickshire and Roxburghshire. Sadly, this eastern side has been marred by a rash of windfarms, and I counted no less than five obtrusive clusters of turbines. If we are to have such intrusions in the landscape, and I accept the contribution they make towards green energy and in the fight against climate change, then they should be spaced a bit more evenly than they currently are in the Lammermuirs and Borders.

These areas are now at saturation point. Climate change has challenged each and every one of us, and it's comforting to know that Scotland fulfils much of its energy needs nowadays from green energy. I don't think massive turbines enhance scenery but I am pragmatic enough to accept their need. My fears about the long-term effects of climate change diminish any concern about having my views spoiled, but the Borders have paid a heavy price.

The route of the Southern Upland Way bypasses the rounded summit of Broomy Law and, as a native-born Glaswegian, how could I ignore such a landmark? Broomielaw being such an iconic Clydeside place name. Only earlier in the day I had been listening to the American singer James Taylor singing about soldiers taking the silver shilling and setting off to war from Glasgow's Broomielaw, and here I was treading the summit slopes of its namesake. I wonder if there is any connection?

From Broomy Law we descended to a pine-lined ridge before climbing the broad path to Brown Knowe, our final top of the day. From there we left the comfort of the path and took to the heather, dropping towards the farm at Williamhope where a long-haired man sat outside a North American-style tepee playing Eastern European music on his violin. It was a moment of pure magic, as was the chorus of curlews and skylarks that accompanied our descent. A tarred road took us to the hamlet of Peel, the site of an old hospital, built to serve the wounded of the Second World War, and past Ashiestiel House on the opposite side of the Tweed. It was here that Sir Walter Scott lived before he moved to Abbotsford, where he spent the seven happiest years of his life.

Our annual Borders trip isn't always about chasing legends and ancient heroes. We like to take little nibbles of some of the finest walking on offer, so we usually head for a favourite spot of ours, Kirk Yetholm and the lovely little campsite in the neighbouring Town Yetholm. Kirk Yetholm's chief claim to fame is an unusual one. It's the northern terminus of the Pennine Way, England's long distance trail that runs up the spine of the country from Edale in the Peak District to the Cheviots and the Scottish Border. A few years ago I chose Kirk Yetholm as the starting point for a route I walked for television, the Scottish National Trail, a 470-mile journey linking a host of existing trails and footpaths to make one continuous route between the Scottish Borders and Cape Wrath.

Kirk Yetholm may be small in size, and dominated by its

larger neighbour Town Yetholm, but it has a second claim to fame. Situated so close to that national border line, it was often used as a refuge for groups and individuals fleeing from one country to the other, particularly gypsies. In the late eighteenth century Scotland's last gypsy king and queen, Charles and Esther Faa Blythe, were crowned here. It's said the coronation carriage was drawn by six donkeys.

Keen to retrace the old route of the Border gypsies, we left the campervan at the foot of the Halterburn Valley, just a mile outside the village, and took to Shanks's Pony, across the burn and up the Pennine Way itself, the grassy path lifting us high above the green pastures and wooded slopes and across the south face of a hill called Green Humbleton. We were heading for the Stob Stones. Known locally as the 'Gypsy Stobs', the name relates to the tradition that the stones mark the spot where the gypsy kings and queens were crowned. They could also be boundary stones, set up to mark the line of the Border. Although the present Border is some distance to the west, this point was regarded as fixed as far back as 1222. Today, an old wall and fence marks the present national border, the man-made line that separates two distinct nations, two distinct cultures and two distinct parliaments. Beyond the Stob Stones we followed the fence line over White Law to the summit of Black Hag, where another grassy track runs downhill to Old Halterburnhead. We stopped for a while by the ruins there before the final romp back to the campervan.

Next day, being so close to the Cheviot in Northumberland, we decided it would be a tad churlish not to climb it. From the Scottish side of the Border you get a largely peat-free ascent, and a much prettier one than from the Northumberland side. Indeed, the walk-in from Sourhope Farm in the

Bowmont Valley near Yetholm is a sheer delight, wandering through narrow valleys that are rich in ancient remains and traversing sheep-grazed slopes by good paths.

We left the campervan at a road junction above Bowmont Water near Sourhope Farm so we could follow farm tracks all the way up to the Border ridge, just south of Black Hag. From there, the ridge carried us over the distinct peak of The Schil, past the Mountain Refuge at Auchope and onto Auchope Cairn, which left just over a mile of peat-plodding to the summit. From there we returned to Auchope Cairn and resumed our ridge-wandering south, over Score Head and King's Seat and onto Windy Gyle, almost ten miles from The Schil. From Windy Gyle a track runs north down Windy Rig to Kelsocleuch Farm and the farm road, past Cocklawfoot and back to the start.

Leaving Kirk Yetholm we headed for Carter Bar, the 1,371-foot-high/418-metre border point between Scotland and England, that is also the historic barrier between Celt and Saxon. From the warm comfort of the campervan we were blasted by the Arctic chill of a northern wind as we squeezed into our boots and windproofs and searched for gloves and warm hats. Warmed up and legs stretched we were better prepared for the wind when we broke free of the trees and tramped over the frozen turf of Carter Fell, where the full splendour of the view burst upon us. To the south the sinuous twists of Redeswire Dale dropped down to the Catscleugh Reservoir, deep in its conifer-covered cradle. Eastwards, straddling the Border, lay the broad slopes of Redeswire, famous for its sixteenth-century skirmish between Border families, and way beyond it, across the crumpled Borderlands, lay the massive bulk of the Cheviot.

Grand as these views were, it was the view north that

was most heart-warming. Yellowed moors led the eye to the Eildon hills. From the Lammermuirs to the Moorfoots to the Tweeddale Teviotdale and Ettrick hills, everything was gleaming brightly fresh in the springtime sun.

H. V. Morton's comments about Elfland came to mind as we rested briefly by the small cairn that marks the summit of Carter Fell, but it was far too cold for any elfin queens so, anxious to keep warm, we continued over the broad whale-back of Carter Fell, following the Border fence but well aware that on one side of the fence hillwalkers can wander freely, and legally, while on the English side we could well have been trespassing. Scotland's laws of access and freedom to roam seem so radical and sensible compared with England's ancient feudal system where trespass is a continuing threat to walkers and ramblers.

Trespassing or not, we were aware that the rough topography below our boots was once scraped and dug and quarried for coal, surely some of the most exposed and wild open-cast mines in the land? Little is left to remember the hardships and labours of those miners of old. The open-cast areas have been scoured and raked by decades of wind and frosts and below, in the headwaters of the Bateinghope Burn, old ruins whispered their industrial heritage from a wild and bleak hillside. An old track led us back along a natural shelf high above Redesdale and back to the car park. It wasn't a place to linger, so we turned our backs on England and headed north for Moffatdale and St Mary's Loch, an area always associated with a favourite author of mine: James Hogg, the Ettrick Shepherd.

If you want to read a tremendous psychological thriller that's been described as a 'famous tale of persecution, delusion, devilish mimicry and tortured consciousness' then

I'd enthusiastically recommend *The Private Memoirs and Confessions of a Justified Sinner*. This is a novel that explores one of the key tenets of Scottish culture, Calvinism, and was written in 1824 by James Hogg, a contemporary of Sir Walter Scott and Robert Burns. Like the national bard, Hogg was a man of the earth, a farmer and shepherd. Sometimes known as the Ettrick Shepherd, he grew up steeped in the traditions and lore of the Borders. His mother recited the tales of Michael Scott the Wizard and his grandfather, 'the far-famed Will O'Phaup', was reputed to have been the last man to converse with the faeries.

Hogg didn't achieve great success in his lifetime, neither as a writer nor a farmer, and he certainly knew what poverty was, but he had an encyclopaedic knowledge of the Borderland and often used its hilly topography in his writing. Just as there was an element of the supernatural in many of his writings, I once experienced a curious touch of serendipity that sparked a little light in my own consciousness, stirring me to try and discover more about a man whose own career so often paralleled that of his great literary hero, Robert Burns.

As so often happens when we're in the Borders, Gina and I found ourselves drawn to Tibbie Shiel's Inn, on the shores of St Mary's Loch. There used to be a wonderfully atmospheric little snug bar but sadly it closed several years ago. If truth be told, there are one or two places close by where we can park the campervan overnight, but Tibbie's certainly had its attractions, not the least being that James Hogg would often meet Sir Walter Scott, his patron, in that same little snug.

From Tibbie's we followed the old Captain's Road to just beyond the farm at Crosscleuch where, on an impulse, we took to the hill. A long grassy ridge followed the forest edge for a while before climbing to the summit of a dumpy wee hill that goes by the curious name of The Wiss. As we wandered down the narrowing ridge between Peat Law and Altrieve Rig I noticed a little farm, deep-set in the cleft of the valley to our right. I'm not sure why, perhaps it was the set of the buildings, huddled against the elements, or maybe because it was so dominated by the surrounding hills, but my imagination went into overdrive, thinking of what it must have been like to live and work there, before the roads and communication we have now. A grim existence I suspect. It wasn't until later, while having a beer in Tibbie Shiel's, that I learned that Altrieve Farm, for that was its name, was where James Hogg spent his final years. The farm had been given to him by the Duke of Buccleuch and he died there on 21st November 1835. Phew, what kind of karma is that?

From Altrieve Rig we dropped down grassy slopes beside Thorny Cleugh to the edge of the forest, and carefully climbed the wall onto a narrow footpath that took us to the head of a wind-ruffled St Mary's Loch. Across the Yarrow lay the old farm at Blackhouse where the Laidlaw family had taken on James Hogg as a young shepherd. More importantly, they had opened their library and its literary delights to him and later, when he began to show some promise as a poet, introduced him to the Sheriff of Selkirk, Sir Walter Scott. This south shore of the loch took us past the farm at Bowerhope, surrounded by an oasis of deciduous trees amongst the dense conifers, and it was easy to imagine Scott and Hogg wandering along here, anticipating an evening by Tibbie's cosy hearth, two men from differing backgrounds bound together by their love of legend and literature.

Despite Scott's patronage, James Hogg wasn't universally approved of. After his death William Wordsworth published his 'Extempore Effusion upon the Death of James Hogg', which includes the lines:

> *The mighty Minstrel breathes no longer,*
> *'Mid mouldering ruins low he lies;*
> *And death upon the braes of Yarrow,*
> *Has closed the Shepherd-poet's eyes.*

A eulogy certainly, and well deserved, but sadly Wordsworth's notes go on to suggest: 'He was undoubtedly a man of original genius, but of coarse manners and low and offensive opinions.' Mmm, perhaps snobbery knew no bounds then, even amongst the nation's literati.

There's a literature connection to another hill in this area. The last time I climbed White Coomb, the jewel of the Tweedsmuirs, the hill was worthy of its name. A spring snowstorm (it occasionally happens, even here in the Borders) had transformed the greens and browns of the landscape and, from the snow-covered summit dome of White Coomb, white-topped hills rolled in every direction. Northumberland's Cheviot appeared as a vast whale-back, shining above its black outliers. The rise of the Pennines gave way to the snowy Lake District fells, and past the pewter waters of the Solway Firth the darker outline of Criffel stood proud. In the north, beyond Hart Fell and Broad Law and across the flats of the Central Belt, the Highland hills rose in a frontier of white, their clarity only slightly distorted by wisps of muirburn smoke.

Closer at hand there were even fewer hints of springtime's arrival. Below the frowning crags of Lochcraig Head the

waters of Loch Skeen were still frozen, although the tumultuous course of its Tail Burn now ran freely to form the Grey
Mare's Tail that drops precipitously down into Moffatdale.
We had followed the course of the cataract from the National
Trust for Scotland car park beside the A708 Moffat to St
Mary's Loch road. Despite the cold there must have been an
element of snowmelt, for the waterfall was impressive and
the burn lively, freed as it was from the freezing ice that had
captured its spirit for much of the winter.

It's so easy to anthropomorphise elements in these wild
places. We mountain writers do it all the time, but poets are
even worse. Indeed, Sir Walter Scott left it on record that
any poet, however poor his attainments, can write about a
waterfall, and many have, some better than others. Norman
Nicholson refers to his 'chain of water, the pull of earth's
centre,' while others anthropomorphise, describing cascades
and cataracts as 'the voice of the mountains'. In his typi-
cally adjectival poem *Inversnaid*, Gerard Manley Hopkins
describes the course of the burn in tumultuous terms: 'His
rollrock highroad roaring down/ In coop and in comb the
fleece of his foam/ Flutes and low to the lake falls home,' a
poem which of course concludes with that emphatic plea for
wilderness: 'What would the world be, once bereft, of wet
and wildness?/ Let them be left/ O let them be left, wildness
and wet/ Long live the weeds and the wilderness yet.'

Although it's not the highest of waterfalls, the crashing
sixty-metre drop of the Grey Mare's Tail above the A708
Moffat to St Mary's Loch road in Dumfries and Galloway
is certainly one of our most spectacular falls, motivating Sir
Walter Scott, despite his literary theories, to pen a rather
grandiose poem about those waters which hurl down the
abyss from 'dark Lochskene/Where eagles scream from

shore to shore.' I guess he used a bit of poetic licence, for I doubt if you'll see eagles there today, although you might see peregrine falcons, and, once the snow melts and the ice on Loch Skeen gives way, black-headed gulls will return to nest on the reedy shores and colourful displays of wild flowers will decorate the ferociously steep banks of the Grey Mare's Tail.

Beyond the waterfall, and above Loch Skeen, the south Tweedsmuir hills cut an empty, desolate quarter of Dumfries and Galloway. Rising between the Moffat Water and the source of the Tweed, these are well-rounded hills with boggy skirts that exude a very definite air of wet and wildness. The place names describe the nature of the land: Rotten Bottom lies between White Coomb and Hart Fell, and Dead for Cauld is just south-west of the Megget Reservoir. I'd love to know the story behind that name, although I got a hint of it as we filmed the views from the summit of the 2,696-foot/822-metre White Coomb for BBC Scotland's *Adventure Show*. A bitterly cold north-westerly had me frozen as I waited for Paul Diffley, our cameraman, to do his stuff, and although I wasn't quite dead for cauld, I was relieved when we could start moving again. Television? Glamorous? You're having a laugh.

White Coomb is the highest point of a network of ridges that lie south-east of the town of Moffat. The ridges are broad, giving way to steep-sided valleys and narrow cleughs, and can be linked to make extensive high-level hillwalks. The whole area is a walkers' delight and it's one of life's curiosities that so many people drive blithely past on the way to the Highlands, while others drive past in the opposite direction as they make for the Lake District.

Beyond the upper reaches of Annandale these southern

Tweedsmuir hills rise in a broad swell between the valley of the Moffat Water and the headwaters of the Tweed. They're big, testing hills that are spared the usual Border disfiguration of forestry plantations, and are more often than not ignored. Several times over the past few years I've found myself swinging the car off the motorway, to find the little minor road from Moffat that creeps up the east side of Annandale to Ericstane, the starting point for a quick romp up Hart Fell. At 2,651 feet/808 metres, this is the apex of several long grassy ridges that run down into Annandale. One of those ridges, bounding the Auchencat Burn, spreads its long finger all the way down to Ericstane from where a good path leads to Hartfell Spa, a chalybeate spring contained in its little beehive-shaped shelter. A local man, John Williamson, is said to have discovered the mineral qualities of the water in 1748, and many were those who climbed into the confines of this narrow glen, eager to test the healing properties of the Hartfell waters.

Beyond the well, steep grassy slopes climb to the crest of the ridge, south-west of Arthur's Seat, although this top is infinitely wilder in its high setting than its namesake in Edinburgh. The Arthurian legends are widespread in the Borders and these hills even have links with Arthur's wise counsellor, Merlin the Magician. The wizard Merlin, it is claimed, once roamed these broad slopes. Indeed, it's said he was able to transform himself into a hart, a small deer often associated with royalty.

The ridge now rolls in a north-east direction, over Arthur's Seat and on to the wide summit of Hart Fell itself, with its long views down Annandale and Nithsdale to the waters of the Solway Firth. From the trig point a line of fence posts march in a north-west direction before turning and heading roughly west over the tops that rise above the Annan headwaters: Whitehope Knowe, Whitehope Heights, Spout Craig, Chalk Rig Edge and the simply named Great Hill. A short distance to the north lies the intriguingly named Crown of Scotland and not far below it lies Tweed's Well, the source of that great river's journey to the North Sea.

From just west of Great Hill's summit, a footpath drops into an ancient glacial gouge that for generations has been known as the Devil's Beef Tub. This great hollow was important in former times as a holding place for the great cattle herds when such livestock were the area's most valuable commodity. Cattle raids were not infrequent. In 'tubs' like this one, the herd could easily be held and guarded until it was safe to release them. Local legend claims that a family called Johnstone used the corrie for hiding stolen cattle in the sixteenth century. Finally, a good footpath runs down the flanks of the Beef Tub to Corehead and the road back to your waiting car at Ericstane, the end of a walk that, while actually in Dumfries and Galloway, is part of the sprawling mass of high ground that gives the Scottish Borders so much of its character.

3

THE LONGEST, THE LOVELIEST
AND THE LONELIEST

Sir Walter Scott first described Glen Lyon in the above terms, and my mentor Tom Weir was fond of using the same alliteration to describe this thirty-four-mile-long glen of Highland Perthshire. He often told me Glen Lyon was his favourite, and for a man who knew Scotland like few others that was a high recommendation.

It is indeed a magnificent place, from its heavily wooded lower glen near Fortingall, where the River Lyon crashes and tumbles through its deep, shadowed gorge, all the way to the bare upper slopes of the glen, a place of desolation and remote mountain grandeur despite the hydro works that have dammed the loch, created a stony tideline around the shores and laced the upper glen with power lines. Notwithstanding the hand of man, Glen Lyon is famed for something else. It is also Scotland's most mysterious glen, a place of myth and legend and, according to some, home to the creator goddess of the ancient Celtic world.

Years ago, I met an old friend of mine here. Laurence Main lives in Mid Wales and has a penchant for New Age thinking. Laurence describes himself as a Druid and has a long-standing fascination with the earth-mysteries and legends of our wild places. He had come north to Glen

Lyon to visit Fortingall, a place he believed may have been the birthplace of Pontius Pilate, the Roman judge of Christ. Two thousand years ago, the legend suggests that Emperor Caesar Augustus sent an emissary to Scotland, to Dun Geal, near modern Fortingall. The emissary's wife gave birth to a baby, and they called him Pilate. He went on to become the fifth procurator of Judea and ordered the crucifixion of Christ.

Laurence was also searching for the Praying Hands of Mary, a large split rock that stands in Gleinn Dà-Eigg, an offshoot of Glen Lyon close to Bridge of Balgie. He also believed that Glen Lyon was the home of the Celtic creator goddess, and was itself a sacred place. Although megalithic remains are found just outside the glen, in Fortingall and near Loch Tay, Glen Lyon is curiously devoid of megalithic monuments. As the home of the creator goddess the glen was sacred by nature and such special sites were normally left untouched by the ancient Celts.

Laurence's revelations aroused my own long-standing interest in such mysterious matters. Just as North American outdoors folk have learned much from the native North American tribes, so I believe we can learn much from our Celtic ancestors, particularly about living in harmony with the land. Laurence's various speculations reminded me of a story I had been told some forty years ago by an old pal of mine, the late Harry McShane, a former warden of Crianlarich Youth Hostel and an erstwhile hillwalking buddy.

Harry told me a story about small stone figures that were apparently taken to a lonely spot near the head of Glen Lyon every spring, and removed again every autumn. He couldn't verify the story and had no idea who moved the stones, but the tale has lodged in the scree slopes of my memory and my conversations with Laurence Main encouraged me to carry out further research. What I discovered surprised and astonished me. This is the story of a pagan shrine dedicated to the Cailleach, in the tradition of the Celtic mother goddess, who once blessed the cattle and their pastures and ensured good weather.

The Cailleach, often translated as the 'old woman' or in this case the 'divine goddess', is a potent force in Celtic mythology, commonly associated with wild nature and landscape. The Celtic creator goddess is encountered throughout the length and breadth of Scotland, an entity taking many forms and represented in a variety of different shapes. Believers would see her essential nature in the harmony and balance of the natural order, the ebb and flow of growth and decay, of life and death itself.

Nearby, in Rannoch, legend names her as the Cailleach Bheur, the blue hag. According to A. D. Cunningham's excellent book *Tales of Rannoch* this old witch was once a familiar sight on Schiehallion: 'Her face was blue with cold, her hair white with frost and the plaid that wrapped her bony shoulders was grey as the winter fields.'

Other ancient forces have been at work in Glen Lyon. Years ago, just before I climbed the Corbett of Cam Chreag, high above the glen, I visited the little church at Innerwick. There's a car park with interpretative signs beside the start of the right-of-way that runs over the hills to Rannoch and the little church is well worth a visit, just to see the ancient bell of St Adamnan.

St Adamnan, also called Adomnan or Eonan, was Irish-born and is famed for his biography of St Columba, whom he studied and worked under at Iona. Adamnan lived mostly in the seventh century and died around AD 704. His bell has been dated to AD 800 and apparently lay in the churchyard of St Brandon's Chapel in Glen Lyon for centuries before being rescued. St Adamnan travelled here from Iona, setting up Christian cells on ancient pagan sites of worship. Another of his churches lies on the shores of Loch Insh, by Kincraig in Badenoch and, curiously, that church also has a bell that apparently belonged to the well-travelled saint. At Loch Insh, according to the legend, St Adamnan used to ring the bell to summon the Swan Children of Lir, a brother and sister who were half child, half swan, to worship. Today, Loch Insh, and its adjoining meadows, is Scotland's principal wintering place for whooper swans. Coincidence?

I recalled these old stories as I climbed towards Cam Chreag, a 2,828-foot/862-metre Corbett that neighbours the Munro of Meall Buidhe above Loch an Daimh. I wanted some photographs of the loch and the wild land beyond it and remembered Cam Chreag as a pretty good viewpoint. I was also aware that the recommended route given in the guidebooks was less than satisfactory and a better route was possible by following the hill's south-east ridge, returning to the start via its lowly neighbour of Meall nam Maigheach, a pleasant horseshoe-shaped route of about nine miles round the glen of the Allt a' Choire Uidhre.

This glen has a bulldozed track running up its length to a corrugated iron hut just below Cam Chreag's eastern face – the guidebook route – but the first bonus of my horseshoe route became apparent as I topped out on Ben Meggernie, at the end of Cam Chreag's east ridge. This little bump offers a fabulous view right down the length of Glen Lyon and is well worth climbing, if only to understand why Tom Weir, and others, have described this as Scotland's loveliest glen.

On one side the peaks of the Ben Lawers range rise high into the sky, the pointed culmination of long, steep ridges. On the other, the blunter Carn Mairg hills rise on equally steep-sided flanks. The glen itself is wooded with the River Lyon flowing through green meadows. Rob Roy's mother was born here, and before that the ancient Kings of Scotland came here to hunt deer.

Lovely as Glen Lyon is, I was more impressed with the views from Cam Chreag itself. To the west, the big Munros stood clear: Stuchd an Lochain and Meall Buidhe, one on either side of Loch an Daimh, and the wild country beyond to the hills of Mamlorn and Orchy. To the north-west, across the Rannoch Moor, Ben Nevis was clearly visible, rising above the hills of the Mamore Deer Forest and the enormous bowl of peat hag and heather, lochs and lochans that make up the vastness of the Rannoch Moor. Only the West Highland railway line offers any sign of man's hand until you reach the A82 Bridge of Orchy road and the A86, away beyond the narrow slit of Loch Treig.

The north-east face of Cam Chreag gave an interesting descent down some old snow patches before Argocat tracks took me over the rounded hump of Meall nam Maigheach to again meet the bulldozed track. Great spotted woodpeckers were drilling in the woods and oystercatchers were piping from the green flats below. I hadn't seen another soul all day: one of the advantages of the Corbetts over the Munros.

Given that St Adamnan, like other travelling priests, would have set up Christian cells on ancient pagan sites of worship it's perhaps not surprising that pagan Glen Lyon was a target for the early Christian missionaries. The name Lyon is thought by many to be a derivation of Lugdunum, after Lugh, the Celtic sun god. Other historians believe that

Glen Lyon was a stronghold of the Picts and suggest that Glen Lyon, rather than Scone, might have been the epicentre of their kingdom. If this is true it could explain why Glen Lyon was thus named. The sun god was normally associated with the king.

St Adamnan is also credited with banishing the Black Plague, which raged through Glen Lyon in AD 664. It's said the saint prayed and, summoning God's help, cast the plague's evil spirits into a hole in a rock. The rock itself is said to lie by the roadside at Camustrachan and is known as Craig Fhionnaidh but I've searched for it without success. However, I did find the Bronze Age standing stone with the carving of a cross that is said to stand close to the spot. Further up the glen, near Bridge of Balgie, is Milton Eonan, said to be the erstwhile home of Adamnan and the site of his original cell.

Encouraged by finding the standing stone I set off in search of the Praying Hands of Mary, the name of which I suspect is a twentieth-century Christian invention. Some say the historic name of the rock formation is Fionn's Rock, the split in the rock created by the supernatural arrow of Fionn MacCumhail, leader of the ancient Fianna warriors.

Cone-shaped hills were important to pre-Christian religions, and that importance possibly dates from before Druidism and the ancient Celts. Glastonbury Tor is one example and the 2,106-foot/642-metre Creag nan Eildeag in Glen Lyon could be another. On its lower slopes, in Gleann De-Eig, a curious rock formation depicts two hands pointing skywards as though in supplication, the fingertips not quite touching. The split, upright stone is balanced on a base rock as though placed there by man's hand. Despite a long search on the Internet I can't find any archaeological research that suggests this is a natural phenomenon and so the assumption is that the formation is man-made.

Having said that, I'm open-minded about its origins. Over the years I've ceased to be surprised at the highly unlikely formations that nature so often produces. However, its position is interesting. If you stand some twenty or thirty metres downhill from the stones and look back at them they appear to be praying towards the most conical aspect of Creag nan Eildeag, a symbol perhaps of the 'primordial' hill, the first hill created on Earth and suggestive of the navel of the Earth. Other interpretations suggest the primordial hill mimics the extended belly of a pregnant woman. In this case it's believed by some ancient scholars that the sun god Lugh had impregnated the Cailleach, hence the cone-shaped hill mimicking her pregnancy.

The shrine to the Cailleach lies in Gleann Cailliche near the head of Glen Lyon, and I realised this was the place Harry McShane told me about all those years ago. The pagan shrine was relatively unknown until recent times when a proposal for a run-of-river hydroelectric scheme threatened to create bulldozed tracks and buildings close to its cherished pasture lands. There were strong objections, largely from local people, and the proposal was abandoned, but the location of the ancient shrine was made known to a wider audience. Ironically, perhaps a better awareness of its situation and its importance will protect it in the future.

On a warm and sunny summer's day I drove to Pubil, close to the Lubreoch dam that holds back the waters of Loch Lyon, and cycled my mountain bike along the north shore of the loch to Gleann Meurain, a northern offshoot of Glen Lyon. Close by lay the entrance to Gleann Cailliche, a lovely green and flat-bottomed glen that would have been an ideal site for traditional summer shielings. There was abundant water and the pastures would have been lush. Several vegetated mounds indicated former settlements and it wasn't long before I climbed into the glen and glimpsed what I was searching for. On the Ordnance Survey map it's called Tigh nam Bodach, the 'house of the old man', but others refer to it as Tigh nam Cailleach. It's a drystone walled structure, about waist-high, with a turfed roof. From a distance it appears tiny, a solitary construct in the midst of an empty glen and, as I approached, I saw there were several water-worn stones, shaped like fat, rounded bodies with heads, lying outside on the grass.

The largest stone represents the Cailleach (old woman), accompanied by the Bodach (old man) and their daughter, Nighean. In what is believed to be the oldest uninterrupted pre-Christian ritual in Britain, the water-worn figures from the River Lyon are taken out of their house every May, faced down the glen, and returned every November. The ritual was formerly performed, until his death, by a local gamekeeper, and others are now continuing the tradition. Indeed, only a few years ago a Crieff-based drystane dyker called Norman Haddow, along with five local volunteers, spent a weekend renovating the ancient house.

Decades of wild winters had taken their toll on the ancient structure and it had become a rather tatty home to house the Celtic creator goddess and her family. The ancient ritual that takes place here twice a year marks the two great Celtic festivals of Beltane and Samhain (Halloween). These festivals represent the annual removal of cattle to the high shielings in spring, and back to the lower glen, and villages, in the autumn. According to local lore the Cailleach, in the tradition of Celtic mother goddesses, blessed the beasts and the pastures and ensured good weather for the summer.

Forty years after hearing about this place for the first time, I was thrilled and excited to sit beside the stones and wonder at all those who had been here before me. The 'servants' who had, throughout the generations, made their way to this spot to take out or put back the figures; those who had come in a form of pilgrimage to pay their respects to the creator goddess, and folk like me, who were merely inquisitive and nourished a curiosity about all things Celtic.

The sun was warm, a soft breeze kept the midges away and the only sound was the music of nearby streams. I dozed softly, aware that Gleann Cailliche was virtually sealed off from the modern world. This drystone structure and the nearby track were the only signs of modern man's hand, and that is how it should be, but I was also aware that the Celtic sun had long since set, the ancient temples and their traditions have vanished, the sacred groves and holy forests have all gone, and the stories of those who performed mighty deeds and miracles have become confused with folk tales and mythology. All that remain are places like this, and the standing stones, forever alert for the sound of Fingal's bugle, heralding his return to the Highlands of Scotland.

Close by Glen Lyon, in Rannoch, lies Schiehallion, the faery hill of the Caledonians. Like Glen Lyon this conical mountain is shrouded in mystery and there are those who would suggest that it could possibly be Mount Zion in the far north, as mentioned in the Old Testament of the Hebrews. When I met my friend, Laurence Main, at the foot of Schiehallion, the stillness and silence of the day were intensified by low clouds shrouding the hill, mists that could well have been the frozen breath of the Cailleach Bheur, the blue hag who according to Rannoch legend rides the wings of the storms to deal out icy death to the unfortunate traveller. The mist didn't perturb us too much. I've lost count of how many times I've climbed Perthshire's Schiehallion and I knew there was a good footpath, built some years ago by the John Muir Trust, which would carry us to the hill's long eastern ridge. Once we reached the ridge it was a simple case of following a compass bearing, more or less due west, to the rocky summit.

Although its name has the cut and thrust of a battle-cry and its conical shape was once used to help calculate the weight of the Earth, Schiehallion, 3,553 feet/1,083 metres, translates into something much less macho, Sidh Chailleann, the faery hill of the Caledonians. Some scholars have suggested the name might mean 'the maiden's pap' or 'constant storm' and that latter interpretation certainly fits with the legend of the Cailleach Bheur. According to A. D. Cunningham's excellent *Tales of Rannoch*, she was once a familiar sight on Schiehallion. The old hag's presence was evident as Laurence Main and I climbed onto the mountain's long whaleback ridge. The air was still, visibility down to a few metres and ice crystals decorated every boulder. There was little temptation to linger in the Cailleach Bheur's cold grasp. You don't have to believe in faeries to experience the chilling fingers of winter reaching out to you. I've had the pleasure of climbing hills in Scotland with all kinds of people – famous mountaineers, television celebrities, pop singers, musicians, artists – but few have been as intriguing as Laurence Main. Before I tell you more about him, let me set the scene, particularly for those who may be unfamiliar with the more mystical aspects of this popular Perthshire mountain.

I've already mentioned that Schiehallion was used to ascertain the density of the Earth. In 1774 the Astronomer Royal Neville Maskelyne chose it for his measurements because of the hill's relatively isolated position and conical shape when seen from Loch Rannoch. The experiment was based on the way the mountain's mass caused a pendulum to pull away from the vertical. The deflection of the pendulum provided Maskelyne with the information to allow him to calculate the mean density of the Earth, from which its mass and a value for Newton's gravitational constant could be worked out.

Now, I'm afraid I have no idea what that actually means, but I do know this: one of the assistants on the project, Charles Hutton, worked out a graphical system that measured areas of equal height. The system later became known as contour lines, and all of us who go to the hills have reason to be grateful for that particular development. But it was discovery of a more mystical nature I hoped for today. In his book, A. D. Cunningham leaves a tantalising message: 'The adventurer who lingers in the secret places of the mountains senses that the Cailleach and the spirit life are still there, and he is aware that enchantment has not vanished from the world.' Wow!

Enchantment has certainly not vanished from Schiehallion. Climb her slopes on a sunny summer's evening and you will most certainly be thrilled by views across the rolling hills of Highland Perthshire to where Loch Rannoch stretches towards the pocked mattress of Rannoch Moor. Descend the hill at nightfall and hear the curious summer sounds of drumming snipe and roding woodcock, or listen to the roars of rutting stags during the chilled days of late autumn. But Schiehallion has an allure that is not always comfortable.

Shrouded in the snows of winter her cold charm is compelling, as she tempts you like a harlot, or an icy blue hag.

The mountain and its immediate area are rich in superstition and legend and it's in Uamh Tom a' Mhor-fhir, a cave in the upper reaches of Gleann Mor on the south side of the mountain, that Schiehallion's faeries are supposed to dwell. Needless to say, I've never come across much evidence of faery folk in the glen but years ago I did climb the hill with old friend Hamish Brown who pointed out a rock with ancient cup-and-saucer ring markings, evidence of hut circles and the remains of shielings: reminders of an earlier way of life when glens like this were used for grazing cattle. Another old pal of the hills, the late Irvine Butterfield, once scolded me for making fun of the faery stories. 'There are things on Schiehallion that shouldn't be mocked,' he warned, and he was being serious.

In his book, *A Highland Parish*, published in 1928, Alexander Stewart suggests the Uamh Tom a' Mhor-fhir cave is in fact part of a huge cave system:

> It has a fairly wide opening which extends for three or four yards. It then contracts and slants into total darkness in the bowels of the earth. Some miles to the east of this there is another opening, which tradition holds to be the other end of the cave. According to the traditional accounts, this cave was regarded as an abode of faeries and other supernatural beings, rather than a hiding place of mortals. The only men who were supposed to have lived there were individuals who were believed to have been in league with supernatural powers.

There are no cattle today and very little evidence of faery folk, but you might well see, and indeed smell, Schiehallion's feral goats. I must confess I haven't seen any goats here for years but, if you do spot some, look out for the Ghobhar Bacach, the lame goat, who according to legend still hirples about Schiehallion, always in milk, with yield enough to supply the Fingalians, the fair-haired warrior giants under the command of Fionn MacCumhail, when they return from Ireland to take Scotland back.

There was little evidence of the Ghobhar Bacach as we crunched across the snows of the hill's eastern ridge but the cold mists clinging to us suggested the Cailleach Bheur was keen to make her presence felt. Her attention was made even more credible because my companion was infinitely more in tune with these curios than I was. Laurence Main was in the second week of a length-of-Britain pilgrimage visiting ancient, sacred sites. He had started his mammoth walk at the Callanish Standing Stones on Lewis and worked his way south via Culloden's Clava Cairns and Aberdeenshire's Bennachie. I had collected him from his lonely camp at the head of Glen Lyon where he had been visiting the old yew tree at Fortingall (probably the oldest living tree in the UK) and the Praying Hands of Mary.

Laurence writes walking guides for a living, and lectures on Earth mysteries. He is a Druid and the purpose of his long walk was to raise publicity for the Vegan Society. 'If we were all vegans we would only need ten-million acres of agricultural land to supply our needs,' he told me. 'That's a quarter of all the agricultural land in England and Wales alone.'

I must confess my ham sandwiches tasted no less fine as I sipped hot coffee from my flask while Laurence nibbled organic chocolate and drank water. He had asked me to accompany him on Schiehallion and, while I was happy to do that, it was obvious his interests were in the hill's legends rather than her status as a Munro. As we crossed the exposed summit ridge, I became a little concerned about him for he had insisted on wearing shorts. The middle of March may be mild in his home territory of Mid Wales but here in Highland Perthshire at three-thousand feet the weather was bitter, and Laurence's non-leather vegan boots didn't appear to be coping with the iced-up rocks. However, he struggled on manfully, and managed to gasp out the reasons why he had been so keen to climb Schiehallion.

'This is one of the world's holy hills,' he told me between deep gulps of frigid air. 'Druids believe there are three primary Holy Mountains: Mount Moriah in Palestine, Mount Sinai in Egypt, and Mount Heredom, although there is no hard evidence to show where that is.

'Schiehallion has always been known as a mystical mountain by Gaelic-speaking Highlanders, and a source of inspiration and revelation to prophets and saints. Other hills in the UK with similar associations are Uisneach, situated at the geographical centre of Celtic Ireland, and Plinlimmon, close to the centre of Celtic Wales. Here, Schiehallion lies at the centre of Celtic Scotland. Could that be mere coincidence?

'What's more, there are those who believe Schiehallion may have been visited by Jesus Christ himself. Between his presentation to the Temple as a child and taking up his ministry at the age of thirty, it's thought he may have travelled extensively in the company of Joseph of Arimathea, a tin trader and merchant and a family friend of Mary and Joseph.

'What we now know as Britain was once the tin-manufacturing centre of the world, so it's not unreasonable to believe that Joseph came here. It's entirely possible the young Jesus came with him. It's also ironic that Christ's judge, Pontius Pilate, was allegedly born just over the hill in Fortingall, the son of a Roman officer.'

I listened to Laurence with a degree of scepticism, but it's also been suggested that after the disastrous Battle of Methven, Robert the Bruce took refuge in a small castle on the north slopes of Schiehallion, where he established the masonic 'Sublime and Royal Chapter of Heredom', a chapter of the Freemasons that had originally been constituted on the Holy top of Mount Moriah in the Kingdom of Judea. But why would the Bruce choose Schiehallion? Apparently because, like Mount Moriah, Schiehallion was thought to be a Holy Mountain, the 'Mount Zion in the far north' as recorded in Psalm 48 in the Hebrew Old Testament.

In his book, *The Holy Land of Scotland*, author Barry Dunford quotes the eighteenth-century writings of the Chevalier de Berage on the origins of Freemasonry: 'Their Metropolitan Lodge is situated on the Mountain of Heredom where the first Lodge was held in Europe and which exists in all its splendour. The General Council is still held there, and it is the seal of the Sovereign Grand Master. This mountain is situated between the West and North of Scotland at sixty miles from Edinburgh.' Could Schiehallion be the Mount Heredom of the ancient scriptures?

Laurence and I originally planned to descend the rocky flanks to the west of the summit, a route that would take us to the head of Gleann Mor and the Tom a' Mhor-fhir cave, but by then he looked half frozen. His long beard was tangled in ice and his knees were blue. He had grazed his leg on a sharp rock and blood poured from the injury. He would have to forsake the delights of Gleann Mor, the cup-and-saucer ring markings, the old shielings and the faery cave at Uamh Tom a' Mhor-fhir for a direct descent back to the warmth of the car. We parted on the promise that he would return and enjoy the spiritual aspects of Schiehallion when the Cailleach Bheur had departed for the summer. I went off to reconsider my initial scepticism and recall the words of an old Perthshire cleric:

> *I love to view Schiehallion all aglow,*
> *In blaze of beauty 'gainst the eastern sky,*
> *Like a huge pyramid exalted high*
> *O'er woodland fringing round its base below;*
>
> *The Bible tells of Hebrew mountains grand,*
> *Where such great deeds were done in days of old,*
> *As render them more precious far than gold*
> *In our conception of the Holy Land;*
> *But every soul that seeks the heavenly road*
> *May in Schiehallion, too, behold a Mount of God*

FROM *Schiehallion* BY REV. JOHN SINCLAIR

Wonderful as Glen Lyon may be, there was initially a strong local resistance to the access provisions of the Land Reform (Scotland) Act 2003, legislation that includes a right of responsible public access. The legislation was a codification of the traditional right to roam that Scottish walkers and mountaineers had enjoyed for generations, but for some time there were hotbeds of discontent amongst some of Scotland's landowning fraternity, many of whom have been trying to interpret the term 'responsible access' to suit their own needs and purposes.

The round of the Carn Mairg hills in Glen Lyon became infamous amongst hillwalkers. A massive metal gate was put across the access track and a notice board, pinned to the gate, spouted forth all sorts of conservationist gobble-dygook about why people shouldn't walk on the hills during the stag-shooting season, the hind-culling season, the deer-calving season and the lambing season. Many walkers inter-preted all that as simply 'keep out'. After considerable work by the Perth & Kinross Access Officer and Mountaineering Scotland, the estate relaxed their opposition to the access legislation and hillwalkers once again enjoy this high-level walk around the Munros of Carn Gorm, 3,376 feet/1,029 metres Meall Garbh, 3,176 feet/968 metres, Carn Mairg, 3,415 feet/1,041 metres, and Meall nan Aighean (sometimes referred to as Creag Mhor), 3,218 feet/981 metres, one of the best expeditions in the area, a walk of about eleven miles.

My mate Steve and I had arranged to meet in Glen Lyon with the intention of walking at least part of the route. The weather forecast suggested a brief lull in the gale-force winds and driving rain that had been battering Scotland all week and we knew that if the weather really closed in we could escape from the route by descending through one of the corries back to the glen. As it was, we didn't have to. What wind there was tore great patches of blue in the cloud layers and thin drifting mists only enhanced the views up and down the length of Glen Lyon. Carn Gorm was snow-capped, and after a long pull over rising moorland and the final steep pull to the summit, we delighted in the prospect of the high-level walk that lay before us.

The broad, rolling nature of these Carn Mairg ridges allows you to stride out purposefully, and navigation is made simple, even in foul weather, by the rusting uprights of an old boundary fence that march their companionable way over the tops. We used them to good effect, for the spells of glistening, clear weather were interspersed with curtains of black cloud that obliterated the views across the deep, tree-lined chasm of Glen Lyon towards the Ben Lawers hills and to the north where the wide open landscape rolls on towards the broad swell of mountains beyond Loch Rannoch. During the clear spells, nearby Schiehallion stood out supreme, not as the bold conical shape it's so often portrayed as, but as a long whale-backed ridge.

It was on Carn Mairg itself that we might have come to grief. The fence posts lulled us into a false sense of security but a sixth sense convinced me we were heading the wrong way, and none too soon. A check with the map and compass confirmed it. A steep crag lies immediately below the summit slopes and it's best to traverse east for a bit from the summit cairn, before descending grassy slopes down to the high bealach above Coire Chearcaill. Our little error was hardly serious, but it did mean we had to negotiate a slope of boulders that were covered in wet, slobbery snow; more ankle-threatening than life-threatening.

Double-topped Meall nan Aighean was our final Munro, the summit of which is the rock-capped north-east top. With black storm clouds gathering in the distant recesses of Glen Lyon we were keen not to outstay our welcome. Taking issue with hostile landowners is one thing, pushing your luck with Biera, the Celtic queen of winter, is another thing entirely. A quick trot down the grassy ridge on the south side of the Allt Coir Chearcaill soon dropped us back at the footpath by the Invervar Burn. We beat the rain by minutes.

Further west along the glen, near the farm at Gallin, a side road crosses pine-studded moorland to a huge concrete dam that holds back the waters of Loch an Daimh. On either side of the dam two big hills rise: Stuchd an Lochain, 3,150 feet/960 metres, the peak of the small loch, and opposite it, across the waters of the loch, Meall Buidhe, 3,058 feet/932 metres, the yellow hill.

Most Munro-baggers combine these two hills by climbing Stuchd an Lochain, returning to their starting point by the Loch an Daimh dam, climbing Meall Buidhe and returning by the same route. I have to admit I've always thought that a rather disrespectful way to treat hills, the style of the list-ticker, but hey, I've done it myself and it's perhaps only when you've climbed all the Munros that you can afford the luxury of visiting them as individuals, taking time to explore their corries and ridges more fully.

You can, of course, climb these hills as part of an excellent circuit of Loch an Daimh, starting and finishing at the dam. This makes a superb twelve-mile circular walk and adds an extra Corbett, Sron a' Choire Chnapanich, 2,746 feet/837 metres to the itinerary. As a bonus, the head of Loch an Daimh is a wonderful spot, splendidly remote and atmospheric.

Stuchd an Lochain can also be climbed from Cashlie at the western end of the Stronuich Reservoir in Glen Lyon via the Allt Cashlie which leads to the plateau between Sron Chona Choirein and the summit, but some believe this route of ascent lacks the character of the north side of the hill. When climbing the hill from this direction you can add two Corbetts to the Munro in a big, circular route.

Sron a' Choire Chnapanich is actually the name of the bold prow that dominates the western end of Loch an Daimh. The hill's summit is unnamed on the Ordnance Survey maps but Sron a' Choire Chnapanich, the nose of the lumpy corrie, is as good a name as any, and a Corbett at 2,746 feet/837 metres. A deep glen separates it from another long 'nose,' the Sron a' Mhill Bhuidhe, which eventually climbs up in a south-west direction to another Corbett, the triple-topped Meall Buidhe. The 2,976-foot/907-metre summit is the most western of the three tops. It's not the most imposing peak in the world but the situation is one of pure empty wildness, with the vastness of the empty Rannoch Moor to the north and good views of Beinn Heasgarnich, king of the Mamlorn hills, to the south.

The best descent from Meall Buidhe is down to the high bealach between the Eas nan Aighean, which drains to Loch Lyon, and the Feith Thalain, which runs down into the head of Loch an Daimh. Descend the ridge to the Loch Lyon dam then follow the road back to your start point at Cashlie.

Some years ago, I chose Stuchd an Lochain for one of my walks on the BBC's *Adventure Show*. With the leaves on the trees beginning to turn, the hill slopes taking on a shade of burnished bronze, the wild geese heading south and the red deer stags at the rut, the seasons were definitely turning. Soon we would be turning the clocks back and that meant shorter days, and I wanted to describe a shorter hill day for the series. Stuchd an Lochain was ideal.

We started from the Loch an Daimh dam, or more correctly, the Giorra Dam. There were once two lochs here, Loch Giorra and Loch an Daimh, separated by a strip of land where there was a farmhouse and a tract of woodland. These were submerged below the waters when the dam was built and the waters raised, turning the two lochs into one. The Hydro-Electric Board has chosen to keep the name Giorra for the name of the dam, although the Ordnance Survey appears to prefer Loch an Daimh.

From the south end of the dam a faint path climbs grassy slopes south to reach the ridge above Coire Ban. A line of fence posts can be followed west to Creag an Fheadain from where a descent into a bealach is followed by an easy climb to Sron Chona Choirein. A broad mossy ridge now leads round the cliffs above Lochan nan Cat to the summit. If you get as good a day as we did, you'll be blessed with a full 360-degree panorama, with views of hills ranging from the Cairngorms to Ben Nevis, and the Buachaille to Ben Lawers. This summit has to be one of the finest viewpoints in the Southern Highlands.

So much for Stuchd an Lochain and its Corbett neighbours, but what about the other Munro of Meall Buidhe? Can you also combine it with a Corbett for a full day's outing? You can. I mentioned Cam Chreag, 2,828 feet/862 metres, earlier; it lies east of Meall Buidhe and is a superb viewpoint in its own right. To the west, the big Munros stand clear, Stuchd an Lochain and Meall Buidhe, one on either side of Loch an Daimh and the wild country beyond to the hills of Mamlorn and Orchy. To the north-west, across the Rannoch Moor, Ben Nevis is clearly visible. Cam Chreag connects easily with Meall Buidhe via a high bealach at the head of Coire Odhar and Meall a' Phuill, Meall Buidhe's south-eastern top.

If you think I'm going to finish this chapter on the storied Glen Lyon and vicinity without another tale you'll be wrong. In 1590, a local laird called Mad Colin Campbell of Meggernie apparently took a perverse delight in chasing a herd of goats over the edge of Stuchd an Lochain into the waters of Lochan nan Cat below. Campbell really earned his nickname as a madman when he tried to throw the shepherd over the edge as well.

4

TO KNOW BEING,
THE FINAL GRACE

Back in the mid-seventies, Hamish Brown urged me to read
a slim book about the Cairngorms. It was titled *The Living
Mountain*, and it was at a time when I was discovering the
Cairngorms for myself. I had just moved to Aviemore and
was thrilled and excited by the qualities of spaciousness
and height and relative remoteness of some of the hills.
The remoteness especially was something I was unused to.
Until then my mountain experience had been on the more
jagged peaks of the west, Lomond and the Trossachs, the
Crianlarich and Tyndrum hills, the Blackmount and Glen
Coe, hills where you can see a road from almost every peak.
The Cairngorms, particularly the Braeriach and Beinn Avon
plateaux, felt extremely remote, almost a land apart.

The author of *The Living Mountain* was Nan Shepherd,
perhaps best known today as the woman on the Bank of
Scotland five-pound note. Nan was a reasonably successful
novelist and poet, a good friend of Neil Gunn and a contemporary of Lewis Grassic Gibbon, but it was her work as a
'geopoet', if I may use such a term, that has been widely
acclaimed by literature experts and academics alike, as
well as many of us who love the hills. The focus of that
work, *The Living Mountain*, published in 1972 but written

during the forties, has enjoyed a resurgence in popularity in recent years, a renaissance championed by respected writers like the author and Cambridge academic Robert Macfarlane. Now, I don't claim to be an expert in literature and I'm certainly not an academic, but I am a writer and a mountaineer, in the broadest sense of the word, and while I find some of Nan Shepherd's writing to be almost impenetrable I've certainly found some aspects of the book fascinating, particularly those sections that chime with my own Cairngorm experiences.

At the time of publication, Nan Shepherd's book cast a new light on these big, burly mountains, and encouraged me to look at mountains, generally, in a different way. I began to focus more on the micro – the lichens, plants and birds – as opposed to simply concentrating on the big picture and the macho determination to bag summits. In many ways Nan Shepherd's writing about the Cairngorms made me open my eyes and refocus.

As I've suggested, there are sections of Nan's book that just lose me. To a lad from Govan, Zen Buddhism was a leftover from the hippy days of the sixties. But having said that, I thought it was worth examining some aspects of her poetic treatise, aspects that perhaps offer food for thought for those of us who climb hills, ideas and notions that, for me, provided a pathway to other works of transcendent mountain literature by the likes of Barry Lopez, Ralph Waldo Emerson, H. D. Thoreau, Aldo Leopold and Gary Snyder.

In recent times *The Living Mountain* has been championed by Rob Macfarlane who knows the Cairngorms intimately. His grandparents spent their retirement years in

Tomintoul, and Rob spent his holidays there as a youngster, wandering the hills by day and poring over his grandfather's mountaineering books at night. Sir Edward Peck enjoyed a long and illustrious career as a diplomat but his heart was in the mountains. When he was eight years old he met the Everest veteran Charles Bruce on the summit of the Dents du Midi in the French Alps, a meeting that inspired a lifetime of mountaineering in the Greater Ranges and in Scotland. His love of wild places was a grand inheritance to pass to his grandson.

Rob wrote a foreword to the most recent printing of *The Living Mountain*, identifying two seminal ideas in Nan's writing: 'We don't walk up a mountain, but into it', and secondly: 'we must abandon the summit as the organising principle of mountains.' There are resonances of John Muir's philosophy at work here. The great conservationist once wrote, 'Going out is actually going in', and Nan takes that thought a little further and eventually reaches the conclusion that the 'living mountain' lives because of our conscious engagement with it. 'As I penetrate more deeply into the mountain's life, I penetrate more deeply into my own ... I am not out of myself, but in myself. I am.'

There's more than a touch of eastern religious thinking here, and that doesn't surprise me. Buddhists, for example, have a far greater awareness of our relationship with nature than any other philosophy or religion, and that was recognised by another great Scottish writer, W. H. Murray, whose books, *Mountaineering in Scotland* and *Undiscovered Scotland*, have hugely inspired so many of my generation – but I'll come back to W. H. Murray later if I may.

There's possibly another explanation for Nan's line of thinking. Because of the very nature of the glaciated, sculpted shapes of the Cairngorms, there is often a sense of 'going in' as opposed to 'walking over.' Consider the cathedral-like An Garbh Coire, or Coire Etchachan, or the great natural cradles that hold Loch Avon and Loch Einich. Inspired by this concept of 'going in' to the mountain, I once made a girdle traverse of Braeriach, a long mid-height journey around and 'in' through the ten great corries of Braeriach. I began in the An Garbh Coire, the big rough corrie, and walking in an anti-clockwise direction stumbled and scrambled through Coire Bhrochain, the Lairig Ghru, Coire Gorm, Coire Beanaidh, Coire Ruadh, Coire Bogha-cloiche and finally Coire nan Clach before climbing out to the Einich Cairn summit of Braeriach.

It was an astonishingly revealing expedition that took me two full days, and my overnight camp by Loch Coire an Lochain gave me a magnificent sunset. By the end of the expedition my right leg felt longer than my left, but I felt I had come to know Braeriach in a much more intimate way than if I had just climbed to the summit. I felt I had truly explored its corries, its ridges, its lochans, its streams, its crags and its plateau, much more than by merely traipsing to the top. I had slept on its flanks too, the ultimate connection. I had a copy of *The Living Mountain* with me on that walk and as I lay in my sleeping bag, close to the edge of the corrie's lochan, I read with some delight that Nan too had visited the same spot:

> On one toils, into the hill. Black scatter of rock, pieces large as a house, pieces edged like a grater. A rough bit of going. And there at last is the loch, held tight back against the precipice. Yet as I turned, that September day, and looked back through the clear air,

I could see straight out to ranges of distant hills. And that astonished me. To be so open and yet so secret! Its anonymity – Loch of the Corrie of the Loch, that is all – seems to guard this surprising secrecy. Other lochs, Avon, Morlich and the rest, have their distinctive names. One expects of them an idiosyncrasy. But Loch of the Corrie of the Loch, what could there be there? A tarn like any other. And then to find this distillation of loveliness.

That journey taught me something else. You don't have to reach the summit of a hill to connect with it. Of all the mountains that I have climbed both here and abroad, my memories of reaching summit cairns tend to be hazy and blurred. On the other hand, I can recall, in glorious technicolour, various events that occurred on the way to the summit. Reaching a ridge, passing through a high bealach, glimpsing patches of moss campion or snow gentian or seeing a golden eagle fly on outstretched wings. These are the diamonds that sparkle in my memory.

Such experiences enrich a mountain day, but our ingrained mountain instincts still urge us to strive for the summit cairn, to reach the top, to conquer the mountain (how I loathe that term, with its military overtones), to achieve. The unwritten rule suggests we can't tick off the mountain name in our (Munro or Corbett, or Graham or whatever) book or boast that we have actually climbed it unless we physically touch the summit cairn, and for many hillwalkers not touching a summit cairn means the day has been a failure.

'To aim for the highest point is not the only way to climb a mountain', Nan Shepherd asserts. 'We must abandon the summit as the organising principle of mountains. The talking tribe, I find, want sensation from the mountain – not in Keats's sense. Beginners, not unnaturally, do the same – I did myself. They want the startling view, the horrid pinnacle – sips of beer and tea instead of milk. Yet often the mountain gives itself most completely when I have no destination, when I reach nowhere in particular, but have gone out merely to be with the mountain as one visits a friend with no intention but to be with him.'

Before you all start throwing your Munros Tables at me it's worth recalling that Nan Shepherd wrote *The Living Mountain* in the forties, although the book wasn't actually published until 1972. By 1949 only fifteen people were recorded by the Scottish Mountaineering Club as having climbed all the Munros. The Munro-bagging phenomenon didn't really begin until later and while folk did 'collect' summits in those early days there was a much greater emphasis on exploration, as Nan Shepherd's exploits in *The Living Mountain* suggest, and there can be few places better for high-level explorations as the Cairngorms. The whole range is rich in what Nan Shepherd called 'The Recesses'. Comparatively few people are impressed by gazing up at the Cairngorms from below, unlike the Skye Cuillin, or the Glen Coe peaks, or the ancient behemoths of Torridon. The Cairngorms require you to expend some effort before they reveal their true glory. It's only when you reach the heights of the high-level plateaux that you can gaze down, over edges and corrie rims into deep chasms and trenches, recesses of rock and scree and the Cyclopean masonry of the granite cliffs and 'fiacaills'.

Recently, during one of those quirky weather changes that characterise our new overheating climate, I took advantage of a good forecast, climbed Cairn Gorm via its Windy Ridge and dropped down snow-covered slopes to the spread of high undulating ground that rises fairly gently towards Beinn Macdui. I had no intention of climbing to any other summit. I simply wanted to wander, to roam freely, linger by an upland burn and, when the opportunity arose, gaze into the dark depths of the massif's recesses.

Coire an t-Sneachda is one of those recesses. Deeply scalloped by glaciation it is typical of the archetypal mountain cirque, complete with not one but two corrie lochans. Although snow still rimmed the corrie edge it was free of cornices, so I had ample opportunity to gaze over the sudden and abrupt rim into a brink of air and space. A thousand feet below me the lochans, still shaded by the high crags of the corrie's headwall, lay like pools of quicksilver in their cradle of boulder fields. I remember skinny-dipping in those lochans in years gone by and wondered if they would still be there by the end of the summer that stretched ahead? In most years at least one of the lochans dries up. In dry summers it's not unknown for them both to vanish.

The plateau tilts towards another rim, less distinct than the corrie's but nevertheless another edge, and another recess, bigger, grander, cradling a stretch of water much larger than those in Coire an t-Sneachda. I can't think of another loch in Scotland that has as grand and wild a setting as Loch Avon, framed as it is by plunging precipices: Stac an Fharaidh, Stag Rocks, Hell's Lum Crag, Shelterstone Crag, Carn Etchachan, Stacan Dubha and Crag Dhubh. The classic view of the loch, from the point where the Feith Buidhe crashes over granite slabs of Creag na Feithe Buidhe is a fine one with the long and narrow loch stretching towards the Strath Nethy saddle, but I prefer to view it in the other direction, from the foot of the loch to its head. Here the square-cut shape of the Shelterstone Crag and the steep silver slabs that form the head of this massive corrie blunt the narrow trench that cradles the loch. It has all the feel and atmosphere of a cathedral, or a throne room of the Cairngorm mountain gods.

A viewpoint that offers a different, and more precarious, stance is from a narrow platform beside the dark gully of Hell's Lum, just south-west of the path that descends Coire Domhain. From here you get more of a sense of height and a distinct notion of the vertical world of the rock climber. It's definitely not a stance for those who suffer from vertigo. A less exposed view is from the flat area above Stag Rocks. Sit yourself on one of the flat granite slabs and peer down towards the loch. Let your eyes roam upwards to the tapering lines of Carn Etchachan and into Coire Etchachan where you will glimpse another deep recess and another shining level: the waters of Loch Etchachan, lapping the 1,000-metre contour.

Beyond lies Beinn Macdui, Scotland's second-highest mountain, with its large, sprawling summit dome. The real character of Macdui lies not in its summit plateau but in its corries. Coire Etchachan is the finest and its close neighbour, Coire Sputain Dearg, is also spectacular. The view south from the latter cliff-girt corrie is magnificent, sweeping down ochreous miles to the verdant green of the Luibeg pines. Above Coire Sputain Dearg another smaller corrie is sculpted from the steep crags and it cradles one of the Cairngorms' four Lochan Uaines, the green lochans.

Across the steep-sided trench of the Lairig Ghru from Macdui lies Braeriach, the bridled upland, and it's an airy place, essentially the apex of at least five distinct corries.

Stand by the summit cairn on a clear day and gaze down the long, empty miles of Glen Dee, past the bulk of Beinn Macdui and the long arm of Carn a' Mhaim on one side, and the angular outline of Cairn Toul on the other, and you'll be overwhelmed by a sensation of space and distance, an emotion that wills you to fly. Launch yourself instead around the rim of this ginormous corrie that fills the space at your feet. This is An Garbh Coire, the big, rough corrie; it's a simple enough name and yet one which manages to evoke all the wildness and barrenness and stark ruggedness of the place.

Follow the rim, with boulder-covered slopes easing off to your right. What utter contrast between those relatively easy slopes and the great cliffs of red granite to your left, thrusting up from the rough corrie in pinnacles and buttresses and spires into snow wreaths which circle the upper tiers until summer. You'll cross the infant Dee hereabouts, a natural miracle in hydrodynamics, a phenomenon that is something of a mystery to me. This great inanimate mound of rock and gravel, scree and moss somehow harnesses the fluids and moisture of the air, soaks it all up like a sponge, then, by unseen energies, forces it though the surface of the ground in the form of a bubbling stream, chuckling at its own unlikely birth here on the roof of Scotland. Half a mile later its voice changes, a forced maturity, as it crashes and surges over the lip of the corrie to begin its long meandering course, passing Peterculter, Nan Shepherd's birthplace, a suburb of the city of Aberdeen, to the North Sea.

In her works of fiction, *The Quarry Wood*, *The Weatherhouse* and *A Pass in the Cairngorms*, Nan portrays the possibilities of freedom for her characters, especially the female characters, and in a sense she does the same in *The*

Living Mountain, this time not for fictional characters, but for herself. At the very end of that book she wrote:

> I believe that I now understand in some small measure why the Buddhist goes on pilgrimage to a mountain. The journey is itself part of the technique by which the god is sought. It is a journey into Being; for as I penetrate more deeply into the mountain's life, I penetrate also into my own. For an hour I am beyond desire. It is not ecstasy, that leap out of the self that makes man like a god. I am not out of myself, but in myself. I am. To know Being, this is the final grace accorded from the mountain.

Early in my career I was invited to give an after-dinner speech to Scottish Natural Heritage. I quickly realised that a large part of my audience, the more scientific, objective types, looked a bit vague as I enthusiastically rhapsodised about the more poetic and philosophical side of the Scottish hills and wild places. One or two respected and well-known naturalists actually became quite rude and dismissive, but their contempt didn't put me off. I know that scientific objectivity and assessment are very important in the work of naturalists and ecologists, but I am also very aware of the more 'spiritual' side of my own relationship with hills and mountains, an aspect of wild places that has been recorded and discussed by generations of writers, including the Scots-born environmentalist John Muir.

His peers often reprimanded him because his writing was too spiritual. As a result of this criticism, some of his papers, where he clearly tried to appeal to the scientific community of the time, were quite dull in comparison to the usual colourful and enthusiastic nature of his popular writing. Another author who was criticised for sounding too spiritual was Scotland's finest writer on mountain matters, W. H. Murray.

Bill Murray was one of Scotland's best climbers in the thirties, so would have been a contemporary of Nan Shepherd. During World War Two he was captured by Rommel's troops in North Africa and taken to a prisoner-of-war camp in Czechoslovakia where he met a young British officer by the name of Herbert Buck who introduced him to the concept of the Perennial Philosophy, 'a perspective within the philosophy of religion which views each of the world's religious traditions as sharing a single, universal truth on which foundation all religious knowledge and doctrine has grown.' Aldous Huxley would later, in 1945, publish a book on the subject.

Perennial Philosophy hugely influenced Bill Murray's writings, and indeed his way of life, so much so that he spent some time training to be a Benedictine monk at Buckfast Abbey in Devon. Some aspects of the priesthood didn't appeal to him, and he eventually took the decision to become a full-time writer instead, one who leaned heavily on the more nebulous aspects of religion that we often define as 'spirituality'. We tend to think that Eastern philosophical influences on the west occurred in the heady, hippy days of the sixties, but it's quite clear that this kind of thinking deeply influenced the likes of Bill Murray and Nan Shepherd much earlier in the century. Indeed, Rob Macfarlane described *The Living Mountain* as a 'sensual exploration' of the range and suggested that it had quite altered his own view of the Cairngorms, an area he knew well. One factor that stands out for me throughout *The Living Mountain* is Nan Shepherd's preference for the journey, rather than her eventual destination. What was important for her was simply to be there. Like Muir and Murray and many, many others, simply being amongst mountains was the main appeal. To know Being, the final grace accorded from the mountain.

'Here then may be lived a life of the senses so pure, so untouched by any mode of apprehension but their own, that the body may be said to think. Each sense heightened to its most exquisite awareness, is in itself total experience. This is the innocence we have lost, living in one sense at a time to live all the way through. At first, mad to recover the tang of heights, I made always for the summits, and would not take time to explore the recesses,' but like Robert Louis Stevenson who said 'I travel for travel's sake, the great affair is to move,' she soon realised the real rewards were to be found in the journey rather than the destination.

> . . . often the mountain gives itself most completely when I have no destination, when I reach nowhere in particular, but have gone out merely to be with the mountain as one visits a friend with no intention but to be with him.

There is no better mountain range in the country to do just that. My very first expedition in the Cairngorms was a long backpacking trip over the high tops and I've lost count of how many camps I've enjoyed on those high plateaux, thrilled by the vast, black skies and stars that took my breath away by their sheer intensity. Remembering Nan Shepherd's advice, I've also enjoyed lower-level expeditions, although in this first case 'lower' levels may be a slight exaggeration. The plan was beautifully simple, to wander around the central massif of the Cairngorms following the trench-like passes of the two Lairigs, the Lairig an Laoigh and the better-known Lairig Ghru. This circular long-distance route can be split nicely over two days but in fact this is no low-level ramble. The summit of the Lairig Ghru is in excess of 2,700 feet/823 metres and it can snow there almost any month of the year.

With strong winds forecast, Gina and I reckoned we might be in for a battering, but what we didn't expect was a battle with raging rivers and unseasonal deep snow. The Lairig an Laoigh is generally regarded as the easier of the two passes, running from the Pass of Ryvoan across high ground to the River Avon and down Glen Derry to Derry Lodge. From there it's about an hour to the Lairig Ghru where our plan was to head north again, to the glacial overflow that goes by the name of Chalamain Gap. From there good footpaths would return us to our starting point at Glenmore Lodge.

The gale-force winds were, unknown to us, having a much more serious effect on the Cairn Gorm snowpack than they were on us. An old song suggests, 'the snow it melts the soonest when the wind begins to sing,' and this wind was singing like a banshee. In turn the snow was melting fast and the levels of the burns and streams were rising fast. As we fought our way closer to the River Avon, we became increasingly convinced we wouldn't be able to make the crossing but, unexpectedly, it was a mere trickle and we stepped across with dry feet. The reason for our good fortune? The source of the river, Loch Avon, was still frozen solid.

With increasing confidence, we climbed over the summit of the Lairig an Laoigh into the head of Glen Derry, where the first of our aquatic barriers appeared. A side stream, the Glas Allt Mor, came crashing down the hillside from Beinn a' Chaorainn, and we had to climb high up the hillside looking for somewhere narrow to cross. Eventually, hanging onto our trekking poles for balance, we entered the crashing waters and sidestepped across. The water was thigh-deep and the pressure threatened to topple us, but climbing the hillside to cross the stream provided one big bonus. The increased elevation gave us a much better view across the glen of the Derry Burn to the beautifully shaped Coire an Lochain Uaine.

I mentioned earlier that there are four Lochain Uaines, or green lochans, in the Cairngorms: one in Ryvoan, one above Coire Sputain Dearg of Macdui, one on Cairn Toul and this one below Derry Cairngorm. In his excellent guide to the Cairngorms, published by the Scottish Mountaineering Trust, the late Adam Watson mentioned a popular Gaelic song, *Aig Allt an Lochain Uaine*, by the stream of the green lochan, a song that was apparently very popular in the 1700s. It was written by William Smith, otherwise known as Uilleam Rynuie, whose name was an anglicised version of the name of his croft in Abernethy, Ruighe Naoimhe, the Place of Saints.

Affleck Gray, in his book *The Big Grey Man of Ben Macdui*, describes him as 'a man of bold and resolute character, with a powerful physique capable of enduring any amount of fatigue and exposure.' Smith was an infamous deerstalker and poacher who, it was said, was fond of raiding the herds of the Forest of Mar. He built a small howff, his 'stalking bothy', close to the burn that trickled down from the green lochan, a place he grew to love. Adam Watson suggested his song should rank as the finest song of the Cairngorms, and Affleck Gray said it was 'declared faultless by the most competent critics of the time', a hymn to these high and wild places. Also known as the Cairngorm

Poet, legend has it that Smith perished in an avalanche in the An Garbh Coire of Braeriach. Other sources suggest he joined the army and served under the leadership of Sir John Muir, eventually dying at Portsmouth shortly after the retreat from Corunna.

Various authorities offer slightly different and fairly unsatisfactory translations of *Aig Allt an Lochan Uaine*, so I asked Scotland's best-known Gaelic singer, Julie Fowlis, if she would translate the first verse for me. This is what she and her friend Jo MacDonald came up with, a meaningful translation of a lovely poem that anyone who has spent a night in a warm and cosy howff would appreciate. My thanks to Julie and Jo – mòran taing.

Aig Allt an Lochan Uaine
Gun robh mi uair a' tàmh
'S ged bha 'n t-àite fuar
Bha 'n fhàrdach fuathasach blàth;
Ged thigeadh gaoth o thuath orm
Is cathadh luath on Àird
Bhiodh Allt an Lochan Uaine
Le fhuaim gam chur gu pràmh.

At the Stream of the Green Loch
I once lived
and although the place was cold
the house was very warm;
Though we might be assailed by wind from the north
and snow coming fast from the Aird,
the murmuring of the Stream of the Green Loch
would lull me to sleep.

77

By the time we reached the shelter of the Scots Pines at the southern end of Glen Derry, the wind had dried us off. We bypassed the boarded-up Derry Lodge and the old house at Luibeg where Bob Scott the keeper once kept a bothy; a sanctuary for the climbers and walkers who began to visit the Cairngorms after the war years. The late Bill Brooker once told me about a visit to Bob's bothy on Hogmanay 1949. The temperature was about twenty below zero, so cold that the hole in the ice on the water bucket had to be reopened every few hours. Despite the weather the bothy was bulging with visiting climbers.

One group, who all insisted on wearing kilts, was christened by Bob 'the Horrible Hielanders'. One of the group was a young student from Aberdeen called Tom Patey, a larger-than-life character who later became one of Scotland's finest mountaineers. From his very first ascent on Lochnagar's Douglas-Gibson Gully in 1950 to his last climb, on the Maiden sea stack in Sutherland, which led to his premature death in 1970 at the age of thirty-eight, he was a major player on the Scottish and international climbing scene. An Ullapool GP, Tom Patey was also a singer, story-teller, songwriter, pianist and accordionist and was always the life and soul of a party, particularly at Bob Scott's. It was a constant source of amazement that Patey could carouse all night but be up and away by dawn to go climbing. He was as hard as Lochnagar granite, aided a little, perhaps, by the amphetamines he allegedly prescribed himself.

I love this stretch of Gleann Laoigh Bheag, to give it its Sunday name, with its red-barked pines, so deeply rooted and solid to the gales and the tumbled slopes of heather and bilberry.

Gina and I crossed another raging torrent, but by a bridge

this time, and looked for somewhere to camp, as we were ready to call it a day. Two weary backpackers were delighted to sink into cosy sleeping bags and enjoy an early night, comforted in the knowledge that our return through the Lairig Ghru would not involve any major river crossings.

The Lairig an Laoigh splits the main granite massif of the Cairngorms and provides a route of great antiquity that once resounded to the movement of cattle. Up in those roads in the clouds, Highland cattle drovers bullied and beguiled their shaggy beasts, so well adapted to the austerity of the high country, over the boulder-strewn screes of the pass to the great trysts of Falkirk and Crieff. Caterans and robbers also knew the route intimately and left their own mark with such place names as Allt Preas nam Meirleach, the stream of the thieves' bush, or Cnapan nam Meirleach, the small knoll of the thieves, close to where we camped.

For our second day we were broken in gently, past Lochan Feith nan Sgor, appropriately the lochan of bog of the rocky hills, and into the Lairig Ghru itself. Beyond the footbridge that crosses the River Dee to Corrour bothy, looking incredibly tiny below the soaring cliffs of Bod an Deamhain, or Devil's Point, the narrow confines of the pass begin to widen out until An Garbh Choire, the big rough corrie, displays itself as a great scooped-out hollow biting hungrily into three Munros: Braeriach, Sgor an Lochain Uaine and Cairn Toul.

As the steep sides of the Lairig began to press in on us we were cruelly reminded that in this Arctic environment life is sustained by slimmer threads. The summit of the Lairig often takes people by surprise. It's a boulder-strewn defile, which often acts as a wind funnel, blowing snow into contorted and confusing shapes. Today so much deep snow covered the pass that we experienced a deep but unspoken relief on passing the Pools of Dee, at the summit of the pass, to begin the long descent to the Chalamain Gap and on to the Glenmore Forest. From there, superb footpaths through the trees led us back to Glenmore Lodge, the end of a wonderful circular route that offers a real sense of the remote grandeur of these Cairngorms passes.

However grand the passes may be, the high plateaux of the Cairngorms are what sets these hills apart from other Scottish mountains, and if there is one Cairn Gorm summit I never tire of visiting, it's Beinn Macdui, the second-highest mountain in the United Kingdom, but a top that is no more than the high point of the sprawling plateau that lies between Cairn Gorm and its southern rim. I've lost count of how many times I've visited the summit but I never grow weary of it. Many moons ago, when I worked for an Aviemore-based company called Highland Guides, I brought folk up here twice a week, every Tuesday and Thursday. I've climbed this mountain more often than any other and I love the place. I love its spaciousness, its vast, open skies and how it drops abruptly into the deep chasm of the Lairig Ghru. I love its views that can be as widespread as Morven in Caithness to the Lammermuirs in Lothian, and I love the fact that you can wander its flanks in any number of different ways; from Cairn Gorm, from Derry Lodge in the south via Carn a' Mhaim or by Derry Cairngorm, or up the steep inclines beside the March Burn from the Lairig Ghru.

The standard route from the car park on Cairn Gorm has so many spectacular views that the walk becomes a series of visual superlatives. Other mountains in Scotland may be steeper, or more pointedly dramatic, but there is nowhere else you can walk at over 3,000 and 4,000 feet for such long periods, with a wide, open sky above you and extraordinary views all around. There simply isn't anything to compare with it in these islands, but the effects of popularity are fast becoming apparent. On our walk from Coire Cas across the Cairngorm plateau by drought-shrivelled Lochan Bhuidhe, my companion, who hadn't been on these slopes for some years, remarked on the increased erosion of the footpaths, the number of unnecessary waymarking cairns that line the route and the number of stone shelters that exist on Macdui's summit slopes and on the ridge leading to the northern top.

Over a dozen years ago the Government agency that preceded the National Park Authority, the Cairngorms Partnership, singularly failed to live up to its promises of removing all these man-made eyesores. The National Park Authority, apparently more concerned with other issues and perhaps unsure of its role in nature and landscape conservation, has fared little better. Many believe these ad hoc shelters and waymarking cairns should be removed and the slopes of this important mountain returned to their natural wild grandeur.

During my six-year tenure as Chairman of the Nevis Partnership we worked alongside the landowners, the John Muir Trust and other stakeholders to clear all the eyeball-searing detritus from the summit of Ben Nevis. Surely, our second-highest summit deserves nothing less. Can the Cairngorms National Park learn lessons from the Nevis Partnership? I'm sure it can.

From the massive summit cairn, and intoxicated by the hot sun and rarefied air at the summit, we made our way down scree-strewn slopes to the top of Coire Sputain

Dearg, searching for dwarf cudweed, the wee brother of the edelweiss. A spring, seeping from the sun-scorched ground, bubbled through a bed of golden lichens before maturing into a series of small, sky-blue pools, the shining levels that are magnified a thousand times in the lower Loch Etchachan, whose stony shores caress the three-thousand-foot contour.

We wondered at the beauty of the place and, in that wonder, there was an instinctive recognition of the existence of order, a determined pattern behind the behaviour of things, a celebration of harmony. For those few hours we felt part of it. In a land where the basic elements of rock, air and water so heavily predominate, it sometimes seems odd that there should be an illusion of welcome. Vast wind-scoured slopes and gashes of glens offer little in the way of comfort or ease but, up here, the untroubled waters and ancient stones cast a spell as calming as they are dramatic. The high lonely lochans reflect the mood of the skies, which in turn dictate the future, ordained by the winds and clouds of Biera, the goddess of weather and storms. Such experiences are very special.

As they did with Nan Shepherd, these places have taught me the simplicity of 'being', uncluttered by everyday things and thoughts. An ascending grace is conceded by these vast lands to all who are prepared to seek. It's a powerful lesson but you must consider something more, equally as important. While these high places are powerful in their own way, they are also sensitive, even fragile. Our tenuous relationship needs to be nurtured. Along with a small sparrow-like bird, the snow bunting, and tiny deep-rooted plants and great granite mountains, we belong to a biotic community and it's only when we view our relationship from that stance that we can begin to understand it and benefit from it.

These Cairngorms lochs, the shining levels, provide another source of wonder. Further on, deep in its own craggy sand-fringed cradle, lay Loch Avon, the unchallenged jewel of the Cairngorms. The path that drops down into Loch Avon's basin is badly worn and dangerously eroded but fails to diminish the Gothic splendour of the place. The sheer walls of the Sticil, the square-cut granite edifice at the head of Loch Avon, above its skirts of tumbled rock and white slabs, casts its dark shadow wide but not wide enough to subdue the joyous songs of the waterfalls crashing from the plateau. The green meadow, the meandering stream, the white sands that fringe the translucent jade of the loch, all contrast vividly with the steep rock walls above. This is a place closed in and jealously guarded by the mountains and of all the landscapes I know this is the one I cherish most. It's here you'll find the Shelter Stone, Scotland's best-known howff.

Prime Minister Gladstone reputedly sheltered below its solid bulk and it's said that the Prince of Wales was fond of bivvying there on school trips from Gordonstoun. Other residents were less salubrious: generations of vagabonds and itinerant rogues on the run from the law of the day, and of course modern climbers and hillwalkers. Crouching over a jumble of boulder scree below the Sticil, the Shelter Stone is an enormous rock that forms a substantial roof over a natural horizontal cleavage, a cave which is reputed to have once held 'eighteen armed men'. The men of yesteryear must have been very small, or perhaps the Shelter Stone has moved and reduced the space below it. I can't imagine more than half a dozen average-sized individuals sheltering in there

83

nowadays, but the fact is that many still do, and indeed enjoy the experience, despite the ghostly legends of many years.

In 1924 a Visitors Book was left in the cavern and many volumes are kept in the Cairngorm Club's library in Aberdeen. Some of the entries make fascinating reading. One party claimed to have experienced a rather strange encounter with the legendary water horse of Loch Avon. Hearing a strange stamping and whinnying during the night, they went outside to investigate and saw 'a great white horse with flashing eyes and a dripping mane. No other than the supernatural Water Horse or Each Uisge from the unplumbed depths of Loch Avon . . .'

In her fine book, *Speyside to Deeside*, published in 1956, Brenda G. Macrow wrote:

> For my own part, I have met a young man who, while spending a night under the Shelter Stone alone, heard a climber approach at about midnight, pause at the entrance, and then go away again. He called, but there was no answer. Emerging quickly from the cave, he could see no sign of anyone (although it was brilliant moonlight) and no footprints in the snow.

An old pal of mine, the late Syd Scroggie from Strathmartine near Dundee, claims to have once sat outside the howff and watched a giant figure walk towards the loch and simply vanish into thin air. Syd believes he saw the image of Fearlas Mor, the Great Grey Man of Ben Macdui, but could it have been the dreaded Fahm, a grisly monster that was once believed to haunt the summits around Loch Avon? James Hogg, the Ettrick Shepherd, in his poem 'Glen-Avin from The Queen's Wake' tells the fearsome story.

To Know Being, the Final Grace

...Yet still at eve, or midnight drear,
When wintry winds begin to sweep,
When passing shrieks assail thine ear,
Or murmours by the mountain steep;

When from the dark and sedgy dells,
Come eldritch cries of wildered men;
Or wind-harp at thy window swells -
Beware the sprite of Avin Glen!

The climb out of the Avin Glen, or the Loch Avon basin, on another steep and eroded path, leads to the grassy extravagances of Coire Domhain and the edge of the plateau before it drops into Coire an t-Sneachda, the snowy corrie with its pools and rock rubble and echoes of climbs in both summer and winter. The memories of those climbing years always embrace me as I descend the Goat Track. This footpath has become so badly worn that it is now potentially dangerous, but despite the underfoot problems I am always overwhelmed by love for these places and how badly I want to see them protected from man's extravagances.

As I left the bowl of Coire an t-Sneachda my whispered prayer, thrown at random to the mountain gods, was that the Cairngorms National Park will overcome these extravagances and contrivances. Like many others I need these places like lifeblood, but the creation of National Parks comes with huge responsibilities. If success is measured in the number of visitors to an area, we must be prepared to repair the unintentional damage caused by the boots of all those visitors.

The Cairngorms will not be worthy of the title of National

Park if we can't protect them from continual degradation. I would urge the National Park Authority Board members, the councillors, the economists, the local entrepreneurs and the community developers, to memorise the words of the late W. H. Murray, Scotland's finest ever mountain writer and conservationist, who said: 'the human privilege is to take decisions for more than our own good; our reward, that it turns out to be best for us too.'

5

SPIRIT OF THE SPEY

Greylag geese grazed in the fields that roll down to the River Spey, and snowdrops and crocuses brightened the road verges. A pale green tint on the birches suggested the promise of spring but, less than a thousand feet above, the snow still lay deep and the wind had a razor edge to it. The breezes that blow off Ben Rinnes, the north-eastern terminal of the Grampians, are legendary.

Nearby Ballindalloch Castle dates from the mid-sixteenth century but a local tale suggests the stonemasons and builders had a hard time during its construction. No sooner had the walls reached a certain height than they were knocked down by some unseen force. This happened so many times that the Laird set up a special night watch to discover who was responsible. Early in the morning, the story goes, a great wind swirled down from Ben Rinnes and not only blew the newly built walls down but pitched the Laird and his cronies into a holly bush. Three times a demoniacal voice was heard above the rushing of the wind, saying, 'Build on the cow haugh'. The Laird, thinking what might happen if he ignored the warning, built his new castle on its present lower, less attractive site instead.

It could have been the same demoniacal voice that was trying to convince me to stay in the warmth of the car rather than expose myself to the raw coarseness of the north wind. The mischievous breeze was already drifting powder snow across the narrow Glack Harness road between Ben Rinnes and Meikle Conval, but tantalising glimpses of blue skies were enough to cast out the demon voice and turn my thoughts to the demon drink instead. Lying just a few miles south-west of Dufftown, Ben Rinnes is positioned in the epicentre of Speyside whisky country. Someone once wrote that while Rome may have been built on seven hills, Dufftown was built on seven stills, and from the 2,756-foot/840-metre summit of Rinnes you can look down on over a dozen distillery towns and villages: Aberlour, Keith, Cromdale, Dufftown, Rothes, Knockando, Ballindalloch, Craigellachie, Carron, Glenlivet, Tomnavoulin and Advie. All are associated with names that stir the blood of any whisky enthusiast: Balvenie, Glenfarclas, Glenlivet, the Mortlach, Cragganmore, Tamdhu, Glenrothes, Glenfiddich, Carndow, Tamnavullin. These are the epithets of the waters of life and lifeblood of the entire regions of Moray, Nairn and Banffshire.

Indeed, this major whisky-producing area extends about fifty miles to the west and twenty-five south of the Moray Firth, nourished by the waters of both the Monadh Liath and Grampian mountains. Not content with this distinction, Speyside whiskies are distinguishable from other malts by being lighter in 'weight' while still carrying their own character on the palate. Not as peaty and heavy as, say, Islay malts, the whiskies of Speyside are still full-flavoured, but in a more subtle, delicate way. Water of life indeed.

Tramping upwards through the snowdrifts it didn't seem too fanciful to imagine the basic elements of this *uisge bheatha* as provision of the mountain: the melting spring snows, the roaring burns, crystal clear and cold, the rolling slopes of peat that were once used to fire the distilleries, and the patchwork fields of barley below me in Glen Rinnes. Rising boldly above the Laich of Moray, Ben Rinnes climbs to a height of 2,756 feet/840 metres and offers magnificent views across the Moray Firth to the mountains of Ross, Sutherland and Caithness. On a clear day you can see Ben Nevis in the west, Buchan Ness in the east and, beyond Corryhabbie Hill on the opposite side of Glen Rinnes, the horizon formed by the outline of Lochnagar and the distinct arc of the Cairngorms.

From Glack Harness a track then a narrower footpath runs all the way to the quaintly named summit, the Scurran of Lochterlandoch, offering a glorious afternoon's walk, the comparative ease of which is out of all proportion to the mountain's height. The name of the hill comes from the Gaelic Beinn Rinneis, which possibly means 'headland hill', but the word 'rinn' in Gaelic means a sharp point and while this north-eastern hill couldn't really be described as pointed it does have distinctive granite tors on its summit which give it a spiky appearance. It's a shapely hill nevertheless, its slopes easing themselves gradually down to the waters of the River Spey on its north side and considerably more steeply on its southern, Glen Rinnes, side.

Ben Rinnes was once known locally as Babbie's Moss. 'Babbie' was a local lass, one Barbara McIntosh who, in the 1750s, lived nearby at Rhinachat Farm, a couple of miles from Aberlour. Sadly, Barbara took her own life after her husband left her. She apparently hanged herself on a tree close to Ben Rinnes. As a suicide, Barbara couldn't be buried in consecrated ground, so the summit of Ben Rinnes was chosen as her final resting place and her grave dug at a spot known then as the Three Lairds Boundaries. The weather was horrendous as the funeral party struggled uphill and Barbara was buried in a shallow grave. A cairn was built over her and she lay in peace until the middle of the following century.

Tradition tells us that a gang of Aberlour loons had doubts about the weird story surrounding the Moss of Babbie and decided to see for themselves the so-called grave of Barbara McIntosh. It was September 1855 when the lads clambered up with picks and spades and high hopes of putting an end to all the granny tales of yesteryear. They dug enthusiastically into the mossy soil till they came upon a coffin. That first ring of steel on wood sent a shudder up their spines. Was Granny right after all? There was only one way to find out.

Wielding their spades in a frenzy they cleared the battered coffin and prised it open to find the corpse of a woman, still remarkably fresh, with most of her features & hair intact. Had it not been for a spade piercing the coffin, the face of Barbara would have been remarkably distinct. Her petticoats and shawl were in perfect condition and the colours of the tartan plaid they had wrapped her body in, all those years ago, was as bright as they day it fell off the loom.

The body was reburied in its lonely grave until another generation with the same doubts disturbed the soil twenty years later. Nothing had changed but, this time, the ghoulish deed didn't go unnoticed by the local constabulary and the nineteenth-century grave-desecrators were severely reprimanded.

After consultations between the Captain of the Banffshire Police and the local authority, a Christian burial was arranged for Barbara in the old graveyard at Aberlour.

Despite my earlier reluctance to face the wintry conditions, it was curiously exhilarating to battle through the snow drifts and clouds and arrive by the summit tor just as the clouds broke. I could empathise with the Reverend James Hall of Edinburgh who, in 1803, also climbed Ben Rinnes on a cold and cloudy day. His written account tells of becoming lost and frightened but, when the mists cleared, he proclaimed the experience 'a secret enjoyment, a calm satisfaction and a religious fervour which no language can express.' Such quasi-spiritual encounters are not unusual in the mountains and I find it curious that even non-religious people often revert to pious language when describing magical encounters like this.

If you can arrange transport, a complete traverse of Ben Rinnes is well worthwhile, continuing west from the summit down the length of the Lynderiach Burn to Bridge of Avon. Alternatively, descend as I did, in a south-west direction to the Hill of Knockashalg before dropping south-eastwards to Wester Clashmarloch in Glen Rinnes and a quiet road walk back to Glack Harness. I think it's also highly appropriate, after climbing such a worthy hill as Ben Rinnes to toast yourself from a hip flask with a dram of the local *uisge bheatha*, the water of life that flows from the flanks of this north-eastern hill. As Robert Burns once wrote:

Freedom and whisky gang thegither,
Tak aff your dram.

I'm fortunate that my own fondness for the *uisge bheatha*, the water of life, has remained just that, a gentle flirtation that has never quite led me completely astray. A close friend of mine, a recovering alcoholic, once suggested to me that some people have a natural tolerance to alcohol, while others don't and can become easily addicted. I make this point because I'm sure there will be those who passionately believe that a celebration of the amber gold has no place in a book about the Scottish outdoors, and I agree . . . to a certain extent. I accept that drinking whisky in the wild outdoors can be irresponsible. It can dull your senses, increase the effects of altitude and make you significantly more prone to dehydration and hypothermia. I accept all these points, but having never knowingly conformed to the majority view in over forty-five years of writing about outdoor topics, I don't intend to start now. I like nothing better than a wee dram of whisky in my tent at the end of a backpacking day, and I don't really care who knows it.

Moderation is the key, and the aim. A measure of whisky, or maybe a couple just to be sociable, can create a very satis-fying ritual at the end of a wild camp meal, when the bones are weary and sleep is calling. It's then that whisky helps the 'connection with nature' process that I and many other backpackers seek. Unlike tea or coffee, whisky is a product of the land that I love and have hiked over and camped on for years. For me, drinking whisky in the wilds is as integral to the outdoor experience as washing your face in the dew or hugging a tree. You see, whisky is a genuine tour de force of nature. Of the water that percolates up through layers of peat that has been formed over centuries in wet and damp conditions, where flooding obstructs flows of oxygen from the atmosphere, slowing the rate of decomposition of the vegetation it is created from.

That water is then mixed with barley, one of the world's healthiest foods, and one that is particularly suited to the Scottish climate. What happens then is a source of consider-able mystique, almost magic. It's said that the first distil-lation of alcohol was discovered in the Middle East when

Arab alchemists were making cosmetics and perfume by distilling flowers. It's where the word comes from: al kuhul, or eye makeup! The Moors then brought the process to Europe, where it eventually spread to Ireland and Scotland and caught the attention of the Melrose-based magician, Michael Scott the Wizard, who some folk recognize as the father of Scotch whisky.

I've never really wanted to learn how whisky is made. I'm happy to let that remain a mystery, and that mystique adds to the notion that what I'm sipping is something rather special, something enigmatic and otherworldly, almost divine. I believe that is why a glass of whisky is so much more satisfying when I'm lying on a Highland hillside, gazing across a view of corrie and crag, listening to the primeval roar of rutting stags or the music of a tumbling burn. It's here, on the hill, that I can add a dash of ice-cold water, straight from a Highland spring, to release the flavour and complexities of the whisky itself.

As far as I'm concerned there are only three ways to drink whisky: neat, with a dash of water or with a lump of ice (although this decreases the temperature of the whisky and inhibits some of the characteristics). I suspect those who drink whisky with lemonade or Coca-Cola are simply trying to hide the taste of the whisky, and would be better imbibing some lesser beverage, like vodka or gin. I very rarely drink whisky during the day. For me it's a ritual that heralds the end of the day, a bedtime luxury that is as soothing and relaxing as anything I know, and as I slowly sip that golden liquid as day turns to night and shadows lengthen across the hillside, I come to understand that God is in his heaven and all is well on the land, as did the Celtic monks of old.

The process of whisky distilling has been explained to me

a number of times, most notably by my good friend, Alan Winchester, chief distiller at the Glenlivet distillery. As part of a television programme, Alan very kindly put together a 'home-made' still to demonstrate but, in the course of his explanation, I became more intrigued by his stories of the early distillers and whisky smugglers. Alan is a great story-teller and partly responsible for the creation of Smugglers' Trails in the Glenlivet area.

While Glenlivet looks to be a thriving agricultural and distilling centre today, two hundred years ago it was very different. The glen was remote and thought to be cold and wild, but it was these same characteristics that made it a haven for illicit whisky stills. Glenlivet bred a bold and self-reliant people who clung jealously to their old traditions.

Before distilling was legalised by the Excise Act of 1832 there were reckoned to be some two hundred illicit whisky stills operating in the confines of Glen Livet, and the smugglers did a roaring trade. Pack trains of laden ponies would regularly leave the confines of the glen, with an armed guard, and make their way to the coast to the ports of Banff and Buckie, or over the high passes of the Ladder Hills into Donside and the Cabrach. It wasn't unusual for the whisky to reach Edinburgh, where it was enjoyed by the nobility who referred to it as the 'Real Stuff'.

When George Smith of Glen Livet created his first 'legal' distillery the local distillers were furious. Death threats were made against him and legend records that he had to sleep for the rest of his life with two cocked pistols, one on either side of his pillow.

Keen to attract walkers to the glen, Alan Winchester, a keen hillwalker himself, worked with the local landowners, the

Crown Estate, to produce three walking routes to celebrate these Smugglers' Trails. The remotest and wildest of them, the Malcolm Gillespie Trail, is named after one of the gaugers, or excisemen. Gillespie used to boast of the forty-two scars he had on his body, all of them from wounds inflicted in skirmishes with the illegal distillers and smugglers. If nothing else, he was enthusiastic in the pursuit of his duties.

His trail begins at the East Auchavaich car park in Chapeltown of Glenlivet and circles the Braes of Glenlivet at the head of the glen. It's a low-level route, so I added on a little link of my own to include the Corbett of Carn Mor, making use of the right of way that runs over the Ladder Hills from the appropriately named Ladderfoot, via the Ladder Burn, and down Glen Nochty to Bellabeg in Donside. It's also one of the high-level routes the whisky smugglers would have followed on their journey south.

A good path runs up the narrow corrie that contains the Ladder Burn, all the way to the shallow bealach called Dun Muir, just to the north-east of the Corbett. It's an easy enough stroll to the trig point on Carn Mor, but the way is torn and ravaged by a series of deep peat hags, miserable for the hillwalker but vitally important for the smugglers. A plentiful supply of peat was essential to keep the stills burning, with as little tell-tale smoke as possible.

Views from Carn Mor are panoramic, from the butt end of Ben Avon in the west to Bennachie in the east, but the eyes tend to rest on the pastoral scenes in Glen Livet below, a direct contrast to the wildness and bare heather slopes that lead to Donside in the south. With its green fields and blocks of conifers it's difficult to imagine the Glen Livet of Malcolm Gillespie's day, when this place was remote and sequestered from society. Today it's a prosperous-looking glen that blends modern agricultural practice with good wildlife management, and the varied landscape provides many opportunities for watching birds and wildlife. You'll see crossbills, siskins, redpolls, goldcrests and long-tailed tits within the woodland areas, and black grouse on their margins. Mountain hares are commonly seen on the hills and red and roe deer can be seen on both the higher slopes and lower woodlands. This mix of countryside and open moorland provides for a variety of different birds of prey including kestrel, sparrowhawk, hen harrier and merlin, while buzzards are frequently observed in the sky.

George Smith's first legal distillery in Glen Livet dominates the area and Josie's Well still supplies it with mineral rich waters. It's sobering, if you'll forgive the pun, to sit by the spring and consider that from this simple source, bubbling up through the ground, over six million bottles of whisky are produced every year.

While the bubbling spring of Josie's Well supplies the distillery, so the other waters of Glenlivet, Glenfiddich, Knockando, Glen Avon, Glen Feshie, Glen Truim and many others feed the River Spey, a river I've lived beside for over forty years. Sadly, I'm ashamed to say, I don't really know it well. I've never really discovered its character or felt at one with it, never been touched by its spirit of place, even though I've fished it, regularly walked its banks, paddled a canoe and packraft on it and wandered its length from source to sea. I've never 'connected' with it in the same way as I've connected with mountains, but perhaps that's not too surprising. It's easier to get to know a mountain than a river, particularly one that is almost a hundred feisty miles in length. The Spey is the fastest-flowing river in Scotland, fed by the waters that drain the mighty Cairngorms on one side and the Monadh Liath on the other.

Until relatively recently, the Spey was known only for its salmon fishing but the advent of tourism, particularly in the latter half of the twentieth century, has promoted it to national significance with all kinds of sporting and recreational activities: hillwalking, climbing and skiing, and wildlife-watching in the bird-rich natural woodlands and marshes of its strath.

Promotion, particularly the high-octane marketing approach of the ski industry, has even given the region a new name. Spey Valley is a crude anglicisation of Strathspey and a source of ongoing controversy. Many deplore the crass commercialism of it, including me. It's a trend that has seen the most prominent of the mountains, Cairn Gorm itself, re-named Cairn Gorm Mountain by interests motivated only by making money. There are other elements of this mighty river that encourage a healthier familiarity.

Any enthusiast of Scottish country dancing or pipe music will be familiar with the 4/4 dance tune known as the Strathspey, and whisky aficionados will wax lyrical over a whole variety of malts. Whatever controversy rages about preferences, Lowland or Islands or the delights of Speyside, there is little doubt that the water of life in this north-eastern part of Scotland has a considerable influence on our economy.

Never a serious dancer, I'm still passionate about the music associated with the river, particularly the fiddle music of maestros like Scott Skinner. I've also enjoyed a few drams in my time, and more than a fair share of them have been Speyside malts, but even those enthusiasms haven't brought me to a meaningful relationship with the river.

Over the years I've come to realise that the only way to get to know a river like the Spey is to spend time *on* the water, rather than walking beside it, so I decided to get into a canoe to see if I could paddle a little closer to uncovering its secrets. Not being a canoeist, I needed help.

River guide David Craig is a great pal of mine who has worked on the river for almost forty years. I doubt if anyone knows it better. A highly qualified outdoor professional and canoe coach, he is passionately involved, caring for its environment and wildlife while all the time remaining respectful of fellow river users such as anglers. It doesn't take long to realise that Dave has an intimate knowledge of the Spey, not only its moods and characteristics but also its natural and social histories.

The Spey is much more than a meandering, hundred-mile course of water. It has had significant influence in the socio-economic history of the areas it flows through, from the twists and turns of its beginnings above the historic Garva Bridge; down through the hydroelectric scheme near Laggan; through the bird-rich meadows of the Spey Marshes and Loch Insh; and along the flatlands between Aviemore and Grantown where rafts of logs from the great forest of Rothiemurchus were once floated downstream to a flourishing ship-building industry at the mouth of the river.

Logging and shipbuilding have gone, but the twin industries of tourism and whisky distilling still give the river a worldwide reputation. However, I wanted to discover something more fundamental. I could learn about logging, whisky making and ornithology from the banks, but I wanted to know a little more about the spirit of the Spey, and I'm not just talking about whisky.

Dave first paddled here in 1964 but it was when he went to

work at Lothian Region's Lagganlia Outdoor Centre, near Kincraig, in 1976, that he thought of running canoe trips from Kincraig all the way to the sea. Those early descents were made in kayaks with vehicle back-up, but he later introduced open Canadian canoes, a self-sufficient way of carrying camping equipment and provisions. As we carried our canoes to the shores of Loch Insh, I asked him what the characteristics of the Spey were that made it so special?

'The Spey has everything you would want in a river,' he said. 'It's beautiful, every day is different, and it's the right length. My trips usually take about five days. It's historic and it's agricultural. You've got flat lands between Aviemore and Grantown as the river meanders through the big flood plain. Once you get to Grantown, moving seaward, you can virtually see it going downhill. Although you have to be a fairly competent paddler to complete a full descent, there's nothing in the river you'd class as life-threatening.

'I tend to think of the river as the Lady Spey. Quite mysterious at times, she's very beautiful, and very endearing. She almost embraces you, but at the same time plays little tricks. Like your ideal woman, she is a bit mischievous with occasionally stormy moods.'

Dave hails from Stonehaven and says his 'home river' is really the Dee but, while he reckons the Grampian river is one of the finest in the country, he's never developed the same kind of relationship with it.

'The Dee's a lovely river but it wouldn't be possible to paddle the whole of it,' he told me. 'You couldn't paddle from anywhere near its source, high on Braeriach, and even beyond the Linn of Dee it's quite turbulent. There are some big rapids at Dinnet, which are possible to paddle, but to me it's not really a touring river. I was first introduced to the

Spey in 1964 and it was as though she embraced me. I just loved her grandeur and majesty so, as a fourteen-year-old, I fell in love for the first time... with a river. Later I was delighted to come and work at Lagganlia because I could paddle the Spey on a regular basis.'

Dave worked at Lagganlia for twenty-five years and became Deputy Principal before leaving in 2000 to run his own river-guiding business, Spey Descent, facilitating open-canoe and camping journeys along the river. As I was to discover, you can learn the basic skills of paddling an open Canadian canoe fairly quickly.

'I get complete beginners coming on a descent. You don't need paddling experience, although it helps if you've done a bit, and it's good if people have a water confidence, but I've had some very nervous customers. People very quickly pick up the strokes and if they get a proper description of how the strokes work, and can learn by doing, it becomes straightforward.'

After spending thirty minutes or so on the flat waters of Loch Insh, Dave felt I was paddling competently enough to head downriver towards Aviemore. I nervously asked him if we would face any white water?

'The lovely thing about the Spey is the variety,' he said, with a reassuring smile. 'I usually start our descents here on Loch Insh, and I refer to the stretch between here and Aviemore as the fun section. It's good for coaching. Then, if you're doing a full journey to the sea, there is the lovely meandering section at Boat of Garten where you can consolidate your strokes. By the time you get to Grantown, where the water gets a bit more turbulent, you're ready. There nothing above Grade 2 on the Spey, apart from the section near the source at Garva Bridge, but there are some rocks and it gets more difficult as the water gets lower, as it is now. You then have more rocks and submerged tree branches to avoid, and it becomes that wee bit more technical. The main section of white water is really between Ballindalloch and Knockando, which calls for concentration.

'There's a big pool in Delfour Estate called Otter Hole, with a huge boulder about the size of a van. In low water it can be quite tricky, a place where one or two boats have been wrapped, and there's quite a dangerous section towards Fochabers where a couple of boats have been pinned as well. In the main though, the Spey is a very safe river but, like I said earlier, she can be mischievous. She wants to test you now and again, but it's as though she wants to test you without actually hurting you.'

More recently, Dave has launched (pardon the pun) another company. 'Spirit of the Spey' blends open canoeing with visits to whisky distilleries and tastings. This journey makes the most of the many top-class hotels with fine dining along the river.

'I discovered that many of my customers loved the canoeing but didn't particularly want to rough it, while others were very interested in whisky and the process of whisky making. So, I started Spirit of the Spey to provide the traveller with an intimate introduction to the River Spey, her history and heritage, her wildlife and the people who live alongside her and, especially, distilleries and Speyside malts.'

Over the years Dave has become highly knowledgeable about the malt whiskies of Speyside, but what is it that made this region so favourable for malt whisky production?

'I guess there was easy accessibility to good barley and plenty of pure water springs. The barley is grown on very rich alluvial plains, and the quality of the barley is important. Although some experts will tell you the quality of water doesn't really affect the whisky, it's rather nice that some distilleries still use their own springs. Well over half the malt distilleries in Scotland are in Strathspey.'

Is David Craig a Speyside malt man himself?

'Oh yes, I have one or two favourites,' he said, without hesitation. 'For me the epicentre of whisky making must be Dufftown. I love the vanilla honeyed flavour of the Dufftown malts, the Mortlachs and the Balvenies and the rest.'

In 1981 the Scottish Canoe Association asked Dave to become a voluntary advisor for the Spey, a job he tackles with obvious enthusiasm. There has been a long history of conflict on the Spey between canoeists and anglers, but things appear to be more settled now.

'I've promoted an ongoing conversation with the anglers,' he told me. 'In Victorian times angling became very fashionable, although very much a rich man's sport. It became a bit elitist, but the Land Reform legislation of 2003 made it clear that we all have the right to use a river like the Spey. I personally think the Land Reform (Scotland) Act is a great piece of legislation and if we embrace it in the spirit in which it was written then it's clear it's also very well balanced. We have a Spey Users' Group, representing anglers and paddlers, access officers from the various authorities, walkers who use the Speyside Way, and rafters. We take a holistic approach and there is more of an understanding of each other's pursuits and interests.

'I try to liaise with other river users, and encourage them to come out on the boats to see and perhaps understand why we paddle, and for them to tell me, from a fisherman's point of view, what they like to do. At the end of the day we are all incredibly privileged to enjoy our chosen activity on such a great river.

'On one of these familiarisation trips, Dr Catherine Wills came with me in my boat. She was enraptured by the views of her Knockando Estates. She had never seen them from the river before and hadn't realised just how remarkably beautiful they are. That was because she was seeing things from a new perspective, and enjoying the opportunity to feel at one with the river. Because you're low down and moving quietly, especially in the open Canadian canoes, wildlife doesn't feel threatened. You see more.

'I remember a wonderful day down towards Carron Bridge where a family of dippers were on a rock and the parents were popping in and out of the water getting grubs. The youngsters were oblivious to us passing. I could have reached my hand out and touched them. Canoes allow you to get that close to wildlife.

'I was on the river last week with some writers when it snowed. We arrived in Knockando to see the Spey dressed in her winter cloak and, while the group was a wee bit concerned, once they got on the river it didn't really matter. They were well togged up. Despite the snow we saw two ospreys, a roe deer on the bank, saw dippers, wagtails, herons and sandpipers. The group loved it. They felt part of the river. They were on it and working with it.'

As we approached the bridge at Aviemore after a very enjoyable paddle from Kincraig I was pretty sure river descents were not always that uneventful. I asked if Dave's Lady Spey ever took him by surprise?

'I think my biggest surprise was one day we were approaching Spey Bay when it was windy. It normally takes us forty minutes to an hour to get from Fochabers to the sea, but into a force seven onshore wind it took an hour and three quarters. When we reached Spey Bay there were seven-foot rollers coming five hundred metres up the estuary, and I've never seen the Bay so wild. We still made it all the way to Tugnet by following a wee sub channel, and that was my biggest surprise on the river. You must be prepared for anything and that little section, the final section, between Fochabers and the sea, can catch you out.

'Perhaps the most surprising thing is just how much you become endeared to the river. I've had folk come back a dozen times. The river draws you in and, once people have descended it, they tend to want to come back and do it again. Like I did all those years ago. They fall in love and can't let go.'

6

THE BRIDGE AND THE BLACKMOUNT

It was during one of my *Roads Less Travelled* television journeys between the Mull of Kintyre and Mallaig that I noticed how much of a frontier feel there was to the tiny village of Bridge of Orchy. Although the A82 goes through the village before slashing its way across the watery wastes of the Rannoch Moor, the hills on either side offer a wild land experience of the kind you might expect much further north.

After wandering along the leafy roads of Glen Orchy I suddenly felt thrust into a new kind of landscape, one that was bigger, wilder and more remote than anything I'd travelled through since Kintyre. Great hills overlook the village on every side. Beinn an Dothaidh, Beinn Achaladair and Beinn a' Chreachain form the Wall of Rannoch, the boundary between the old Pictish Kingdom of Alba to the east and the Dalriadic Kingdom of the Scots in the west. Beyond the sparkling waters of Loch Tulla lies Stob Ghabhar and Stob a' Choire Odhair, the outliers of the Blackmount Deer Forest.

Deep in the shadow of Stob Ghabhar lies the remote home of ecologist Llinos Proctor, her deerstalker husband Calum and their two young children. For the television camera I took a walk with Llinos along the track to Loch Dochard, one of her favourite places, while she described her love of this area and what it means to her. Llinos is from North Wales and came to Scotland to work in Glen Coe and the Cairngorms, but she now feels very much hefted to the Blackmount. It was her unbounded enthusiasm for the area that encouraged me to revisit some of the hills I hadn't walked for years.

Stob Ghabhar was one of my very first Munros, a hill that my old pal Hamish Telfer and I treated in an abominably disrespectful way when, as brash teenagers, we tackled it via its central south-east-facing Coire na Muic. The slopes of the corrie were piled high with fresh snow and we were blissfully unaware of the possibility of avalanche. With our brand new Aschenbrenner wooden ice-axes we ploughed up the middle of the corrie, a very direct *directissimo*, to the summit, where we celebrated our first winter mountain. In retrospect we were fortunate to survive. Some years later my old friend Tom Weir, by then one of Scotland's most experienced mountaineers, was avalanched in the Upper Couloir of Stob Ghabhar, a narrow gully situated high on the hill's rugged east face. That was my first indication that lethal avalanches could occur in the comparatively low hills of Scotland.

Since then I've come to know Stob Ghabhar in all seasons and have climbed her gullies and ridges by various means: on foot, on ski, and with all the paraphernalia of the winter climber. And a fine hill she is too. The Scottish Mountaineering Club guidebooks suggests that for 'complexity of form and for the splendour of its corries and glens, this hill has few equals in the Central Highlands.'

I can say amen to that, but this time I left the car near

Forest Lodge, adjacent to the West Highland Way, crossed over the old Victoria Bridge and turned left to follow a riverside track as far as the Glasgow University Mountaineering Club hut at Clashgour. From there a muddy track runs north beside the Allt Toaig to the high bealach between Stob Ghabhar and its Munro neighbour, Stob a' Choire Odhair.

Initially, my plan was to climb Stob a' Choire Odhair first but, toiling up the muddy path, I had a notion of climbing Stob Ghabhar by the ridge that encloses Coire na Muic on its west side. This would take me directly to a tight and narrow ridge called the Aonach Eagach that linked with the main summit. Returning the same way, I could drop to the high bealach between Stob Ghabhar and Stob a' Choire Odhair and climb the latter hill too.

Having managed to cross the waters of the Allt Toaig dry-shod, I scrambled through the crags of Creag an Steallaire to reach the rocky ridge which rises at an easy angle all the way to the top of the Couloir Buttress. From here the steepest face of Stob Ghabhar glowers across Coire Ba towards the flat anonymity of the Rannoch Moor. It's an impressive face, steeply buttressed and gullied with the Upper Couloir cutting a deep-set groove just below the summit. It was first climbed by the united efforts of A. E. Maylard, Professor and Mrs Adamson and a Miss Weiss in 1897.

Ahead lay the narrow arête of the Aonach Eagach, the notched ridge, an airy and narrow spine of rock with big drops on either side. On a ski traverse of these hills a few years ago with another pal, mountaineering instructor Steve Spalding, this ridge posed a formidable obstacle. Its snow was beautifully sculpted with a double cornice, and I remember tiptoeing very tentatively across it, skis lashed to my pack, nervously aware that a misplaced footing could have serious consequences. How I longed for the comfort of a rope that day.

Once across, a well-worn path leads to the summit cairn and wide views in all directions. Ben Nevis stood out in the north that day, and closer at hand the hills of the Blackmount Deer Forest unfolded in shimmering shades of grey towards the highest of them all, Ben Starav.

Still feeling fresh I retraced my steps over the Aonach Eagach and dropped down a badly eroded path to the high bealach between the two Munros, a wild and rocky spot and an ideal place for lunch. The climb to Stob a' Choire Odhair was straightforward, and the summit gave a grandstand view across the rumpled mattress of the Moor towards Schiehallion and the Atholl hills. The descent from Stob a' Choire Odhair was straightforward and in no time at all I was waltzing down the zig-zags of the old stalkers' path to the muddy path beside the Allt Toaig, thinking of my first cold pint in the Bridge of Orchy Hotel.

That fine establishment, so beloved of West Highland Way hikers, lies in the shadow of Beinn Dorain, a mountain forever associated with Duncan Ban MacIntyre, Fair-Haired Duncan of the Songs, one of Gaeldom's finest bards. I'd been following his footsteps literally for years, climbing all the hills close to Bridge of Orchy, and cerebrally, thanks to a wonderful new translation of his greatest poem, 'Moladh Beinn Dobhrain', 'In Praise of Beinn Dorain'.

MacIntyre, or Donnchadh Ban nan Oran, was born in Glen Orchy in 1724 and enjoyed a mixed career as a gamekeeper and forester before abandoning the Highlands to become a soldier in the Argyll Regiment of Militia, and eventually a veteran policeman with the Edinburgh City Guard. Despite having fought at the Battle of Falkirk on the Hanoverian side, MacIntyre had sympathy for the Jacobite cause, and was greatly alarmed by the atrocities that followed the Battle of Culloden, the carnage that heralded the beginnings of the Highland Clearances. He reluctantly left his native Glen Orchy for the capital in 1767 and it didn't take him long to record his feelings of loss:

> *The meadows so beloved*
> *And forests so plentiful,*
> *How could I have ever left them.*
> *My thousand blessings forever upon them.*

During his exile in Edinburgh he composed several prize-winning poems, mostly about his native Argyll, but his best known was 'In Praise of Beinn Dorain', the mountain that dominates the view from his birthplace at Druim Liaghart on the southern shore of Loch Tulla. This is a significant work in the canon of early Gaelic poetry because of the author's awareness of the aesthetic values of the hill, a rare acknowledgement in those days.

> *Praise over all to Ben Dorain –*
> *She rises beneath the radiant beams of the sun –*
> *In all the magnificent range of the mountains around,*
> *So shapely, so sheer are her slopes, there are none*
> *To compare; she is fair, in the light, like the flight*
> *Of the deer, in the hunt, across moors, on the run,*
> *Or under the green leafy branches of trees, in the*
> *groves*
> *Of the woods, where the thick grass grows,*

And the curious deer, watchful and tentative,
Hesitant, sensitive: I have had all these clear, in my
sight.

As mentioned earlier, forming part of the Great Wall of Rannoch, Beinn Dorain and its near neighbour, Beinn an Dothaidh, along with Beinn Achaladair and Beinn a' Chreachain form the ancient boundary between the old Pictish Kingdom of Alba to the east and the Dalriadic Kingdom of the Scots in the west. The hills also form part of the ancient Druim Alban, the watershed of Scotland, and it never fails to surprise me that the spine of Scotland should lie so far to the west. To the west of these hills, the rivers Orchy and Etive take short, steep and tumultuous courses to the sea while, on the other side, to the east, the River Lyon flows from Loch Lyon along a rather peaceful and meandering route to its confluence with the Tay, which in turn enjoys a rather stately course to the Firth of Tay at Dundee.

A well-tramped footpath runs up the hill from Bridge of Orchy railway station, roughly following the course of the Allt Coire an Dothaidh. The final few hundred metres to the bealach between Beinn Dorain and Beinn an Dothaidh steepens considerably and the erosion of the path here shows how popular this route has become. With the bealach reached, things improve and a reasonable footpath runs off to the right, climbing steadily to a wide plateau before climbing again over rocky ground towards the long and broad summit ridge of Beinn Dorain. A large cairn appears to signify the summit but beware, the true top is another 200 metres further on. I wonder how many people have been caught out in misty weather and believed they had reached the summit?

At the true summit cairn, with mountains flowing off in

1. Winter, a good time
to take the longer view

2. Ben Starav, fabled land of Deirdre of the Sorrows

3. On Quinag, one of the finest hills in the glorious North-West

4. Approaching the summit of The Wiss, above St Mary's Loch

5. On The Schill, Scottish Borders

6. The summit of the Eildons, formed by the De'il himsel'

7. The Three Brethren

8. Laurence Main, guidebook
author and Druid

9. The Praying Hands of Mary in Glen Lyon

10. The Tigh nan Bodach, Glen Cailliche

11. The east ridge of Schiehallion, Loch Tummel in the background

12. Loch Avon, the jewel of the Cairngorms

13. Walking into the Northern Corries of the Cairngorms

14. Gina at the summit of Ben Rinnes

15. David Craig, river guide on the Spey

16. Craig Dubh at Jacksonville, left to right: John MacLean, Ian Nicholson, Jimmy Marshall, me, and Tam the Bam

17. Buachaille Etive Mor, the epitome of fine mountains

18. Below Na Gruagaichean, in the Mamores

19. The North Face of Ben Nevis, Bill Murray's winter haunt

20. Path repairs on the Ben above Glen Nevis

21. With Bill Murray at his home in Lochgoilhead

22. A frosty Glen Affric

OPPOSITE:
23. Dick Balharry in his element

24. The winter cliffs of Coire Ardair

25. Taking time to ponder at Rowchoish bothy

all directions like waves on the ocean, it's good to sit with a flask of hot tea and consider Fair-Haired Duncan of the Songs. Away below, in the upper reaches of the Gleann Achadh-innis-Chailein lie the remains of the house where he lived when working as a forester. The surrounding hills, rivers and woods inspired him, as did the red deer on the hill. Most of his poetry is descriptive and, despite the Jacobite upheavals that wracked the Highlands, it was his experiences as a keeper and forester in Argyll and Perthshire, in the employ of the Earl of Breadalbane, and later the Duke of Argyll, that had the greatest influence on his poetry. The significance of Duncan Ban's wildlife-themed poetry shouldn't be underestimated. It has been described by scholars as 'the zenith of Gaelic nature poetry'.

There have been a number of translations by such luminaries as Iain Crichton Smith, Hugh MacDiarmid and Derrick Thomson, but a more recent translation by Alan Riach, professor of Scottish Literature at Glasgow University, and published by Kettilonia, is in my opinion the finest yet. It beautifully captures the different flows and tempos of the pibroch, the classical music of the Highland bagpipe, the model on which the original was composed. Indeed, Professor Riach's translation has been applauded by the eminent Gaelic writer Aonghas MacNeacail, who believes the work has delivered Duncan Ban's poetry to the twenty-first century.

'The sustained richness of language, rhythmic drive and flow of thought mirror the original in such a way that non-Gaels are allowed unusual access to the real MacIntyre, while demonstrating that he is as much of our time as of his own.'

There is a vibrant freshness about Alan Riach's translation that I find hugely appealing, a rhythmic and rhyming quality that stands out against the rather stultified and literal interpretations of many older translations. If you ever get the chance to read it, consider this. Duncan Ban MacIntyre remained illiterate throughout his life. His native Glen Orchy had no school and he simply memorised his own poetry. He received help from the minister of Lismore, Donald MacNicol, and his poems were later printed by his son, but I find it astonishing that such work could be created by someone who lacked the ability to write it down. A lack of formal education was no barrier to MacIntyre's genius.

Fair-Haired Duncan of the Songs is buried in Greyfriars Kirkyard in Edinburgh, where he died in 1812, beside a memorial erected by friends and well-wishers. Another memorial, an extraordinary granite monument some forty-four feet high, stands on the Old Military Road from Inveraray to Dalmally, raised by public subscription in 1859, overlooking Glen Orchy, and Loch Awe and its islands.

Grand as such memorials may be, away below, at the foot of the long, steep slopes of Beinn Dorain, lie the remains of the house I have always considered to be Duncan's true memorial. It's cruelly ironic that the ruins of his former home, Ais-an-Sidhean in the Auch Glen, now shelter sheep, for MacIntyre detested the beasts, just as he detested the Clearances. He blamed the introduction of sheep for the eviction of so many people from their homes and his disgust is given full rein in another of his poems, Oran Nam Balgairean:

> *My blessing be upon the foxes, because that they hunt the sheep,*
> *The sheep with the brockit faces that have made confusion in all the world.*

The Bridge and the Blackmount

I don't believe you can fully appreciate MacIntyre's wonderful poem if you don't know the landscapes that inspired him. With that in mind I took to the slopes of a mountain that is in many ways the centrepiece of these big, broadly muscled hills to the east of Glen Orchy. The hill of the monk, Beinn Mhanach, is generally considered as one of the Bridge of Orchy Munros but is also universally cursed by Munro-baggers because of its awkward position.

It lies amidst its four near neighbours, Beinn Dorain, Beinn an Dothaidh, Beinn Achaladair and Beinn a' Chreachain, in the hollow of the curving Wall of Rannoch that they form, and you can't really add it to that round without a big descent and re-ascent. Having said that, I've always thought it's better climbed on its own, either as an out-and-back from Bridge of Orchy, as I did a number of years ago on skis, or as part of a big circular walk that also takes in the Clan MacGregor coffin route between Glen Lyon and the Auch Glen, which passes MacIntyre's Ais-an-Sidhean.

That particular ski trip was memorable. Taff Bowles, an old pal who is now director of Outdoor Education for Yorkshire, and I skied in from Bridge of Orchy over the bealach between Beinn Dorain and Beinn an Dothaidh. Deep snow gave us good running to the head of the Auch Glen which we rounded into the head of Gleann Cailliche. A long rising traverse took us to the shallow col between the two tops and from there it was an easy glide to the summit of Beinn Mhanach. The return in first-class snow conditions was even better, and I recall a long easy schuss from the pass before we had to climb back to the Beinn an Dothaidh bealach and descend in rapidly diminishing light to the warm glow of Bridge of Orchy.

*

More recently I took the old familiar track from Bridge of Orchy station to the Dorain/Dothaidh bealach before dropping down the wet grassy slopes towards the head of the Auch Glen. Realising how long a pull coming back the same way would require, I had a notion to return via the Auch Glen itself, but I really didn't fancy a three-mile walk along the A82 dodging cars, trucks, buses and caravans. It wasn't until I took a wee break and had a look at the map that I remembered the West Highland Way.

How could I have forgotten it? The route parallels the West Highland rail line between Auch and Bridge of Orchy, three miles of easy and flat walking at the end of the day. I was delighted that I wouldn't have to climb back to the high bealach again, and subsequently descend the muddy and eroded path. So, somewhat rejuvenated and with the day's plan of action in hand, the rest of the climb was a delight, with the views growing in scale higher up the steep slopes of Beinn a' Chuirn, the western top of Beinn Mhanach. Less than a mile of easy walking separates the two tops, a delightful mossy stroll with far-flung views in every direction. All the Crianlarich hills stood out clear, Beinn Laoigh was visible down the length of the winding Allt Kinglass and, closer at hand, Beinn Dorain and Beinn an Dothaidh showed off uncharacteristic traits not seen from the A82 side, their steep and rugged north- and east-facing corries.

Although they are long and relatively steep, I decided to drop down the southern slopes of Beinn Mhanach on grassy slopes that had me slithering on my backside several times. Despite that, I was on the Glen Lyon track in just over an hour. This bulldozed track follows part of an old coffin route once used by the MacGregors as they walked from

Glen Lyon to bury their dead in the graveyard at Auch, once a MacGregor stronghold.

Some way down the Auch Glen I passed the sheep fank that in former usage was the home of Duncan Ban himself: Ais-an-Sidhean. It was in a sorry state. Some of the original walls still stand, topped by a galvanised roof in place of the turfs that would have sheltered the MacIntyre family. The place stank of sheep shit and the door was held in place by a length of plastic rope. I had it in mind to stop here for a brew and to contemplate what life here would have been like, but a sense of rural deprivation and squalor chased me on. We're often told that farmers are the guardians of the countryside, but I would query that. The amount of plastic that litters such areas is inexcusable.

It didn't take long for my spirits to rise again. I had just crossed the boundary between the old kingdoms of Alba and Dalriada and, with the immaculate conical shape of Beinn Dorain towering regally above, crossed the waters of the Allt Kinglass on an old arched bridge and took the military road north, a track that now echoes to the army of West Highland Waygoers rather than the calls of soldiers.

I passed several groups of hikers, all suffering because of badly fitting boots. My advice to them all was the same: you really don't need boots on a route like the West Highland Way. Lightweight trail shoes are much more comfortable, especially if you're not used to wearing heavy and stiff footwear, and I couldn't help but wonder what Fair-Haired Duncan of the Songs would have made of them all. I also wonder what he would have made of people like me who climb hills for nothing more than recreation, or to test ourselves?

*

It would be remiss of me to write about this lovely area of Breadalbane without mentioning a hill-round that is possibly the finest the Corbetts have to offer, a hill-round that is my own personal test-piece.

We climb hills for different reasons. To tick off lists from a guidebook, or to release ourselves from everyday routines. For some years the round of the five Corbetts just north of Tyndrum was my little proving ground. If planning a big trip abroad, or a trekking expedition to the Himalaya, I would come here to discover just how fit I was, or wasn't. The round of Beinn Odhar, 2,955 feet/901 metres, Beinn Chaorach, 2,685 feet/818 metres, Cam Chreag, 2,903 feet/885 metres, Beinn nam Fuaran, 2,645 feet/806 metres and Beinn a' Chaisteal, 2,907 feet/886 metres is only about twelve miles in terms of distance, but the traverse of all five involves a whopping 6,500 feet/1,980 metres of climbing. That's about one-and-a-half times Ben Nevis! The hills are situated north of Tyndrum and to the south-east of the Auch Glen. The first hill of the round, Beinn Odhar, impresses as the rather fine conical peak you see as you drive towards Bridge of Orchy from Tyndrum on the A82. Indeed, many people mistake it for Beinn Dorain, the Munro to the north.

This is the only Corbett grouping that will earn you five ticks in your book, but give yourself plenty of time. Beinn Odhar gets the legs working but the descent to the bealach below Beinn Chaorach is considerable. The 400 metres of climbing to Chaorach's summit ridge is a good, steady pull and from the trig point you'll get a chance to enjoy the views of the Bridge of Orchy hills, as you will all the way down the wide ridge to the bealach below Cam Chreag. This hill never really feels like it belongs in the group. Its natural home is with the Mamlorn hills of Creag Mhor and Ben Challum, but at least its long north ridge gives access to what is always the toughest hill of the round, Beinn nam Fuaran. It's a long climb, about 400 metres, from the bealach to the summit but it feels longer when you know you have another hill to climb afterwards. It's also a difficult hill to descend because by this time your legs are likely to be turning to rubber. Beware of several little rock bands that require extra care.

The final climb to Beinn a' Chaisteal, thankfully, isn't too steep but it feels long. The best plan is to enjoy the view across the Auch Glen to dark and craggy Beinn Dorain as you plod upwards. Don't even think of the steep descent that comes after the summit, which will come soon enough. By the time you reach the top you'll know why this is one of the toughest hill-rounds in Scotland, and it's in an area that is surprisingly close to the Central Belt. You don't need to go all the way to the Northern Highlands to test yourself in wild, uncompromising country.

Travel north from Bridge of Orchy, beyond the waters of Loch na' Achaise with its glorious views towards the Blackmount, and ease round the familiar left-hand bend that opens out to reveal the squat pyramid of Buachaille Etive Mor. Turn left just in front of the Buachaille and you will enter one of Scotland's most beautiful glens, the gateway to some of the best hills in the Central Highlands.

With steep-sided hills rising on either side, a single-track road runs from its high point on the Rannoch Moor for some fourteen miles to the head of Loch Etive, a sea-loch that bites its way greedily into the jumbled landscape of Argyll. Its glorious river is a cascading, tumbling watercourse that has been described as the finest canoeing river in Scotland, commanding cult status among Scotland's paddlers.

Two hundred and sixty years ago the glen was considerably more inhabited than it is today, when a track made its way down the south side of Loch Etive as far as Taynuilt. From 1847 a steamer service from Oban sailed up Loch Etive to the now derelict pier where the modern road ends. It's certainly a quieter place today, but the old jetty at the head of the loch is still a magnificent place to linger and consider the scene before you. Savagely steep slopes lead to the Munro of Ben Starav on one side, and the Corbett of Beinn Trilleachan on the other, while ahead rises the equally steep slopes of another Corbett, Stob Dubh.

Further up the glen the classic view of the two Buachailles, the twin herdsmen of Etive, with the Lairig Gartain separating them, dominates everything else, and the big hills of the Blackmount Deer Forest spread out on your right. On the other side of the glen the Stob Coire Sgreamhach edge of the Bidean nam Bian massif gives way to the long ridge of Beinn Maol Chaluim and the Munros of Glen Creran, Beinn Sgulaird and Beinn Fhionnlaidh. Few glens in Scotland offer such a phenomenal wealth of hillwalking in a hugely inspiring landscape.

While most hillwalking visitors to Glen Etive will head for the Blackmount or Glen Coe, this is one area where the Corbetts are every bit as interesting, and challenging, as their higher counterparts. Stob Dubh is a good example.

This 2,897-foot/883-metre hill rises from Glen Ceitlin in lower Etive and has been described as 'steep, dark and intimidating'. You have to climb virtually from sea level, and its summit always seems to be an extraordinarily long way above the glen, a phenomenon created by the steepness of its slopes. To emphasise its reputation as a serious mountain, its slopes become steeper the higher you climb.

The Bridge and the Blackmount

As I tramped along the Coileitir track, in the lower glen, the hill reared up in front of me in such a threatening manner that I questioned whether I really wanted to climb it. Its top third was covered in snow and dark clouds hung like funeral curtains over the distant summit, adding to the potential threat and making me doubt my own ability to climb the damned thing.

Some hills are like this, with an almost overpowering air of oppression, a perception usually created by weather conditions at the time. Indeed, as I crossed the footbridge over the Allt Ceitlin, sunshine suddenly burst through the clouds, bathing the slopes with such a delightful flood of light that all sense of oppression immediately vanished. High above Glen Ceitlin, the tops of the neighbouring hills pushed their snow-covered summits and ridges above the cloud: Stob Coire an Albannaich, Meall nan Eun and Meall Odhar, all sparkling bright while, behind me, Ben Starav and Beinn Trilleachan still cowered under their cloak of grey.

The lower slopes of Stob Dubh may be steep but their ascent is a straightforward upward haul, all sweat and heaving lungs, and it wasn't until I reached the higher crags that I was faced with what might be some difficulty. The slopes between the crags and rocky bluffs were still snowbound and, although the snow was soft enough to kick steps into, the ground below was still iron-hard after several weeks of sub-zero temperatures. Exchanging trekking poles for an ice axe, I tried several times to hammer the pick of the axe into the ground for security but it merely bounced off the frozen turf. It was like trying to cut steps in concrete!

Uncomfortably aware of the precipitous slope, I understood that a slip would see me sliding hundreds of feet downhill, not stopping until the ground became soft enough

119

to sink the ice axe in. Such ground was a long way below and by the time I reached it considerable momentum would have built up. Such knowledge prompts a keen feeling for self-preservation, and I literally tiptoed up the remaining few hundred feet until the slopes were leaning back in a more reassuring manner. I was glad to reach the summit cairn.

Rather than return the same way, I carefully traversed the summit ridge to neighbouring Beinn Ceitlin, before slowly creeping and sliding down the southern slopes towards the bealach between the Allt Ceitlin and Allt a' Chaorainn headwaters. Even on these south-facing slopes, and by this time the sun was shining with appreciable warmth, the ground was still so iron-hard I half expected sparks to fly as I hammered in my ice axe. Only when well down the slope could I relax enough to descend in a normal fashion.

Close to the head of Loch Etive lies Beinn Trilleachan, with its sweep of granite crags, known to rock climbers as the Etive Stabs. The famous boiler-plates contain some of the most surreal climbs in Scotland. Etive slab climbing is friction climbing, tiptoeing upwards through a steep ocean of granite, relying on the sandpaper roughness of the rock, and is not for the faint-hearted.

Another Etive Corbett, Beinn Mhic Chasgaig, is also protected by steep and craggy slopes, but it's not as isolated as Stob Dubh or Beinn Trilleachan, and has the advantage of being connected to the Creise/Clach Leathad ridge of the Blackmount Deer Forest by a high-level bealach. It is easy enough to tag this one onto a round of those two Munros. Indeed, for many years peak-baggers were forced to take this route because of a fortified gate across a bridge over the Etive near Alltchaorunn. In pre-Land Reform Act days, the gate to the bridge was barricaded with a padlock and barbed wire, but in these more emancipated times the barriers have been removed to allow access to what is a marvellous route to the hill.

One word of warning though. A sign reminds walkers that under the Land Reform Act householders can expect 'reasonable privacy', so try and avoid walking immediately past the house at Alltchaorunn. Break off the track that runs to the house at the first gate you encounter and follow the line of a deer fence uphill until you reach a stile. Cross it, and you'll soon pick up the Allt a' Chaorainn path again.

On another visit to Beinn Mhic Chasgaig I tackled the hill's western nose head on, a steep and uncompromising climb that had me twisting through crags and rock barriers until I reached the summit plateau in a lather of sweat and frayed nerves. I've since found an easier and lovelier route that follows the Allt a' Chaorainn to its junction with the Allt Coire Ghiubhasan, where a single-plank bridge crosses the latter stream to access a footpath on the other side, a path that runs through a narrow and magnificent gorge.

The glen of the Allt Coire Ghiubhasan is a narrow defile below the steep slopes of Aonach Mor and Mhic Chasgaig, with the footpath contouring the slopes above a tumbling burn. A Scottish Mountaineering Club guidebook suggests it has the character, if not the scale, of the Himalaya, and with the distinct V-shape of the glen framing the pointed, snow-capped peaks of the Bidean nam Bian range, such a suggestion isn't in the least bit fanciful.

It's possible to follow this narrow path all the way to the head of the glen where steep slopes climb to the Mhic Chasgaig/Creise bealach, but it's better to vary the route, cross the burn and take to the grassy slopes beside a wide and imposing gully. Here lies the hard work of the day, but an hour or so of hard effort will give you enough height to enjoy the views across the Blackmount hills and down Glen Etive. It won't be long before the angle of the slope eases back onto the wide upper slopes and the rock-strewn summit plateau.

The summit cairn, at 2,835 feet/864 metres, lies at the east end and the views are breathtaking. Beyond the blunt nose of Creise, the watery mattress of Rannoch Moor spreads towards the east, while closer at hand the squat, rocky form of Buachaille Etive Mor looks very different from the famous pyramid shape normally seen from the A82 Glencoe road. To the west and south the big hills predominate: the Bidean hills, Ben Starav, the Blackmount tops, Clach Leathad and Stob Ghabhar, all big, bright and brash. After the climb the descent to the high bealach that links with Creise, and down steep slopes to the head of the Allt Coire Ghiubhasan is pure magic. The temptation to linger by the clear pools and falls of the upper burn can be too much to resist. Deep in the cusp of the hills, this is as perfect a spot as you'll find anywhere, even in the Himalaya.

You'll encounter very few hillwalkers on Beinn Mhic Chasgaig, and likewise you'll find few walkers on another fine Etive Corbett. Hidden away in a cleft of wild mountainous land between Glen Coe and Glen Etive, Beinn Maol Chaluim, 2,975 feet/907 metres, does not attract large numbers. Its proximity to the popular Munros of Glen Coe tends to keep it relatively free of people, and those hillwalkers who do take the long single-track road down Glen Etive are usually intent on bagging Ben Starav.

The Bridge and the Blackmount

With every car park in Glen Coe full to overflowing I decided I wanted a quiet day on the hill, and I knew from experience that I needn't go far in search of it. Glen Etive, unusually, was also busy, but with paddlers not hillwalkers. Every little waterfall had half a dozen stubby, brightly coloured canoes waiting to take the plunge, and the grass verges were full of cars and people camping for the Easter weekend. Despite the general air of busyness, I was confident of a quiet day on Beinn Maol Chaluim.

A large herd of red deer grazed close to the road as I parked the car just past Inbhir-fhaolain, opposite the wind-ruffled waters of Lochan Urr. I momentarily thought of dropping from the road to the loch-side to take a photograph of the twin Buachailles of Glen Etive with the loch as a foreground but, being an extremely lazy photographer, decided that the light was too flat. And it was! Dark clouds tickled the summits of the highest peaks and it felt unseasonably cold. There was a greyness in the day that suggested winter hadn't quite yet finished with us.

Despite the chill it didn't take long to get sweating on the lower slopes of Creag na Caillich, en route to Beinn Maol Chaluim's southern ridge. The slope is unrelentingly steep, but the upside is that you gain height quickly. Within twenty minutes I was getting a hint of what the views would be like later in the day. The twin Buachailles looked magnificent and behind me the steep slopes of Stob Dubh fell into the glen as a scree-scarred curtain. Further down the glen I caught the silver sparkle of Loch Etive, trapped in a cleft between the hills.

Once you reach the broad south ridge of Beinn Maol Chaluim only a steep, short climb separates you from the magnificent high-level ridge that leads to the summit. It's straightforward enough until you reach the top, where the summit is protected by a long wall of vertical red porphyry. You can avoid these crags by traversing right for some distance but there are one or two breaches in the wall where even non-scramblers can clamber through. Beyond, some minor tops lead to the summit ridge, on this occasion fringed with snow.

What a marvellous high-level romp this produces. On one side steep slopes lead to another ridge that connects with the Munro Sgorr na h-Ulaidh, and on the other even steeper slopes drop into the bare fastness of Gleann Fhaolain, the narrow glen that separates Beinn Maol Chaluim from the Bidean nam Bian massif. I had harboured tentative thoughts about descending into Gleann Fhaolain, climbing steeply to Bidean and following its ridge east to Stob Coire Sgreamhach before descending back into Glen Etive, but dark clouds were on the way and there was a dusting of new snow on the higher tops. Discretion being the better part of valour (I didn't carry an ice axe) I loitered for a while before dropping out of the wind for a scenic lunch break and returning to Glen Etive the way I had come. As a reward the sun shone for a while on the descent, illuminating some of the finest views you'll see in this magnificently mountainous part of highland Scotland, but was the hill as quiet as I expected? No, not quite. I saw three other people. Not bad for an Easter Saturday.

While there are definable subtleties attached to the ascent of Beinn Mhic Chasgaig and Beinn Maol Chaluim there is nothing subtle about the ascent of Glen Etive's best known Munro. The climb to the summit from the head of Loch Etive is brutal. You have to earn every inch!

The Bridge and the Blackmount

There's a definite inequality about some of our Munros. You can wander up the Cairnwell, for example, from the Cairnwell Pass at 2,199 feet/670 metres, which doesn't leave much of the mountain. The Drumochter hills start from the roadside at 1,500 feet/457 metres, and even the two Buachailles of Glen Coe rise from the loftiest part of Rannoch Moor. But wander through the Lairig Gartain, between these two hills, and the ground soon falls away at your feet, all the way to sea level where the tidal floods of Loch Etive lap the skirts of Ben Starav. From those damp skirts there is a full 3,541 feet/1,078 metres of climbing.

Near the summit a narrow crest billows eastwards and down to a high bealach from where you can descend to a lower saddle that gives access to another Munro, the outlying Beinn nan Aighenan, the peak of the hinds. This is one of those tops that always seems destined to be left for another day. It looks far out on its rocky limb and the temptation is to ignore it and bash on to Glas Bheinn Mhor. So many Munro-baggers build up a list of such solitary, isolated hills, all left for another day – but don't make Beinn nan Aighenan another.

From the outlying summit retrace your steps to the high col that gives access to the south-west ridge of a third Munro, Glas Bheinn Mhor. Follow the ridge over a grassy subsidiary top and climb the rocky ridge to the summit. It's from here that Ben Starav really shows its classic form, with no fewer than five narrow ridges culminating in its blunted peak. Under snow cover it looks positively Alpine when its sweeping cornices reflect the low-lying sun.

Take care on the descent from Glas Bheinn Mhor. It's best to drop down eastwards to a col from where you can descend easily to the head of the Allt Mheuran and a footpath back to Coileitir. Tired you may be, but I have no doubt that like Deirdre of the Sorrows your heart will have been well and truly captured by Glen Etive and it won't be long before you are planning a return visit.

7

THE HEARTLAND

Every time I drive through Glen Coe a shudder of awe and wonder runs through me. I don't think many hillgoers would argue that the Coe is a very special place. Glistening crags fall down from a sequence of high, glaciated corries on one side of the road, while the notched, jagged wall of the Aonach Eagach rises dramatically on the other. In certain weather conditions, like anywhere else, the glen can give the impression of being a dark place, even gloomy, but over the years I believe commercial tourism has done it a disservice, bestowing on it the rather silly title of Glen o' Weeping.

The fanciful nickname recalls the 1692 massacre, when Hanoverian forces murdered their MacDonald hosts, but as Highland massacres go it was far from being the worst. In 1577, the MacLeods of Dunvegan lit a huge fire at the mouth of a narrow cave on Eigg where 400 members of the Clan MacDonald were hiding. They all died from suffocation. The following year the MacDonalds took revenge. Under cover of a thick mist they set fire to Trumpan Church on the Vaternish peninsula on Skye while it was full of worshipping MacLeods. Only one person escaped.

The Glen Coe affair didn't match that level of retribution, although it was bad enough. Thirty-two men, women and children died at the hands of their guests, government soldiers, who rose quietly and murdered them during the hours of darkness. This 'murder under trust' became indelibly etched in the pages of history as the Massacre of Glen Coe and, even today, over three hundred years later, there are those who want to preserve the site of the infamy as a memorial to those who perished.

Life was comparatively cheap in those days and, while we should never forget the 'murder under trust' element, I've always felt it was unfortunate that such an emotionally charged nickname as Glen o' Weeping should have been coined for what was little more than a marketing campaign. It paints too grim a picture of what is one of Scotland's finest natural landscapes, a heartland for hill-going folk and, arguably, the cradle of Scottish mountaineering. As I sat on a high eyrie above the glen, with a clutch of memorials to other mountaineers lying around me, climbers who loved Glen Coe, I couldn't help think of the generations who have been thrilled and inspired by the place, and who never considered it to be a 'dark place', but one of light, joy and wonder.

I sat up there, enjoying the last rays of the winter sun, close to a howff built years ago by some lads from the Squirrels, a climbing club in Edinburgh. The memorial plaques scattered around were moving in their simplicity. One read: 'These are my mountains, and I have come home', a sentiment many of us appreciate, the sense of belonging, the 'duthchas' of the Gael that means a community not created by clan lineage but by a commonly held love. In this case it is a love of place, far removed from the notion of 'oigreachd', which signifies feudal ownership and inheritance, concepts that are foreign to most climbers and hillwalkers.

Three great craggy prows dominated my view: Beinn Fhada, Gearr Aonach and Aonach Dubh, collectively known as the Three Sisters of Glen Coe, their cliffs tumbling down into the narrow glen where river and road squeeze through the mountains, leading to the glorious west. If such a view was not enough to whet your appetite you might also catch a tantalising view of the peaks that make up the classic round of Stob Coire nan Lochan, Bidean nam Bian and Stob Coire Sgreamhach.

Bidean nam Bian, 3,773 feet/1,150 metres, the centrepiece of this round of Glen Coe peaks, is not only the highest mountain in the county of Argyll but the name of an entire massif, and a complex one at that with several pointed tops and deep-cut corries. There are a variety of routes to the summit which, in winter conditions, can be very challenging. Great rock crags like the Diamond and Church Door Buttresses add drama and a sense of history. The first climbs were put up by some of the great pioneers of rock climbing in Scotland: Norman Collie and Harold Raeburn at the end of the nineteenth century and, later, Dr J. H. Bell. These famous climbs were preceded, by a couple of decades, by what is believed to be the first recorded rock-climb in Glen Coe.

In 1868, Neil Marquis, the son of a local shepherd, clambered up the north Face of Aonach Dubh above Loch Achtriochtan to reach the long vertical slit in the rock that's commonly known as Ossian's Cave. Years later I tried to repeat the climb but the experience wasn't a good one. It became one of my greatest hillwalking disappointments.

At the time I was infatuated with the heroic sagas of the Celtic Twilight, in particular James MacPherson of Balavil's controversial translations of *The Poems of Ossian*, first published in the mid-eighteenth century. MacPherson claimed the work was a record of ancient oral poetry told to him in Gaelic during his travels through the Highlands and Islands but, after publication, he was roundly criticised by the London Tory Dr Samuel Johnson, who denounced the work as a forgery. This was the Samuel Johnson, literary critic and poet, who once remarked: 'The noblest prospect which a Scotchman ever sees, is the high road that leads him to England!'

The belittling of Scotland and the Scots appears to be a Tory tradition but despite the learned doctor's scorn, other academic studies suggest MacPherson's work may have been genuine. Sadly, the harm was done, and to this day history recalls James MacPherson as a fraud.

Fraud or not, *The Poems of Ossian* offer a wonderful account of the ancient sagas of Fionn MacCumhail, his Fingalian warriors and their heroic battles. Ossian was the bardic warrior son of Fingal himself and his poems, despite Johnson, had an enormous impact on eighteenth-century European society with the idea known as the 'Celtic Twilight'. Admirers included Robert Burns, Sir Walter Scott, William Wordsworth, W. B. Yeats and even Ludwig van Beethoven. It's been claimed that the book was a favourite of Napoleon Bonaparte, who carried it into battle. It's said he read passages from it every night and was inspired by the combination of North European cultural mythology and Celtic identity.

In an introductory note in the 1926 printing, John Gregorson Campbell of Islay suggests: '...the groundwork of much that is in Ossian certainly existed in Gaelic in Scotland long before MacPherson was born. The chief characters figured in Gaelic compositions centuries ago, and in Gaelic songs by well known ancient bards. There are so many allusions to Fionn, the Feinne, Oisin (Ossian) and the heroes of the Ossianic cycle, that there is absolutely no standing ground left for this (Johnson's) theory.'

The patriotic view still held by a limited number of Scots is that Ossian's poems are historical; that the Gaelic is genuine ancient poetry composed by a bard of the third century who witnessed many of the exploits recorded; and that to all intents and purposes MacPherson simply gave us, in more or less sequential narrative, an anglicised version of traditional lore.

> *Blest be thy soul, son of Semo. Thou went mighty into battle. Thy strength was like the strength of a stream: thy speed like the eagle's wing. Thy path in battle was terrible: the steps of death were behind thy sword. Blest be thy soul, son of Semo, car-borne chief of Dunscaith. Thou hast not fallen by the sword of the mighty, neither was thy blood on the spear of the brave. The arrow came, like the sting of death in a blast: nor did the feeble hand, which drew the bow, perceive it. Peace to thy soul, in thy cave, chief of the Isle of Mist.*

'The Death of Cuchulin',
FROM THE POEMS OF OSSIAN

The legends of Fingal and Ossian are commemorated in place names throughout the Highlands and Islands, and goodness known how many Fionn Coires there are. As a young climber Ossian's Cave beckoned to me with all the magic of a Druid's command and I succumbed to the call.

The cave itself is a vertical slit two-thirds of the way up the north face of Aonach Dubh, the big crag that gazes down on Loch Achtriochtan and the busy A82. It was formed when a column of basalt collapsed some time in the dark and distant past, and the long and narrow slit it left frequently grabs the attention of folk driving through the glen. It is like the dark entrance to another world.

Hamish Telfer and I clambered up through vegetated gullies, over loose crags and along faint meandering sheep trails, searching for a route known as Ossian's Ladder. Whether we found it or not we'll never know, but after a wet and miserable scramble we stood below the final short, greasy-looking climb to the cave itself. It was here, according to Fingalian legend, that Ossian was born, the son of Fionn MacCumhail, chief of the Fianna warriors, and a half-woman, half-hind by the name of Sadh. The couple met when Fingal was hunting with his hounds, Luath and Bran. There was one hind the dogs wouldn't chase, and when Fingal called them off it turned into a beautiful woman. Later, the call of the wild proved too strong for her, and she returned to the steep and lonely places to give birth to a son in this cave above dark Loch Achtriochtan. Fingal never met the boy until a chance encounter on Ben Bulben in County Sligo, on the west coast of Ireland, seven years later.

On our high stance we considered whether to attempt the last section to the mouth of the cave but eventually decided against it, not because of the difficulty of the final pitch but because it was clear from where we stood that it wasn't really a cave. A ledge sloped upwards at an angle of about forty-five degrees from the opening to the top, and it was running with water. A disappointed and dispirited pair of youths slipped and slithered their way back down to the A82.

Despite that early setback, Hamish and I enjoyed many other adventures in Glen Coe. We became members of the Lomond Mountaineering Club and spent weekend after weekend on its crags and cliffs, exploring the corries and ridges, connecting with these landscapes as we connected with no other. Becoming familiar with the geology of Glen Coe, we learned the difference between its various kinds of schist, quartzite and granite, and began to recognise plants such as lady's mantle, willow scrub and sundew. Often, they were hung with watery diamonds. We learned to differentiate between ring ouzel and blackbird, skylark and meadow pipit, and learned why a buzzard is often called the 'Englishman's eagle'. We became familiar with the local meteorology, enough to anticipate what the weather would do if the wind suddenly changed, and we learned the names of the peaks, ridges and corries and what they meant in English. It was a transformative period for us, and I often wonder if we could have connected as we did if we had learned our craft on an indoor climbing wall?

Today, on fairly infrequent visits to Coire nan Lochan above the River Coe, Ossian's 'dark Cona,' I like to visit the little howff that was our Glen Coe doss all those years ago. Within the damp walls of this little structure I slide into a dwam of nostalgia, recalling early climbs on the East Face of Aonach Dubh and early, excited tramps to the high tops. From here I first summited Bidean nam Bian. On a dank wet day that made the rock too slippery to climb, we went for a pad instead, up the length of the corrie, past the glaciated lochans and over boulder scree to reach the foot of Stob Coire nan Lochan's east ridge, where it levels out to become Gearr Aonach. A rocky scramble took us to the summit, from where a southerly ridge sweeps downwards into a fine bow-shaped col. Little did I see that day of the great crags of Dinner Time Buttress and Church Door Buttress as we made our way up the other steep side to the rocky summit.

Bidean, the peak of the mountains, couldn't be better named. Its summit is the culmination of four great ridges which give way to no less than nine separate summits and cradle three deep and distinctive corries. It even has a secondary Munro, since Stob Coire Sgreamhach was promoted to Munro status in the 1997 revisions. A number of alternative routes ascend Bidean nam Bian but my usual route is this one, by Coire nan Lochan and its eponymous Stob.

The linking of Stob Coire nam Beith offers a pretty good route of descent if you've had enough, down to to Achnambeithach at the western end of Loch Achtriochtan, but there's a glorious ridge awaiting your attention to the south-east, with wonderful southern views down the length of Etive, beyond the fabled lands of Deirdre to the peaks of Cruachan. It skirts the head of steep-sided Coire Gabhail before climbing the boulders and screes of the new Munro to provide another great spot to sit and while away the time. Gaze across at the twin ridges of the two Buachailles, or pick out the tops of the Blackmount Deer Forest, its clutch of fine Munros and the square topped peak of mighty Ben Starav.

From here you can descend north-east, down the two-mile length of Beinn Fhada, although this route can be awkward and difficult, especially in snowy conditions. Escape from the Fhada ridge can be effected by dropping steeply down into Coire Gabhail, but you have to backtrack quite a distance to avoid a deep chasm that lines the upper corrie floor. Better to return down the north-west ridge of Stob Coire Sgreamhach towards Bidean, and then carefully descend the loose scree-filled gully in the steep headwall of Coire Gabhail itself. After further scree slopes the corrie begins to fan out, and a footpath offers easier going over the incredibly flat pastures that may once have fed hidden cattle. Legend suggests the MacDonalds of Glen Coe once hid stolen cattle up here. A great jumble of boulders fills the woodlands at its mouth, but follow the track to the right to avoid it, cross the stream and continue to the footbridge over the River Coe.

Listen now, and brace yourself for the modern madness of the roadside car park and the A82. You might hear a tinker/piper playing a lament and likely as not the car park will be filled with tour buses, its passengers photographing the peaks and crags of the Glen o' Weeping. The smile of contentment on your face may cause them to question that nickname.

While the south side of Glen Coe is made up of a complex system of corries and a succession of individual peaks, the remains of a supervolcano that erupted some 420 million years ago and the subsequent processes of glaciation during the last Ice Age about 10,000 years ago, the north side of the glen consists of one single feature, the great wall of the Aonach Eagach, the notched ridge.

The last time I traversed this wonderful ridge I was in the company of John Manning, then my deputy editor on *The Great Outdoors* magazine. Managing to escape the *TGO* office for a day we headed north to the Coe. John had been keen to tackle the ridge but rumours and tales of steep and awkward scrambling had always held him back. The traverse of the Aonach Eagach is one of the classic scrambles of

Scotland, but the tightrope route along its narrow crest has been the nadir of many a Munro-bagger's career.

When we arrived on the summit of Am Bodach at the eastern end of the most awkward section of the ridge I began to share John's concerns. The serrated edge looked as if it was tearing the clouds apart as the wind blew them over the crest. Swirling mist curled into the sky and each time a gap was torn in the cloud, the long fin of rock, grass and scree appeared dramatically before us. On the best of days the Aonach Eagach can be a daunting sight. On a day like this it looked positively threatening. However, as we left the summit cairn I optimistically suggested that other than the initial descent onto the ridge the rest of the route was a doddle. It's curious how selective the memory can be.

Almost four kilometres in length, the Aonach Eagach boasts four summits, two of which are Munros. There used to be a sign warning hillwalkers not to descend from the ridge but it appears to have vanished, and we nipped down the ledges and grooves of the descent from Am Bodach onto the ridge like mountain goats. Generally considered the crux of the route, it is in effect a sixty-foot drop-off that looks much worse than it actually is. We were on the crest in no time, striding purposefully along an easy gradient to a top beyond which lie the slopes of Meall Dearg, at 3,127 feet/953 metres. This was the last Munro summit of the Reverend A. E. Robertson, the first person to climb all the 3,000ers, just over one hundred years ago. It's said he kissed the cairn, then, as an afterthought perhaps, his wife.

Between Meall Dearg and Stob Coire Leith, a series of rocky towers known as the 'Crazy Pinnacles' bars any straightforward progress. While the path and the crampon marks of generations of climbers make route-finding relatively straightforward, we soon realised we weren't going to get things all our own way. The rocks were greasy and slippery and the narrow chimneys and gullies, so delightful in dry, summer conditions, were muddy and wet. Everything seemed steeper and harder than I remembered, but the exposure and the scrambling were exhilarating and we were both mildly disappointed when, with the last of the pinnacles behind us, all that was left was a rather steep trudge on to Stob Coire Leith. From there it was an easy walk to the second of the ridge's Munros, Sgorr nam Fiannaidh, 3,173 feet/967 metres.

From the Peak of the Fianna there are several descent options but, with the sun piercing the grey clouds, we elected to stay high and continue to the logical end of the traverse at Sgorr na Ciche, the Pap of Glencoe. We weren't being purist. A reasonable path runs down to the old Glencoe road from here, and it is preferable to the steep, scree-scabbed, knee-wrenching descent that runs parallel with the Clachaig Gully. The only advantage to that route, the normal descent route from Sgorr nam Fiannaidh, is that it takes you to the front door of the Clachaig. That said, I'd rather enjoy my post-walk pint with my knees intact.

A few weeks later I received a call from a friend and member of the Glen Coe Mountain Rescue Team, Davy Gunn. A recent spate of accidents and two fatalities in the past two years have highlighted a growing problem for hillwalkers. Davy pointed out that the real hazard of the Aonach Eagach doesn't arise until the western end of this three-thousand-foot descent, and there were about twenty call-outs each year for cragfast walkers. It would appear they try to avoid the notoriously loose and unstable path, but are often frightened, late, or tired (often all three) due to underestimating the route or attempting it in foul weather.

The sheer volume of walkers descending directly to the A82 from the Sgorr nam Fiannaidh end meant the slopes had become unstable and there was a risk of rockfall. Davy said the ground to the east of the Gully had become eroded, especially the track that descends to Loch Achtriochtan, even though restoration work had been carried out. The implications of missing this rather vague path from Stob Coire Leith have led to a lot of rescues. Unsurprisingly, the Clachaig Inn, at the foot of the Gully, is a magnet after a day on the ridge, but the direct route is now pretty dangerous. The safest way to a pint is via the col that lies south of the Pap of Glencoe and down to the old Glencoe road. This route, although longer, is much safer. From the col, a path descends to the road between the Inn and the village, but it's sensible to give yourself as much time as possible to traverse the ridge, allowing plenty of daylight so that the need to escape is less urgent.

Part of the problem on the Aonach Eagach is that some Munro-baggers are not sufficiently experienced, or competent enough in scrambling skills, and take a long time to nervously negotiate its various difficulties. If you're determined to get those two Munros ticked off there are other options available.

Many walkers hire a guide to take them along the Cuillin ridge in Skye, so why not here too? If you're a little nervous about such steep, rocky terrain then it's no shame to hire a qualified mountain guide who will not only ensure your safety, but give you a superb day out. Alternatively, you can tackle Sgorr nam Fiannaidh directly from the route I've suggested for descent. This Munro can be climbed from the north, from Caolasnacon on the B863 Kinlochleven road, where Stob Coire Leith and Meall Dearg/Am Bodach can also give two shorter but equally good days avoiding the awkward Aonach Eagach pinnacles. Incidentally, these routes offer safer escape options at the start and end of the Pinnacles. Once down to the B863 you'll have to hitch-hike back to Glen Coe but that's a small price to pay for safety. The northern slopes and corries of the Aonach Eagach are quiet and tranquil, and are really delightful. They also give access to the Corbett Garbh Bheinn.

Although not strictly in Glen Coe, Stob Dearg of Buachaille Etive Mor is generally considered to be one of the glen's clutch of Munros. It also happens to be one of my favourite mountains in Scotland. I've always loved W. H. Murray's notion that this peak has the 'stateliness of tall trees on a broad lawn'. Bill Murray was our greatest mountain writer, a climber who spent so much time on the steep flanks of the Buachaille that he referred to the mountain as an 'old friend'. His comparison between the mountain and trees is spot on, capturing the harmony of vertical and horizontal in a way that few mountains do. In the Buachaille's case it's because the mountain dramatically upthrusts from the bare flats of Rannoch Moor, dominating everything around, standing guard over both Glen Etive and the gaping jowls of upper Glen Coe. Its squat base, pyramid shape and sharp peak are the very epitome of a dream mountain... or a nightmare.

Charles Dickens didn't like it at all. He suggested it was an awful place, 'haunts as you might imagine yourself wandering in, in the very height and madness of a fever'. William Wordsworth described it as: 'A huge peak, black and huge, as if with voluntary power instinct, upreared its head.' I'm not altogether sure what he meant but I think he was a little overawed.

Most climbers in Scotland regard the Buachaille as an old friend. Its close proximity to the A82 Glasgow to Fort William road makes it easily recognisable and most, at some stage in their career, will have tackled some of the routes on its steep flanks. As a youngster I used to spend weekend after weekend bumming around them, camping below and testing my nascent climbing skills on easy scrambles like Curved Ridge or D Gully Buttress. Later I moved on to some of the comparatively easy rock-climbs like January Jigsaw and Agag's Groove, followed by some of the harder John Cunningham routes like the Hard VS (Very Severe) Crow's Nest Crack.

Such familiarity with the mountain engenders a sense of belonging, a kinship if you like, and when I left the car park at Altnafeadh to film an ascent for the BBC's *Adventure Show* I had a real sense of coming home. Camera operator Paul Diffley and I had decided to take the hillwalkers' route up Coire na Tulaich, above the little whitewashed Scottish Mountaineering Club hut at Lagangarbh, before making our way up the broad, stony ridge to the summit of Stob Dearg, 3,350 feet/1,021 metres. What a summit it is! I can't think of any other mountain peak in Scotland where you get such a sense of immense spaciousness. From the cairn, you gaze across the flatness of Rannoch Moor, stretching towards the Wall of Rannoch in the south and Loch Rannoch and Schiehallion in the east. It's an extraordinary sight and all the more remarkable when you consider that you could drop the entire Lake District National Park into it and still have space to spare.

With the sun shining and more hillwalkers than I've ever seen on a Scottish mountain there was an air of festivity about, a relaxed and happy group of people simply enjoying being there on a glorious day. The Buachaille's mountain gods are not always so benevolent. The previous winter three hillwalkers were killed in an avalanche just below the lip of Coire na Tulaich. These were hillwalkers, not climbers tackling one of the notorious gully routes on the Buachaille's north-east face. Hillwalkers taking the normal hillwalkers' route. Although the route up Coire na Tulaich is the easiest way up, it does pass through a notorious avalanche spot, reinforcing the fact that winter hillwalking in Scotland is no less demanding than mountaineering. Walkers who tackle routes like this need the skills of the mountaineer, including avalanche awareness. The thought of it brought a chill to an otherwise perfect day.

Mountain filming takes time, and we were keen to laze around on the summit, so we simply descended the way we had come, while most Munro-baggers will want to climb the Buachaille's other tops.

From Stob Dearg a superb high level promenade runs in a rough south-west direction, linking together three other tops, each of which are worthy of Munro status. Just over a mile away, Stob na Doire's conical north-east face looks particularly impressive while, beyond it, the ridge twists over stony ground on the gradual rise to Stob Coire Altruim. The Buachaille's other Munro, Stob na Broige, 3,136 feet/956 metres, is easily reached over a series of undulations and offers extensive views down Glen Etive towards Ben Starav. To return to your starting point you're best to head back over Stob Coire Altruim to the bealach between it and Stob na Doire. From here, rough slopes, many of them badly eroded, lead into the Lairig Gartain where a muddy footpath returns to Altnafeadh and the A82.

Here's another thought from W. H. Murray and his description of Buachaille Etive Mor: '... it is a form profoundly satisfying to the eye; for it fires the mind with thoughts of the eternal, and we call that fire the love of beauty, and the emotion it arouses the awe of God.' The awe of God, I suspect, would have been a long way from the minds of a bunch of Clydeside climbers who made the cliffs of the Buachaille their own particular testing ground.

The Second World War had a completely different impact on mountaineering in Scotland from the Great War. Rather than devastating a complete generation it almost had a positive effect. Along with a new awareness of physical fitness, many young men had been trained in survival skills and mountain warfare. If the war brought any real positive benefit to mountaineering, it was surely in the shape of better equipment: nylon ropes, better karabiners and Vibram-soled boots, though most climbers had to wait several years to see any of these.

These Vibrams, named after their inventor Vitale Bramani, were moulded rubber soles and they, according to Bill Murray, began to replace traditional nailed mountaineering boots from about 1947. Not everyone liked them. Controversy raged about their effectiveness. On wet grass and lichenous rock, or on hard snow and ice, they were potentially lethal, lacking the natural bite and grip of Tricounis and nails. Conversely, they were lighter in weight, warmer, clung tenaciously to dry rock, and required less repair. They gradually replaced traditional boots, although the Aberdeen climbers, some would say deliberately, sequestering from the main opinion of Scottish mountaineering, continued to use nailed boots well into the late fifties.

The other great breakthrough came with the advent of the nylon rope. Climbers caught in freezing winter weather couldn't untie the hawser-like knots of conventional rope, and would frequently have to remain tied until it thawed out, often only after reaching their car, hut or hotel. Nylon rope virtually ousted manilla as soon as it became available in 1946–7. Its greater strength and elasticity offered additional safety, and its water-shedding properties ensured a much welcomed suppleness.

During the war years a certain amount of activity still took place in the mountains. Syd Scroggie's exploration on the Eagle Ridge of Lochnagar bore fruit with Jimmy Bell later adding a direct finish, a route that was to be regarded as one of the best ridge climbs in the country and is still regarded as a classic. Other explorations by Bell in the North-East revealed the great potential of Cairngorm granite, soon to be opened up by the Aberdeen school. In the west, Brian Kellett's Gardyloo Gully and Minus Two Buttress on Ben Nevis gave an indication of things to come.

In the years immediately after the war, Murray's book, *Mountaineering in Scotland*, popularised the sport in a way that no book, before or since, had done, and provided a stimulus to many young men whose freedom had been curbed and existence dominated by rationing and strict discipline. In the late forties he also began preparing the Scottish Mountaineering Club's first rock climbing guide to Glen Coe, so encouraging a host of climbers in new explorations.

It was at this time that Scottish climbing began to experience the onslaught of the Creagh Dhu club, the direct antithesis to the comparatively affluent, middle-class SMC. The Creagh Dhu was founded in 1930 in Clydebank, a working-class ship-building town, and its early members were genuine all-rounders who hillwalked, climbed and travelled the byways of the Highlands in an escape from the Depression. They made no real mark prior to the outbreak of war, but after the war it was a different story. Localising much of their activity in the Arrochar area, on the Cobbler and Beinn Narnain, the Creagh Dhu introduced artificial climbing, or continental tension-climbing, to Scotland, a technique used on the big walls of the Italian Dolomites in the thirties and popular in the Alps. The Creagh Dhu was characterised by this new and exciting style and was always willing to adopt new ideas and techniques, making breakthroughs where almost all their Scottish predecessors had failed. For the first time, Scottish rock climbers were creating standards which compared with, and were often in advance of, what was happening south of the Border!

Indeed, the Creagh Dhu members made the biggest impact on Scottish climbing since the golden days of the SMC. They were soon followed by Aberdonian climbers under the inspiration of Bill Brooker and Tom Patey, with the Squirrels from Edinburgh arriving later still. Names such as John Cunningham, Bill Smith, Charlie Vigano, Mick Noon, Patsy Walsh, John McLean, George Shields and Hamish MacInnes would virtually monopolise West of Scotland climbing from the late forties to the middle fifties, putting up climbs which forty years later are still regarded as serious routes.

An old friend of mine, Yorkshireman Dennis Gray, for many years the General Secretary of the British Mountaineering Council, lived for a time in Scotland and climbed with the Creagh Dhu. He recalls those days in his autobiography, *Tight Rope*, published in 1993 by the Ernest Press.

'This was also a golden era for the Dhus,' he wrote, 'and on my journey with them I grew to appreciate fully the initiative of working-class climbers in escaping from their awful inner-city environment, which appeared then to be a sea of slums and saloon bars, terribly depressing to a newcomer, but there was nothing depressed about my gregarious Glasgow friends, who joked and sang all the way to Arrochar. Every Dhu sported a flat cap, and they looked like the original "No Mean City" gang. Their accents were so thick that I could barely follow their conversations, but it soon became apparent that, when the Dhus took a dislike to anyone it went deep, and in that era (like my own friends in the Bradford Lads) this dislike was directed towards the climbing establishment, which in Scotland then meant the SMC. However, they were not afraid of turning the joke on themselves, and I laughed until I cried at the misfortunes that had befallen them.'

Dennis told me a story about two Creagh Dhu members discovering the fresh carcass of a deer which had been killed by a passing vehicle. Somehow they managed to stuff the remains into a rucksack and took it back to Glasgow, convinced that one of the city hotels or restaurants would buy it, but it wasn't the 'venison season' and no-one was interested. Realising that if the police discovered the remains in their possession they would be accused of poaching, they cut it up and put the pieces into a suitcase which they then deposited, under a false name, in the left-luggage room at Glasgow's Central Station. A number of weeks later, in the middle of a summer heatwave, a headline in the *Glasgow Herald* proclaimed, 'Body found in suitcase in station's left-luggage.' An attendant had noticed the strong pong and called in the Health Inspector who, in turn, discovered the source of the niff. Convinced it was a human body, the police were called in and it took several days for the decomposed remains to be identified as non-human.

Unusually, the Creagh Dhu gave an honorary membership to an Edinburgh climber, one of Scotland's finest ever mountaineers. Jimmy Marshall first came across the club on little Ben A'an in the Trossachs. Despite the myths that later suggested the Creagh Dhu were an introspective, aggressive bunch, Marshall's first recollection was how friendly they were. Friendly, but wild.

> 'They always climbed on Ben A'an because it was handy to get to from Glasgow. They took the bus over to Aberfoyle then they'd hike over the Duke's Pass to the Trossachs. And they had these tremendous thrashes there as well. They had a particularly famous one when they had this huge piss-up and they had a battle in the bar and they stole the targes and swords off the walls and they were running around in the snow, smashing the place up and thinking, "this landlord's a bloody great guy, he's not doing anything about this." The truth was that the police had become stuck in the snow on the way over. Of course they were then barred from there forever!'

Dennis Gray also suggests that John Cunningham, in company with Joe Brown, was in 1951 *the* outstanding rock climbing pioneer. This reputation was created by the evidence of his many first ascents, including Gallows Route and Guerdon Grooves on the Buachaille's Slime Wall, the latter a route far in advance of its time. Consider that Gallows Route, which was strenuous and poorly protected, was first climbed in 1946 in plimsolls. Today it's graded at E1 5b!

Edinburgh climber Kenny Spence, writing in *Mountain Magazine* in the mid-eighties, suggested that if 'modern' in rock climbing means athletic and technical, as opposed to the romance of summits, sunsets and routes which finish on tops, then Cunningham's Gallows made him Scotland's first modern master. Guerdon Grooves, climbed with Bill Smith in 1948, is still a Hard VS and the original ascent was apparently watched by forty other members of the Creagh Dhu, some claiming it to be unjustifiable such was its degree of difficulty.

John Cunningham served his time as a shipwright in John Brown's shipyard on Clydeside, a background shared by many of the Creagh Dhu. He was, perhaps, difficult to get to know. Allen Fyffe, later to be a colleague at Glenmore Lodge, said that if you got on with him he was great. If he didn't like you, then beware. This was a characteristic shared by many of his fellow club members.

Like most of his contemporaries, Cunningham climbed mainly in summer in those early days of his career, preferring to ski in winter. It wasn't until much later, when working with the Antarctic Survey in Antarctica that he began experimenting with 'front pointing' techniques on ice. As Hamish MacInnes later recalled: 'He studied ballet at one time and used these skills to climb intimidatingly steep ice with razor-keen crampons and an ice dagger.'

On his return to the UK, while working as an instructor at Glenmore Lodge, Cunningham was one of the major technical innovators in the development of winter climbing, using two axes and the front points of crampons. Tragically, he was killed in 1979 while attempting to rescue a pupil from drowning off the cliffs of Anglesey in North Wales.

After the publication of Murray's *Rock-Climbing Guide to Glen Coe* in 1949, activity fell away for a few years, but picked up again in 1954 with a series of impressive routes by Creagh Dhu members. Walsh and Vigano put up Brevity Crack (Hard VS) on the Buachaille, followed by Cunningham and Noon's Boomerang (VS) on Aonach Dubh, Walsh and Smith on Mainbrace Crack (Hard VS), and Walsh and Cunningham on Pendulum (E2), both on the Buachaille. The following couple of years saw a blitzing of routes in Glen Coe, including a number of new routes on Slime Wall by Patsy Walsh including Bloody Crack (Hard VS), Revelation (VS) and Bludger's Route (Hard VS). Possibly the finest route of the time was Carnivore (E2) on Creag a' Bhancair, by Cunningham and Mick Noon in 1958, which Dennis Gray later claimed to be the hardest route he had ever climbed.

During the forties a young man from Greenock noticed that one of his neighbours rode off on his motorbike every Friday night, not returning till late on Sunday. Intrigued, he asked the man where he went, and discovered he was a climber. The next weekend he went along as a pillion passenger, and that chance encounter began a career which has been one of the most enduring in Scottish mountaineering. Hamish MacInnes became a Creagh Dhu member and, with his engineering background, was responsible for many technological advances, not only in equipment but also in climbing techniques. In the early fifties he put up his share of new rock routes on the Cobbler, with routes like

Ithuriel's Wall (Hard VS), Gladiator's Groove Direct (Hard VS), Whither Wether (VS), and Whether Wall (VS).

In 1953, a chance meeting with the young and inexperienced, but extremely self-confident, Chris Bonington led to a first winter's ascent of Agag's Groove (Grade V), on the Rannoch Wall of the Buachaille, and Raven's Gully (Hard VS). Bonington later described MacInnes as 'already a legendary figure in Scottish circles, although he was only in his early twenties'. MacInnes had spent his National Service in Austria where he had developed a taste for pegging routes: hammering pitons into cracks in the rock, clipping in a karabiner and using the peg either as a running belay or for tension climbing. He soon developed a reputation for using pitons and earned himself the sobriquet of MacPiton.

This habit did not endear him to the SMC and many of climbing's traditionalists, but Hamish was never one to let public opinion upset him. He later moved to Glen Coe where he founded the glen's first official mountain rescue team. He also began designing and manufacturing ice axes, tools that helped take Scottish winter and mixed climbing to an internationally acclaimed level. Meanwhile, while the Creagh Dhu's primary contribution was to Scottish rock climbing, in winter many club members took to skis and eventually grasped the initiative in ski development in Scotland, particularly at the White Corries in Glen Coe and Coire Cas on Cairn Gorm.

The Creagh Dhu are still active but perhaps their greatest memorial is a low, slightly squalid-looking building on the south bank of the River Coupall below the north-east flanks of the Buachaille. There have been numerous threats to Jacksonville, the Creagh Dhu club hut, over the years, not least by the National Trust for Scotland, but it has been claimed apocryphally that if they dismantled Jacksonville then some NTS properties might accidentally catch fire.

I became aware of its importance to the Creagh Dhu club when I presented a BBC television series called *The Edge – 100 Years of Scottish Mountaineering*. Two club members, Jimmy Marshall and big John McLean, were to climb a route for the cameras, which would, actually, be a combination of two routes: Bludgers and Revelation. As we stood chatting in the car park a car pulled up, and two young hillwalkers got out and passed the time of day with us. Jimmy and John couldn't have been more pleasant and wished them a great day. However, as the lads left us I noticed them watching over my shoulder. The hillwalkers crossed the River Coupall and turned towards Jacksonville. Jimmy and John were ignoring me by now, their eyes pinned on the two hillwalkers. As soon as the two lads tried to push open the door of Jacksonville they went ballistic. 'Get the fuck out of there, you bastards,' they yelled at the top of their voices. 'That's private fucking property,' they roared, 'Get tae fuck you bastards . . .'

Needless to say the two hillwalkers scampered off, with verbal abuse ringing in their ears. I was equally taken aback by the sudden change in the jovial McLean and the normally quiet architect from Edinburgh, Jimmy Marshall. Jacksonville's reputation as the private domain of the Creagh Dhu Mountaineering Club remains to this day, and long may that continue.

8

LOVELESS LOVELINESS

Mountaineer Hamish Brown once wrote a poem about Ben Nevis in which he described the mountain as a harlot, a mountain of 'loveless loveliness'. I know exactly what he meant.

Ben Nevis is not only Scotland's highest and arguably finest mountain, it also tempts the unwary and the inexperienced like no other. Brooding over Lochaber, the Ben appears as a round-shouldered half-dome of a hill, often gaunt and dark, a mountain of many faces and diverse character. For most, Ben Nevis represents a simple and unique challenge – to walk up to the highest summit in the country – but that is not a challenge that is necessarily easily met. It involves a long and tiresome toil up a rough track that is often exposed to Arctic winds, to a summit area littered with the ruins of an old weather observatory, a corrugated iron shelter, several memorial cairns and the detritus that visitors tend to leave in such prominent places as 'the highest'.

For many thousands of tourists every year, folk who are not by any stretch of the imagination mountaineers, reaching the summit of Britain's highest mountain is a once-in-a-lifetime experience, an achievement to be recalled with pride, and an enticing introduction to the high and wild places of Scotland. For some, it can be a life-changing experience but, for others, the Ben presents an even greater challenge.

Consider this. The brooding, round-shouldered aspect of the hill is really a façade, a screen that protects the real guts of the mountain, its backside if you like. The north-east-facing cliffs, buttresses and gullies dominating the high corrie above the Allt a' Mhuillin present a radical contrast to the rest of the mountain. For many, this, the most formidable mountain face in Britain, is the real Ben Nevis.

The high cliffs are riven and seared by gullies, prominent ridges, towers and buttresses. From the early pioneers in the eighteenth century, generations of climbers have pioneered long and difficult routes on these vast cliffs and, when winter snows change its face, the climbers return to enjoy a type of mountaineering that is world-renowned. Scottish winter climbing is a masochistic blend of rock climbing, winter scrambling and balancing on tiny snow-filled footholds while you endeavour to bury your ice axe into a ledge of frozen turf. All this while the wind throws down showers of fine, powdery spindrift, and the cold throbs through your body like toothache. The north-east face of Ben Nevis attracts climbers from all over the world, eager to experience what has become internationally known as 'Scottish mixed climbing'.

The origin of the name Nevis is obscure, but the general belief is that it means 'terrible', from the old Irish Gaelic word *neamhaise*, or the Highland Gaelic word *nimhaise*, meaning 'no beauty'. Another school of thought believes it derives from *nimheis* which could be 'heaven'. The late writer Seton Gordon suggests the name has been taken from the river and glen below, which had a bad reputation in former times. According to a sixteenth-century bard:

> *Glen Nevis, a glen of stones,*
> *A glen where corn ripens late,*
> *A long, wild, waste glen,*
> *With thievish folk of evil habit.*

A track runs from from Achintee in Glen Nevis, all the way to the summit of the Ben. This so-called 'tourist track' is actually the old pony track to the meteorological station on the summit. Be warned, it is long and tedious, and to climb Ben Nevis without seeing the north-east faces is like going to the beach and not seeing the sea. Try climbing the hill via Carn Mor Dearg and its airy arête, a walk that will take you through some of the finest mountain scenery in the country and is probably the most memorable way of walking up Britain's highest hill. Alternatively, a stiff climb from Glen Nevis into Coire Eoghainn, via the waterslide at Polldubh, gives a hard, but spectacular, route to the Carn Mor Dearg Arête from where the summit can be easily reached.

It may involve a lung-bursting climb of over a thousand metres, a relentlessly steep ascent with very little respite, but the route from the Polldubh car park has a lot going for it. The ascent fits nicely with an excursion over the slim crescent of the Arête to Carn Mor Dearg itself, and the day can be rounded off with a wander through upper Glen Nevis, once described as the 'finest half-mile in Scotland'.

There are many more adventurous routes that trace their way by gully and buttress, ridge and groove, up the massive north-east face of the Ben. The classic Tower Ridge for example, or the wonderful line of the North-East Buttress . . .

but these are essentially climbers' routes. The route from Polldubh, beside the great waterslide that rushes down from Coire Eoghainn, is steep, there's no doubt about that, but the views of the upper Glen are superb. The last time I used this route it was seen through the pale green tracery of early summer, when the birchwoods and lower slopes looked freshly minted, alive and resonant with new life.

In Coire Eoghainn, the soft and lush world of the glen vanishes from sight, and there is a harsh edge to the scene up here, a stone desert and very much imbued with the stark, elemental beauty of Hamish Brown's loveless loveliness. Stone and sky, sky and stone, and mountains rolling into the horizon.

The east ridge of the Ben drops from the summit and within a few hundred metres abuts the graceful curve of the Carn Mor Dearg Arête . . . but that's for later. For now, the summit lies immediately above, beyond the lines of abseil posts placed to guide climbers to the summit plateau during the icy winter months. I won't dwell on the dubious attractions of the summit – the ruins, the rescue hut, the orange peel and banana skins, which have been well documented elsewhere – and, besides, the highlight of the day lies below. Return to the start of the Arête and make your way across this thin fin of curved stone, one of the most beautiful and graceful features anywhere in the Scottish hills. It is a scramble, but it's not difficult and, if the crest is too airy for you, it's easy enough to take a less exposed route on the east side of the ridge. Soon the views of the great buttresses and ridges and gullies of the north-east face begin to open up.

This is the real heart and soul of the mountain, the Ben Nevis that attracts mountaineers from across the world. The character of the mountain is now laid bare before you, and there is no better vantage point, no better upper circle to watch this particular theatre from, than the summit of Carn Mor Dearg.

Once you've drunk your fill from both the view and the flask, descend Carn Mor Dearg's narrow east ridge to the head of Coire Giubhsachan. Fitter walkers might consider adding both Aonach Mor and Aonach Beag by climbing the steep slopes east of Coire Giubhsachan to the col between the two, but that would be a big day for most. I always enjoy the wander beside the free-flowing waters of the Allt Coire Giubhsachan to the ruins at Steall.

The valley drops to a meadow where the stream meanders in relaxed fashion before picking up speed and dashing over a steeper section. Past Steall, the Water of Nevis performs a similar act, flowing gently across the tranquil Steall Meadows before squeezing between rock walls into the deep cataract of the Nevis Gorge. You can enjoy it all as you wander along the footpath through pines and birches high above the crashing waters.

Whatever way you choose, bear in mind Hamish Brown's description. Ben Nevis occasionally shows its nasty side, so choose a good day and don't be tempted by such descriptions as 'tourist tracks'. That particular route was never designed for tourists.

If you get the opportunity, and time is on your side, sit by the cairn on Carn Mor Dearg and gaze at the phenomenal array of ridges, buttresses and gullies that make up the north-east face. This is one of the great climbing arenas of the world, particularly in winter, and some of the climbs are simply world class.

Climbers have explored this vast face since the eighteenth

century. Norman Collie made the first ascent of Tower Ridge, while Harold Raeburn has left his name on some classic first ascents. He joined the Scottish Mountaineering Club shortly after its formation but was something of a maverick in his time, leaving new routes on mountains all over the Highlands. Amongst his greatest winter achievements were Crowberry Gully on Buachaille Etive Mor in 1893, Green Gully in 1906 and Observatory Ridge in 1920, these last two on Ben Nevis. He also made a solo summer ascent of Observatory Ridge.

W. H. Murray made a winter ascent of Tower Ridge his last route in Scotland before going to fight in the Second World War. This has become a classic, the longest route on Britain's highest mountain, and in his graphic description (to be found in his wonderful book, *Mountaineering in Scotland*) Murray expertly weaves a spiritual dimension into the simple, physical act of climbing, an experience that comes to a climax as he walks across the summit plateau after completion.

> Later, when we walked slowly across the plateau, it became very clear to me that only the true self, which transcends the personal, lays claim to immortality. On mountains, it is that spiritual part that we unconsciously develop. When we fail in that all other success is empty, for we take our pleasures without joy, and the ache of boredom warns of a rusting faculty.

As part of our BBC television series, *The Edge – 100 Years of Scottish Mountaineering*, broadcast in 1994, we recreated that route on Tower Ridge. In absolutely perfect conditions of snow and ice, three mountain guides, Graham Moss,

Alasdair Cain and Mark Diggins, dressed in the gear of the thirties to play the parts of Murray and his companions, Jimmy Bell and Douglas Laidlaw. The film later won a BAFTA award but, and infinitely more memorable, I had the absolute pleasure of spending some time with Bill Murray himself, interviewing him about his life and career as a climber and writer. It was one of the great days of my life.

Over fifty years after the Tower Ridge climb, Bill, then aged eighty, remembered the details of the route with almost total recall.

'I was with Jimmy Bell and Douglas Laidlaw, a brilliant young climber who later joined the RAF and was killed in the war,' he told me in the sitting room of his home in Lochgoilhead. 'We were led on, unsuspecting, by the appearance of the ridge which was heavily covered in snow. We had a late start, and climbed to the crest of the ridge by way of the Douglas Boulder, a big 700-foot/213-metres buttress which sits at the foot of the ridge. This took some time because of the conditions, and when we reached the crest it was becoming very windy indeed. The ridge is, I suppose, the better part of 2,000 feet/610 metres, and the way is barred by two towers. At first progress was easy, but it increased in difficulty as the ice and snow thickened. When we reached the Great Tower, it was beginning to get dark, and we had to try and reverse round the east side of the Tower rather than attack it direct. The rock was covered in verglas (thin rock-ice) but eventually, after a lot of very difficult ice climbing, we arrived in the Tower Gap, which is between the Great Tower and the final rocks that lead to the summit plateau. We were aware of two things, the wind, which was roaring through the gap like an express train, and the sunset, which was absolutely fabulous. The sun was going down in a welter of cloud; there was a brilliant reddish sky and we were halted despite ourselves.

'When we tried to climb out of Tower Gap the rock was so covered in thin ice that we couldn't get up, and the wind had become a hurricane. We had to hang on just to keep standing. After long delays and talk of retreat, one of the others suggested I try and lasso a spire which resembled a canine tooth, that rose above the Gap. So, as a last desperate measure, I tried it and to our utmost surprise it caught on a little bulge at the top.

'When we reached the summit plateau there was complete calm. The wind below was striking the cliffs and shooting vertically upwards, leaving us in completely calm conditions. We all felt a profound relief and a deep sense of peace. It is always a very happy feeling getting to the top of any hard climb, and one of the great things about mountains is that the memories are always good.'

Twenty years after Bill Murray's ascent of Tower Ridge there was something of a boom in new routes, in both summer and winter, on the north-east face of the Ben. Amongst the main protagonists were two leading climbers from Edinburgh, Robin Smith and Jimmy Marshall. However, towards the end of the decade Marshall became disenchanted after a long run of wet weekends, and decided to ease off his climbing and concentrate on building his architect's business. Before that though, and before he got married, he wanted to enjoy a final fling in the mountains.

In his excellent history of climbing on Ben Nevis, author Ken Crocket suggested: '...in one week of sustained effort [Smith and Marshall] were to bring to a climax the end of a decade of exciting developments in Scottish mountaineering. In one sense, they were to gain a pinnacle of achievement which can never be bettered.'

Ken has since described that week as 'pivotal', seven days that saw the two mountaineers make the first ascent of Great Chimney on Tower Ridge, giving it a Grade IV, the first ascent of Minus Three Gully, Grade IV, the first ascent of Gardyloo Buttress via Smith's Route, Grade V (which had to wait eleven years for a second ascent), the first winter ascent of Observatory Buttress, Grade V, the second ascent of the notorious Point Five Gully, Grade V, the first winter ascent of Pigott's Route, Grade IV, on the Comb, and finally, the first long awaited ascent of Orion Face, Grade V, a route which W. H. Murray later suggested was 'an important advance in Scottish mountaineering,' a route up a great face demanding a wide range of climbing skills that seemed to augur the shape of things to come.

It was later described by Jimmy Marshall as a 'super week's climbing', but Ken Crocket believes it to be of much greater significance.

> The first winter ascent of the Orion Face was the climax of an incredible week of mountaineering on Ben Nevis. The partnership of Smith and Marshall had joined with ideal conditions, but it was more than that. In the ten years that followed other fine and equally hard routes would be won by step cutting. No other climber would come near to repeating such a sustained effort, nor to writing about it with such sustained feeling. Just as Murray had been a source of inspiration to them, so they would be for those who followed.

Even today, Jimmy Marshall looks back on that week with great fondness, but doesn't believe it was anything special. He has even taken Ken Crocket to task for giving it undue significance. I've had the great pleasure of meeting Jimmy a number of times throughout the years and, since he moved north to Speyside a few years ago, I occasionally bump into him and his wife, Maggie, in the supermarket in Aviemore. In 1994 I interviewed him at length for the BBC television series *The Edge* and, aware of that significant week in 1959, asked him what events had brought it about?

'I had become so pissed off with the weather that summer,' he confessed. 'It rained, rained and rained, so I thought "to hell with this". I had become fed up going north and I just thought I'd get my business started properly and get married. I had no intention of packing climbing in, but I had had enough of this crap of going off every weekend into the rain. As it happened, once I got married I was away every second weekend, and went to Ben Nevis shortly after I did get married. We'd just moved into this top-floor flat in King Street in Edinburgh, and I went off to the Ben and there had been a huge thunderstorm which seemed to go around the country.

'This had terrified Maggie, who of course was alone in the flat, so the neighbours, lovely people, looked after her and told her just to go to bed and tuck herself in and she did that. I arrived home very late on the Sunday and I just couldn't wake her up. I had no keys to the flat, so I had to throw pegs and karabiners through the letterbox to try and waken her. I was shouting through to her and eventually I decided just get out my sleeping bag and doss down on the landing. And that's where I was when the neighbours found me in the morning. One of them actually said, "Oh dear, have you fallen out already?"'

Jimmy and Robin Smith completed so many great routes in that week of climbing, I asked Jimmy if one stood out more than the others?

'Oh it had to be Orion,' he answered instantly. 'We had no targets as such, we had so many things we wanted to do. At the time we were sort of messianic about Scottish winter climbing. It was such a tremendous thing to us, dramatic, exciting, and we were a bit nationalistic about it, like the Germans on the Eiger, the romantic and daft way we thought about it. Because of that we said we would write about it and try and set people winter climbing. Well, I think it had the reverse effect. It stopped them climbing because they thought these things were too difficult. I think that was the effect it had. But we originally wrote to get people interested, and it took a long time before people did.'

I asked him if he was immediately aware of the significance of that week?

'No, we were only pleased with having done the Orion. Smith knew about it and had heard about it from the Currie Boys who had let the information slip, so he thought that would be a great thing to do, but the idea was that it would be the ultimate of fine lines to climb in winter. It was different from things that had gone previously, although it now transpires, historically, that it's not really very different from all the other things that were going on elsewhere.'

Sadly Robin Smith never reached his full potential as a mountaineer. He was killed on comparatively easy ground on Peak Garmo in the Pamirs at the early age of twenty-three, but Jimmy continued to climb and was partly responsible for encouraging another young member of the Currie Boys. His name was Dougal Haston and, with Doug Scott, he was one of the first two Brits to climb Everest.

Jimmy Marshall would be surprised by the number of climbers repeating these old routes of his today, and even more surprised to learn that over 160,000 people ascend Ben Nevis every year. That's not counting the climbers, but only those who tackle it by the Achintee track. Many of them are hillwalkers, Munro-baggers and hill enthusiasts, but the majority will be charity walkers and tourists, folk who simply want to climb to the highest point in the United Kingdom. All those feet put enormous pressure on the mountain and not only on the footpath. Volunteers and rangers have to collect and get rid of tons of rubbish every year, rubbish that is left behind by people who should know better.

Nathan Berrie is a local lad from Fort William and he is the John Muir Trust's Conservation Officer on the Ben. I asked him about the effect of all those pounding boots on the mountain.

'Thanks to the Nevis Landscape Partnership and Heritage Lottery funding, the Ben path is very much fit for purpose and capable of containing the movements and actions of 160,000 individuals,' he told me, much to my surprise. Not overly worried about the track, his overriding concern was with litter and irresponsible behaviour due to increased visitor numbers, and that a large number of them see the Ben as a challenge rather than 'a day out in nature'.

Ben Nevis attracts many thousands of challenge and charity walkers, often combining it with ascents of Scafell Pike, the highest hill in England, and Snowdon, the highest hill in Wales. Such 'Three Peaks' charity efforts raise millions of pounds annually, but are thought to have a detrimental effect on the mountain environment.

Others take on different challenges. The annual Ben Nevis Hill Race is immensely popular; wheelchairs are frequently carried and pushed to the summit, and the late Don Whillans once rode a motorbike to the top. Early last century a Model

T Ford was driven, pushed and carried up and, on the centenary of that event, in 2011, a team of sixty volunteers carried up the dismantled replica of a Model T. Such is the madness associated with our highest mountain, but beat this... Two fell runners from Fort William once carried up a piano! Its remains were later discovered buried deep within a cairn.

Isn't it strange that charity walks are not organised on Ben Macdui, our second-highest mountain, and no-one to my knowledge has attempted to carry a piano to its 4,300-foot/1,311-metre summit? The crazy stunts are reserved for the highest hill, and the highest hill only, so how best should the mountain be protected? Nathan answered without hesitation. It was something he had given a lot of thought to.

'It might be good if those who use Ben Nevis for commercial purposes donated a small percentage of their income to the Nevis Partnership for upkeep of the mountain. A good example is the Ben Nevis Ultra race, which donates one per cent of its profits to the John Muir Trust to mitigate any environmental impact they may cause. We work closely with them and they voluntarily undertake an independent environmental impact assessment of their race. Granted, this is because it takes place on unmarked routes and sensitive habitats, but nevertheless it is a good example.

'If a donation is not possible, these groups might consider including a litter pick into their walk, an approach which I believe would be very good PR for them while benefitting the mountain at the same time.'

Others have suggested a permit system for walkers using the Achintee track in an attempt to reduce numbers, but I think that is not only a long, long way off but also contradictory to Scotland's access legislation.

The Ben's iconic status puts special pressure on footpaths, and footpath work is expensive. On Royal Deeside for example, car park fees (ring-fenced for footpath repair and maintenance) bring in about £50,000 annually. That sounds a lot, but last year over £1.5 million was spent on footpath work in the area. That 'donated' money helps Upper Deeside Access Trust raise grants or matched funding, so it actually goes a long, long way.

However, Nathan has his own ideas about dealing with the problems. He calls it 'slow adventure'. 'This might play a big part in the upkeep of Ben Nevis,' he told me. 'If we educate individuals, and promote slow adventure more widely, we might be able to create more mindful visitors who are there to experience Ben Nevis as a wild place rather than a mountain to be "conquered".

'Educating people is key to this, and while many feel it is a lost cause I believe that if we are not educating people we are only treating the symptom and not the illness. Although the issues of litter and irresponsible behaviour are increasing, the JMT do not believe the situation is critical. Through the help of local groups, mountain guides and especially our dedicated volunteers, Ben Nevis is regularly monitored and litter is managed. It is debatable whether this approach is sustainable with more visitors each year, so education is key in creating more responsible behaviour. The challenge of finding the best channel for education is critical. Ironically, social media, which is often blamed for an increase of visitors to remote locations, might have an important role to play.'

I rather like Nathan's notion of 'slow' adventure, which could be described as the opposite of adrenaline-pumping experiences like rock climbing, BASE jumping, extreme whitewater kayaking or fell running. More of an immersive journey, slow adventure has us living in and travelling through wild places and cultural spaces, experiencing nature in its seasons and appreciating cultural aspects of the area like song, folklore and history. Come to think of it, exactly what this book is about!

While I hugely enjoy revisiting the hills that I've climbed in my youth, the prevailing emotion I've felt has been one of frustration, an irritation borne of the painful knowledge that I can no longer treat these hills in the cavalier fashion I did when I was younger and fitter.

Take the wonderful Mamores ridge, for example. This nine-mile long mountain crest has long been considered one of the great hillwalking outings of Scotland, with Glen Nevis separating it from the Grey Corries in the north and long slopes running down to Kinlochleven in the south, all well served by a marvellous network of stalkers' paths. The ridge itself is narrow, serpentine and sustained, Alpine-like in snowy winter and spring conditions. The full traverse, well over twenty miles for the round trip from Mullach nan Coirean in the west to Sgurr Eilde Mor in the east, is a big day out, but one I enjoyed as a fit twenty-something-year-old. It was my first visit to the Mamores and, along with my old pal Roger Smith, we galloped along the ridge, dodging in and out of cloud and mist, collecting ten Munro ticks on the way and ending the glorious day with a long, weary trudge back along the glen in the dark. I certainly couldn't do that today.

In some ways it doesn't matter. I'm just thankful that I can still get onto the tops and, here's another thing, as I've become older I've learned the value of compromise. The concession in this case is breaking the long ridge into bite-sized chunks, a series of shorter days that can be enjoyed at a more leisurely pace.

The most challenging of these concessions takes in the dramatically named Devil's Ridge, along with four of the Mamores' Munros: An Gearanach, 3,222 feet/982 metres, Stob Choire a' Chairn, 3,218 feet/981 metres, Am Bodach, 3,386 feet/1,032 metres, and Sgurr a' Mhaim, 3,606 feet/1,099 metres. The Devil's Ridge lies between Sgurr an Iubhair and Sgurr a' Mhaim and, despite its name, is far from evil, although in winter conditions it can give several heart-stopping moments.

This section of the range goes by the dramatic title of the Ring of Steall as the route follows the high ridges around Coire a' Mhail, whose waters feed the Grey Mare's Tail which, in turn, falls abruptly onto the Steall meadows. The route traverses three other 3,000-feet tops including Sgurr an Iubhair, which was demoted from Munro status by the Scottish Mountaineering Club in a bout of 'adjusting' a few years back. Ten miles and over 4,000 feet of climbing offer an unforgettable day with close-up views of Ben Nevis and the Aonachs.

Even the preamble to this route is memorable. From the Polldubh car park a well-worn trail weaves through the trees above the roar of the Himalaya-like Nevis Gorge, once described by Bill Murray as the 'best half-mile in Scotland.' I certainly wouldn't disagree. Suddenly the path is squeezed into a flat, green meadow through which the Water of Steall flows gently, as though unaware of what the Nevis Gorge has in store for it. At the head of the meadows, a glorious slash of water falls for 300 feet and, close by, a hawser-wire bridge crosses the river to a footpath which runs east past the Steall hut. This is below the Grey Mare's Tail and a tree-clad buttress into Coire Chadha Chaoruinn.

Once past the Allt Coire Chadha Chaoruinn, another path climbs in long zigzags, eventually carrying you to the north-west spur of An Gearanach, which roughly translates as 'the complainer'. Perhaps because it used to be unmarked on the Ordnance Survey map! A short ridge runs south to An Garbhanach from where another ridge continues in a south-west direction before rising to the scree-covered summit of Stob Choire a' Chairn. The long ridge now undulates towards Am Bodach, before swinging west and north-west to reach the peak of the yew tree, Sgurr an Iubhair.

The drama increases as you approach the Devil's Ridge. From its high point at Stob Choire a' Mhail the ridge narrows in its link with the southern stony slopes of Sgurr a' Mhaim. At the slimmest section, a footpath drops down on the east side and avoids the rocky difficulties before making a scrambled return. The final test-piece is a steep descent of slabs to a narrow bealach where the slopes open on the wide quartz-covered summit of Sgurr a' Mhaim before, again, descending a lovely curving ridge, usually beautifully corniced well into the spring, above Coire Sgorach. The final knee-destroying descent down the nose, Sron Sgurr a' Mhaim, takes you back into Glen Nevis about one-and-a-half miles west of the car park at Polldubh.

The finish point at Achriabhach is also the starting point for another Mamores expedition, the round of the two western Munros, which contrast beautifully with each other. Stob Ban, 3,278 feet/999 metres, is the epitome of ruggedness, with a craggy, seamed and precipitous north-east face, while Mullach nan Coirean, at 3,081 feet/939 metres, is the flat culmination of a number of grassy ridges, corrie-bitten and round-shouldered. What it lacks in bare ruggedness it makes up for in its position high above Loch Linnhe, with panoramic views towards Ardgour and Mull. All the while the huge, humpbacked bulk of Ben Nevis broods just across the glen.

These western Munros can be accessed from Coire a' Mhusgain, and as an entrée to the main course it's difficult to beat this approach. After its initial steepness the footpath levels out before climbing gently through the old birch woods above the tumbling waters of the Allt Coire a' Mhusgain (check out its pools on some hot and sunny day). Just past the woods the footpath checks itself, performs a switchback and climbs a series of zigzags before swinging back into the upper corrie. About here you begin to *feel* the presence of Stob Ban, its scalloped north-east corrie seared and riven by great scree runnels that split its vegetated cliffs into a dramatic series of gullies, buttresses and crags, the upper ones sparkling quartzite white.

The head of Coire a' Mhusgain is enclosed by the pivotal ridges of Sgurr an Iubhair, one running out to the white quartzite screes of Sgurr a' Mhaim and the other forming the high-level link with Stob Ban itself. The corrie head is a wonderful spot, especially with its glacial lochan. I camped here a long number of years ago when walking a big loop around Glen Nevis and remember it as an atmospheric, deer-haunted place. The footpath crosses the stream well below the lochan and zigzags its way up steep slopes to reach the eastern ridge of Stob Ban. Another well-worn path slavishly follows the edge of the east ridge, gradually becoming steeper before it deposits you on the surprisingly rounded summit. The cairn is perched near the cliff edge of the north-east corrie.

A narrow switchback ridge runs out to Mullach nan Coirean, moving from the micaschist of Stob Ban, the white peak, to the pink granite of Mullach nan Coirean. Four main ridges radiate from the Mullach's summit so, before you leave, check your compass to be sure that you take the east ridge.

A few years ago, I stayed overnight at the rather Gothic-looking Mamore Lodge. After giving a talk at the excellent Ice Factor in Kinlochleven, I took advantage of my decrepit but lofty digs to climb another couple of the Mamore Munros, Na Gruagaichean and Binnein Mor.

In the Scottish Mountaineering Club guide to the Central Highlands, author Peter Hodgkiss suggests that few hills of comparable stature are so little climbed in their own right. While Na Gruagaichean (the maiden) is certainly impressive from Kinlochleven, Peter suggests 'its grace of form and the complexity of its twin tops are only revealed when approaching along the main ridge'. A stalkers' path reaches the said ridge less than a mile north-west of the summit, and starts, very conveniently, about half a mile north-east of Mamore Lodge.

The climb through Coire na Ba was straightforward, if a little slippery, but higher up great snow fields covered the stalkers' path, so it wasn't much help. Instead, I took a direct line up steep snow slopes and reached the main ridge in about ninety minutes. Hard snow and *névé* covered the rocky ground but was susceptible to kicked steps up the ridge's twists and turns. Visibility was very poor, but I was aware of a cornice edge close beside me. It would be fragile, and potentially lethal, so I kept my distance while at the same time welcoming its presence as a navigational aid. Provided I kept it on my left I was going in the right direction.

A steady pull to the first of Na Gruagaichean's summits was followed by a steep 200-foot descent into the black and rocky defile between the two tops. By the time I reached the main summit the wind had lost its edge and for that I was thankful, as the ridge east of Na Gruagaichean, to the unnamed top between Binnein Mor and Sgor Eilde Beag, is knife-edged and not a place to be with the wind playing games.

In good conditions this section of the Mamore Ridge is a real highlight, a curving knife-edge with steep drops on either side. I might have heard the sound of rutting stags rising from the deep corries but all I could be sure of was the relentless roar of the wind. The ridge rises to a subsidiary top before veering north along a rockier crest to Binnein Mor where the tiny square-cut summit is formed by curved ridges and corries into a classic, archetypal mountain shape.

From Binnein Mor I returned along the ridge to its south summit, where I should have been able to gaze back along the flowing crest, but a grey, billowing cloak of cloud obscured everything. The favourable views today were not of wide, sweeping panoramas but of the microscopic: lichens, quartz shapes in the rocks and the moisture patterns of the clouds. A broader ridge carried me to Sgor Eilde Beag from where a wonderfully engineered stalkers' path dropped me back down to the track and Mamore Lodge.

That same track will also carry you from the Lodge, or from Kinlochleven, to my final, and favourite, Mamore Munros, Binnein Beag and Sgurr Eilde Mor. Of the ten Munros that make up the ridge, these two are probably the most awkwardly placed. All the other tops are laced by high, interconnecting ridges but the ascent of this eastern pair involves a big descent and re-ascent. I vividly recall climbing Sgurr Eilde Mor as part of that mammoth Mamores ridge walk I mentioned earlier, arriving at the summit on legs of jelly. In more recent years I've climbed the hills in more gentle fashion from Kinlochleven.

One glorious spring day, I left the car park beside St Paul's Episcopal church and made my way up the wooded hillside to the track that runs between Mamore Lodge and Luibeilt. There's a good network of footpaths around Kinlochleven, many of which can be utilised to reach the upper slopes around the village. I made good use of one that carried me high above the village, with wonderful views down the length of fjord-like Loch Leven. It doesn't take long for the surroundings to convince you that this highland village, once a centre of intense industrial activity, is one of the most scenically situated villages in the whole of the Highlands.

Just west of Loch Eilde Mor a stalkers' path left the main track, an old and well-used trail with signs of overuse in its lower stretches. Higher up though, as it traverses the south slopes of Sgor Eilde Beag, it tightens considerably before zigzagging three or four times into another traverse that dropped me into the incredibly atmospheric hollow cradling the blue-green waters of Coire an Lochain. Beyond the corrie, the perfect cone-shape of Binnein Beag rose as a foreground to the Aonachs and Ben Nevis. I climbed its steep slopes to the summit before retracing my steps back to where the pyramidal summit slopes of Sgurr Eilde Mor cast their dark reflections into the waters of the loch. I swapped the easy-angled footpath for the screes and boulders of the north-west ridge, a steep and rough route to the narrow summit, and a spectacular panoramic view of all these wonderful hills, as well as the Easans and the great water-logged mattress of the Rannoch Moor.

More rough slopes took me down the south ridge to the lochan where I picked up the outward path and made my way, reluctantly, through the dimming light to Kinlochleven. It had been one of those days when less is better than more, and taking time to stand and stare allows the sense of wonder that often escapes us in the impetuosity of youth. I guess it fitted in well with Nathan Berrie's description of 'slow adventure'. We only live once, but if we do it right, once is enough.

9

THROUGH THE GATES OF AFFRIC

The Gaelic has it well. The dappled, or mottled, ford is from *Ath-Breac*, and carries a suggestion of overhanging trees and flowing waters glinting in sunlight. Think of pinewoods and a sprinkling of other species like birch, rowan, aspen, bird cherry and wood hawthorn. Willow and alder grow in the wetter, damper areas, and a lush covering of lichens and mosses spreads its green carpet over the woodland floor. Juniper and heather live alongside bilberry and cowberry, and wintergreen chickweed and orchids have their beauty unlocked by the golden sunlight of summer.

The glen of that dappled ford is rarely considered in such a woodsy, watery context. Some claim it is Scotland's most scenic glen, and I wouldn't argue. Glen Affric wears its hallowed reputation well, a rich tapestry of loch, forest, mountain and something else that is not quite visible to the human eye, something that only the soul can understand.

Whenever I visit Glen Affric, and neighbouring Kintail, I experience a sense of deep-rooted belonging, and a gnawing realisation of what is important. That perception is most strong during the seasonal crossover from autumn to winter, when the rising sun offers only an illusion of warmth as it casts its glow over the frosted leaves, and you can delight in the vibrancy and sharpness of the chilled air. Beyond the trees and over the river a curiously welcoming pall of smoke hangs above the mountaineering club hut known as Strawberry Cottage. Beyond it, etched against the ice blue of the sky, a sharp horizon runs east to west, familiar hill shapes in unfamiliar shades of early winter.

Those are the shapes that tempt me here time and time again, the summits of a long serpentine ridge that begins on the high spine between Loch Beinn a' Mheadhoin and Loch Mullardoch and rises over the Munros of Toll Creagach and Tom a' Choinich. Sweeping round the head of Gleann na Fiadh and over Carn Eige and Mam Sodhail, the ridge curves west over the diminutive An Socach before running out to Sgurr nan Ceathreamhnan. Off-shooting ridges to the north stretch to two, further, solitary Munros: Beinn Fhionnlaidh and Mullach na Dheiragain.

Blocking the far end of the glen are two more Munros, Beinn Fhada and A' Ghlas-bheinn, separated by the atmospheric Bealach an Sgairne, the pass 'where the stones make noise'. That's a loose interpretation of the Gaelic and may refer to the wind 'sighing' or 'murmuring' through the rocks. Ghostly apparitions have been seen and heard here. On the trail that winds its way up from Strath Croe in the west, some walkers once passed a tall, thin man with a white beard, hand in hand with a small girl wrapped in a cloak and hood. After making local enquiries they were convinced they had met the ghosts of Osgood Mackenzie, the great botanist and creator of the Inverewe Gardens, and his daughter Mhairi Mackenzie who had died some thirty years previously.

The south side of Glen Affric may not be as Munro-rich until you hit the big hills of Kintail, but I will always hold a candle for two fine Corbetts that lie to the south-west of Cougie Lodge, a popular and hospitable place well known to *TGO* Challengers (the annual backpacking trip across Scotland organised by *The Great Outdoors* magazine): Aonach Shasuinn, 2,913 feet/888 metres and Carn a' Choire Ghairbh, 2,837 feet/865 metres. Both hills can be accessed from the track that runs beside the Allt Garbh from just south of Affric Lodge, rising above an intricate network of glens, sinuous burns and crag-girt corries.

These two hills boast the most precious of mountain gifts. Solitude. It's very rare to meet other walkers on Affric's Corbetts.

While the Munros are popular, many of Glen Affric's other mountains remain unsullied. They dominate and enclose the glen, their frowning presence contrasting with the tranquillity of the forest's lower reaches. Protected as a National Nature Reserve, Glen Affric boasts the third-largest remnant of the once vast Ancient Forest of Caledon, whose stands of Scots Pine have been reduced over the centuries to just one per cent of their original cover. Glen Affric is also home to such important species as the Scottish wildcat and pine marten. Red squirrels scold you from the lower branches of the pines while Scottish crossbills use their curious beaks to poke seeds from gnarly pine cones.

In the 1950s the remnants of the forest were in poor condition but one man had a powerful vision for the Glen Affric pinewoods. Finlay Macrae, one of Affric's first Forest Managers, was inspired by the idea of the large, spreading woodlands he had seen on the Continent, forests of ancient trees over 300 years old with plenty of young seedlings growing beneath them. Having persuaded his senior colleagues of his vision he began to plant native trees in Affric, trees grown from indigenous seed collected in the glen.

Finlay and his teams planted about eight million trees

and he took a very open approach: 'When the regeneration started, it wasn't just pine but birch, rowan and aspen too. I accepted anything that came in as part of the natural sequence of events.'

Finlay's approach was radical. At a time when deerstalking and shooting were considered the only viable land use in the Highlands and Islands, Finlay encouraged local stalkers to shoot more deer around the fenced-off reserve to prevent the animals eating young shoots.

Fighting off the criticisms of the countryside 'establishment', he later admitted he had not anticipated how hard it would be to control the deer, but he succeeded, and one man with the vision and courage to go against the thinking of the day created something very special. Rewilding in its truest form, decades before anyone dreamed of the term.

Today Finlay's life work is continued by Forestry and Land Scotland and the excellent Trees for Life charity. If you want to see for yourself how trees and mountains blend together in natural harmony, climb the slopes of Am Meallan, close to the main Forestry and Land Scotland car park, which offers one of the best views in the glen, down the length of Loch Affric to the high peaks of Affric and Kintail. I can well understand why many people believe Glen Affric is the loveliest glen in Scotland. It's becoming increasingly popular with walkers and I felt honoured when invited to officially open a new walking route that runs through its heart.

Originally it was to be known as the North Highlands Way, but I'm delighted the name was changed to incorporate two of the most inspiring place names in Scotland. Starting in Drumnadrochit on Ness-side, the Affric Kintail Way climbs gradually through Glen Urquhart into Strathglass at Cannich to meander through magnificent pinewoods by Loch Beinn a' Mheadhoin and Loch Affric before crossing the watershed and dropping through Kintail to Gleann Lichd, eventually to finish at Morvich on the shores of Loch Duich. It's a route that people have enjoyed for generations, but it's now signposted, and has its very own dedicated map and website.

The opening of the route was described to me as the 'culmination of a dream' for local man Ian Mure, Chair of the Strathglass Marketing Group. Ian told me the project has seen the successful partnership of a number of organisations including Forestry and Land Scotland, the National Trust for Scotland and Glen Urquhart Community Council.

'By extending the already popular trek through Glen Affric to the east via existing forest paths along Glen Urquhart to Drumnadrochit, walkers have the added option of extending the Affric Kintail Way to or from either Inverness or even Fort William,' he told me. The Affric Kintail Way runs through a wilder landscape than the Great Glen Way and invites a stop-over at Scotland's most remote Youth Hostel at Alltbeithe in Glen Affric.

The forty-four-mile route begins in Drumnadrochit, a fascinating place with all its associations with Loch Ness and Urquhart Castle and a plethora of ancient Pictish sites on the surrounding hills. High above the village, beyond Garbeg Farm, lies one of the largest of all Pictish burial sites. The Pictish heartland was always thought to be in Highland Perthshire but increasing evidence re-evaluates the importance of northern Picts. Here at Garbeg there are no fewer than twenty-three round and square barrows, thought to cover single long cist burials, and the immediate landscape is rich in prehistoric field systems, groups of hut circles and a series of burnt mounds that are thought to predate the Pictish period. Further up Glen Urquhart, walkers can easily divert from the route to visit the Corrimony chambered cairn, a fine example of a passage grave which is thought to be about 4,000 years old. Nearby there are no fewer than eleven standing stones. Walkers on the Affric Kintail Way tread on very ancient history.

Once known as Invercannich, Cannich is the only village of any real consequence between Drumnadrochit and Morvich. There has been a settlement here for hundreds of years, but the present village owes its more recent growth to the hydroelectric schemes in Strath Glass which date from the 1940s. There is a campsite in the village and an excellent café, full of the kind of things that hungry hikers enjoy, like good coffee and home baking. Beyond the village the trail climbs into the woods of Comar, following forestry tracks before descending to the road and the River Affric at the Dog Falls, a majestic waterfall in a very dramatic gorge setting. Here you begin to appreciate the ongoing work of Forestry and Land Scotland, and it is splendidly evident that their programme for protecting and encouraging this great remnant of the Caledonian Pine Forest has been a huge success. Walking through parts of that ancient forest is certainly one of the highlights of the Affric Kintail Way.

Beyond the Dog Falls, the Way meanders through the trees with frequent glimpses of lovely Loch Beinn a' Mheadhoin and its islands, which were created by the raising of the water levels during the construction of the hydroelectric schemes of the early 1950s. Loch Affric, graced by its shadowed banks of pines, birch and rowan, reflects the grandeur of the surrounding hills and crags but, beyond the loch, the character of the glen changes. You leave the pines behind and the landscape becomes more open, more spacious with more than a hint of wildness. A sense of 'cianalas', a form of sadness, might invade your consciousness as you pass the old settlement at Athnamulloch. The last family left in the 1950s, though cattle were brought here to graze from Strathglass for another two decades. The area between here and Alltbeithe is littered with the ruins of settlements. This part of the glen was once densely populated, but beyond the SYHA hostel the only signs of habitation are the bothy at Camban in Fionngleann and Glenlicht House below Beinn Fhada. The route finishes on a track that leads to Morvich near Loch Duich.

For the more adventurous there is a superb alternative finish to the Affric Kintail Way, which is to take to the high tops beyond Alltbeithe, a wonderful high traverse over Beinn Fhada. This 'long hill' is about the same length as the Five Sisters of Kintail and my old friend, the late Irvine Butterfield, in his superb book *The High Mountains of Britain and Ireland*, describes it as having 'unrelenting slopes of merciless proportions . . .'

It's about ten miles from Alltbeithe to Morvich and a memorable walk it is, climbing high above Gleann Gniomhaidh below the slopes of Sgurr nan Ceathreamhnan before treading around the rims of Fhada's big north-east-facing corries: Coire an t-Siosalaich, Coire Toll a' Mhadaidh and Coire Thuill Sgailceich. These big corrie-bitten flanks are best seen from the slopes of neighbouring Ceathreamhnan but to tiptoe along the rims on a still autumn day, thrilling to the deep-throated roars of rutting stags, is an experience not to be missed.

While those north-east-facing corries are wildly impressive, so are the north-facing pair of Coire an Sgairne and

Coire Chaoil above Gleann Choinneachain. Steep and rocky buttresses separate these two northern cirques and a quick glance at the Ordnance Survey map reveals a confusing array of tightly packed contour lines, suggesting very difficult ground. In fact, the ascent of Beinn Fhada by Gleann Choinneachain and Coire an Sgairne couldn't be simpler. Before we look at that though, a second glance reveals another curiosity. Unusually, the map-makers offer a phonetic attempt at the name of the hill. The hill is named as 'Beinn Fhada or Ben Attow', on the 1:50,000 series, a throwback to the nineteenth century when early map-makers were trying to find the correct spelling for the place names. At that time the Gaelic language was dying as people left the glens, either because of the Clearances or due to poverty-enforced emigration. It's maybe time for 'Ben Attow' to be left off future editions.

Hillwalkers formerly accessed Beinn Fhada from a parking place at Dorusduain in Strath Croe, but in recent years the National Trust for Scotland has created a good path from Innis a' Chrotha on the south side of the river, to the end of the Affric Kintail Way. I am convinced this route could challenge the West Highland Way in terms of popularity, while unashamedly celebrating one of Scotland's finest and most beautiful glens.

About thirty-five years ago, inspired by an article in the *Scots Magazine*, I set off from the summit of Ben Nevis to walk over the Munros of the Aonachs, the Grey Corries and the Mamores and back to the summit of the Ben within twenty-four hours. I didn't quite make it. What was meant to be a twenty-minute nap on the bealach below Stob Ban turned into a five-hour bivouac and by the time I reached the road in Glen Nevis I couldn't bear the thought of climbing to the summit of Britain's highest hill again. What I didn't know at the time was how such a round, first completed in 1964 by the late Philip Tranter, son of the novelist Nigel Tranter, was to become known as a 'challenge' route. And a challenge it certainly is, of some forty miles with 20,600 feet/6,297 metres of climbing.

Later, the Tranter Round was superseded by the Ramsay Round when East Lothian fell runner Charlie Ramsay added the five Munros that surround Loch Treig: Beinn na Lap, Chno Dearg, Stob Coire Sgriodain, Stob a' Choire Mheadhoin and Stob Coire Easain. This made a neat-sounding route of twenty-four Munros in twenty-four hours, an astonishing distance of fifty-six miles with 28,000 feet/8,534 metres of ascent.

My own challenge efforts didn't go much further than my original walking attempt, but fell runners have continued to expand their twenty-four-hour horizons. The summer of 1987 saw what was considered to be the maximum number of ascents possible within twenty-four hours in the Lochaber area when Cumbrian Martin Stone ran no fewer than twenty-six three-thousand-foot summits, a remarkable achievement. While Lochaber is historically the arena for such fell running extravaganzas, more recent attempts at collecting as many Munros as possible within twenty-four hours moved north to Glen Shiel.

The new challenge route started at the Cluanie Inn and traversed the South Glen Shiel ridge, followed by a sudden descent to almost sea level before a tough re-ascent to take in the Five Sisters of Kintail and the ridge of Ciste Dubh. The runners then turn to the big hills north of Glen Affric before finishing across the five summits of the Cluanie Horseshoe. In

July 1988, Jonathon Broxap ran the seventy-eight-mile route in twenty-three hours twenty minutes. He climbed over 33,000 feet/10,058 metres of ascent, almost four thousand feet more than an ascent of Mount Everest from sea level, and completed a grand tally of twenty-eight Munros. Since then, Adrian Belton has equalled this total of Munros in the Lochaber area, but it took him slightly longer. In a similarly amazing feat in July 2017, Jim Mann ran thirty Munros in the southern Cairngorms/Glenshee/Lochnagar area within 24 hours. He started and finished at Invercauld Bridge and his circuit included Cairn Toul and Macdui. Astonishing achievements.

There was a time when I might have accused such runners of missing out on some of the great benefits of the hills because they dash round at such a pace, but I know Martin Stone and Charlie Ramsay and a number of other fell runners and accept that their love of the mountains is as deep-rooted as those who wander at a slower pace. I confess to a slight envy of their fitness.

It must be wonderful to know the freedom of untrammelled movement, unburdened by packs or even heavy boots, as you jog over the hills of Lochaber and Glen Shiel. If only my knees didn't protest so much.

In my rather long-winded way, I'm trying to make the point that the area around Glen Shiel is as rich in Munro-pickings as any other part of Scotland. No fewer than twenty-one can be accessed from the stretch of the A87 that runs down its length. With the celebrated Five Sisters of Kintail on one side (only three of them are Munros) and the Munro-rich South Glen Shiel ridge on the other (seven Munros), the area is a Shangri-la for list-tickers. The glen is about nine miles in length, from sea level at the village of Shiel Bridge, where the waters of Loch Duich bite into the land fjord-style, to the Cluanie Inn (708 feet/216 metres) at the western end of Loch Cluanie, and the march with Glenmoriston. Snaking down its entire length is the legendary Road to the Isles.

There's history here too. The Battle of Glen Shiel, an encounter between British government forces and an alliance of Jacobite supporters and Spanish mercenaries in 1719, took place about half-way down the glen. It's said to have been the last close engagement of British and foreign troops on mainland British soil, and ended in victory for the government. It's the Spaniards who are commemorated by a hill name though. High above the northern side of the glen lies Sgurr nan Spainteach, the peak of the Spaniards.

Although Glen Shiel boasts such a multitude of Munros, I want to describe a couple of Corbetts in the area. Lower hills they may be, and less popular than the Munros, but they are not less in character and enjoyment. One involves a fairly long walk-in but the other is easily accessed from Glen Shiel village.

Sgurr Mhic Bharraich is 'the peak of the son of Maurice'. I'm afraid I've no idea who Maurice was and why his son has been celebrated in a mountain name. His deeds have been lost in the passage of time and not even Peter Drummond's informative book, *Scottish Hill Names*, can assist, so let's assume that this fellow MacMaurice had an eye for a hill, and a better eye for a view.

It's often suggested that the Corbetts offer better views than the Munros, being surrounded by bigger hills, and in the case of Sgurr Mhic Bharraich that is certainly true. With the Five Sisters of Kintail, An Diollaid, the Knoydart tops and Beinn Sgritheall all rising close at hand it's difficult to find a better viewpoint in the whole area. I'll note here that the anglicisation of An Diollaid to the dull and unimaginative soubriquet of The Saddle is one of those thankfully rare occurrences when the native Gaelic name has been lost to its English translation. A habit not to be encouraged!

On a clear day the Cuillin of Skye etches its saw-toothed profile across the western horizon but, even better, the ascent of Sgurr Mhic Bharraich offers a delightful few hours in glorious scenery if tackled from the east, and that's the way we went. Parking the campervan at the Shiel Bridge campsite, we used a footpath that crosses a rib of high ground before dropping down into the lovely Gleann Undalain.

Cuckoos greeted us as we crossed the bridge and made our way past the remains of old shielings. In days gone by this path was the main route between Shiel Bridge and Glenelg, via Moyle and Gleann Mor, and I've wondered if cattle drovers would have used it, herding their beasts south from the Skye crossing at Kylerhea. At one time up to 8,000 cattle a year would swim across the Kyle at slack water, usually in groups of five, tied together nose to tail using heather or straw rope. From Glenelg the route to the cattle trysts at Crieff and Falkirk wouldn't have been any less arduous. Long and difficult journeys in harsh conditions.

Despite the forecast of a frigid north-easterly wind we warmed in the sun, skirting the steep eastern and southern flanks to take the line of least resistance to the summit. It was only beyond the high Loch Coire nan Crogachan, when we had to leave the luxury of the footpath, that we faced about a thousand feet of steep climbing through crags. In such surroundings it was no real hardship. We took our time, rested often, and gazed into the bowels of Coire Uaine opposite, a massive glacial scour complete with classic lochan, that lies between An Diollaid and its neighbour Spidean

Dhomhuill Bhric. As we climbed, the Munros of Knoydart, Luinne Bheinn, Meall Buidhe and Ladhar Bheinn all came into view but, the best view of all, across the tumbled, forested Glenelg peninsula, was of the complex ridges and corries of Beinn Sgritheall, Gavin Maxwell's hill. It was in the shadow of this mountain that he wrote his classic *Ring of Bright Water*.

After the steep climb, a shallow dip on the summit plateau led to a sharp climb and the large summit cairn, perched on a plinth of rocky outcrops. Time to sit and take in an amazing panorama of mountain views, from the South Glen Shiel hills behind us, out to Rum and Skye, and north, to the silver quartzite tops of the Torridon mountains glittering in the sun. We ate our lunch beside the cairn, drank from our flask and toasted the son of Maurice, whoever he was, until with some reluctance we tore ourselves away from the best viewpoint in Glen Shiel and made our way carefully down the steep east ridge back to Gleann Undalain.

My other Corbett isn't strictly within Glen Shiel but Sgurr Gaorsaic is a Corbett surrounded by giants and well worth the longish walk-in. To the west the big Munros of A' Ghlas-bheinn and Beinn Fhada dominate the views while to the east Sgurr nan Ceathreamhnan, a real tongue-twister of a hill, is joined at the hip, so to speak, by a high bealach just south of Coire Thuill Easaich. Sgurr Gaorsaic is no more than a western top of Sgurr nan Ceathreamhnan but, because the bealach that connects them is more than 500 feet below the Gaorsaic summit, the hill qualifies as a Corbett.

While it comfortably qualifies as a Corbett, it only just qualifies as a Sgurr. This Gaelic word translates as a sharp, rocky hill or rocky peak and Sgurr Gaorsaic is anything but. It's a comparatively dumpy, flat-topped hill with a few

185

rocky stretches on its north-east and western slopes. Slightly disparaging as these comments may be, the ascent of Sgurr Gaorsaic, which curiously translates as the peak of horror or the peak of thrills, is noteworthy because it necessitates a walk through the superb Bealach an Sgairne, referred to earlier, 'where the stones make noise'.

I've already reported that the ghost of Osgood Mackenzie and his daughter were seen here, and not very far away lies a bealach where the mountaineer Frank Smythe had a strange experience in 1942 when, while a Squadron Leader in the RAF, he taught commandos mountain warfare in the Cairngorms. He wrote of seeing 'a pitiful procession' coming towards him and went on to describe a band of people climbing up a narrow defile when 'concealed men leapt to their feet and brandishing spears, axes and clubs, rushed down with wild yells on the unfortunates beneath. There was a short, fierce struggle, then a horrible massacre. Not a man, woman or child was left alive: the defile was choked with corpses.' Smyth was convinced he had been given a backward glimpse into some ancient page of Highland history, a kind of psychic experience that is comparatively widespread amongst hill-going folk.

Spectral apparitions apart, I think this is one of the finest passes in the country. Parking at Morvich, just along the road from Shiel Bridge, I followed the road to the houses at Innis a' Chrotha. This is the road referred to earlier as terminating the Affric Kintail Way. With hillsides looming on both sides I entered Gleann Choinneachain. Rocky slopes tumbled down from A' Ghlas-bheinn in the north and from Coire an Sgairne in the south, from where a subsidiary footpath climbs to the summit slopes of Beinn Fhada. Here the footpath squeezes through a narrow gap to descend into broad Gleann Gaorsaic with its lochs and burns that feed the main river. These water courses drain the slopes of Beinn Fhada, A' Ghlas-bheinn and the magnificently sculpted Sgurr nan Ceathreamhnan. All that water is captured in a narrow stream and directed into a rocky cleft about three miles to the north. These are the Falls of Glomach, a series of waterfalls that plunge for some 400 feet, twice the height of Niagara, into a deep, black chasm.

The Bealach an Sgairne is like a portal into another world, one of the Gates of Affric, a beautiful place formed by the dog's leg where Gleann Gaorsaic and Gleann Gniomhach meet. The green slopes of Sgurr Gaorsaic rise in the cleft of that dog's leg and its flat-topped summit is dominated by the south ridge of Sgurr nan Ceathreamhnan. The route to Gaorsaic crosses some pretty waterlogged ground and skirts the south banks of Loch a' Bhealaich, where it joins another footpath and continues east to the Youth Hostel at Alltbeithe. Half a kilometre or so after leaving the loch we departed the footpath to climb the fairly steep grassy south slopes of Sgurr Gaorsaic. It's not a demanding climb, most of the hard work had been completed in the ascent to the Bealach an Sgairne, and as I wandered across the summit plateau towards the spiky cairn I found myself gasping at the beauty of the big, surrounding hills. It was a very contented Corbett-bagger who wandered happily back through the Gates of Affric towards Glen Shiel. No records broken but a wonderful day in one of the finest hillwalking areas of Scotland.

Directly opposite Sgurr Gaorsaic lies one of the most remote Munro summits in Affric, Sgurr nan Ceathreamhnan. Hamish Brown once told me about a friend of his who suggested that, when he died, he would like his ashes scattered on its summit. If nothing else, it would give his friends a good long walk, which was very decent of him I'm sure. Indeed, if that was his altruistic intention then he chose well. The 3,776-foot/1,151-metre peak is comparatively remote and all approaches to it tend to be long overland treks. The ascent can be shortened by hiking into Alltbeithe Youth Hostel, which conveniently lies at the foot of the mountain, and staying overnight. Otherwise you'll have walk-ins of six miles from Cluanie Inn or eight miles from the head of Loch Duich. Probably the shortest approach is from Glen Elchaig in the north, which has the added advantage of climbing past the spectacular Falls of Glomach. Once above the falls you continue up the Allt Coire-lochain to the ridge on the west side of Coire Lochan, which eventually leads to the summit.

Most Munro-baggers climb Sgurr nan Ceathreamhnan along with its neighbours, An Socach 3,018 feet/920 metres and Mullach na Dheiragain, 3,222 feet/982 metres, although the latter, lying out on a long and rugged limb to the north of Ceathreamhnan, is one of those Munros that tempt you to leave it for another day. There is some justification in climbing Mullach na Dheiragain on its own from the north, from Glen Elchaig and the Iron Lodge. Long grassy slopes up Coire Aird give easy access to the rockier north-west ridge and, a short distance after that, to the summit cone.

A longer alternative is to tackle the entire horseshoe circuit of Gleann a' Choilich, the long and curved glen which separates the Beinn Fhionnlaidh/Carn Eige/Mam Sodhail massif from the Ceathreamhnan/Dheiragain ridge. This entails about twenty-five kilometres of walking with about 2,000 metres of climbing. It's a big day by any standards, and you have to get to Loch Mullardoch before you set foot on the hills.

Alltbeithe Youth Hostel can be reached fairly comfortably through the An Caorann Mor from Cluanie Inn. The route tends to be boggy in its upper reaches and lower down in Glen Affric. A footpath follows the line of the Allt na Faing into the higher, rocky reaches of Coire na Cloiche and onto the bealach just west of An Socach (unnamed on earlier Ordnance Survey maps). This hill is dramatically dwarfed by its bigger neighbours, and it's hard to believe it's of Munro status. It's often climbed on its own from Affric Lodge via the Bealach Coire Ghaidheil. The ridge that runs west from An Socach narrows appreciably and offers an interesting route over Stob Coire nan Dearcag, high above Coire nan Dearcag with its high-level lochan, and over Sgurr nan Ceathreamhnan's east top to finish on the suitably rocky summit of the Munro, one of the great hills of the western Highlands.

Oh, and by the way, it's skoor nan kerrevan.

Five sinewy ridges radiate from the summit block that forms the apex of five well sculpted corries. The longest of those ridges runs in a north-east direction towards the end of Loch Mullardoch and slap-bang in the middle of that ridge lies Mullach nan Dheiragain. Although given Munro status it is, in effect, no more than an outlier of Ceathreamhnan.

I've mentioned the Falls of Glomach several times. No visit to Affric or Kintail is complete without a tramp below the Meall Dubh shoulder of A' Ghlas-bheinn and down to the top of the falls. It's difficult to suggest the best time of year to visit, but this impressive cataract tempts hundreds of walkers and I have a suspicion that later in the year is as good as any, before the ground becomes too soggy from winter's snows and when the midgies have vanished for another blessed insect-free interlude.

The last time I saw the Falls of Glomach was on a long walk from Fort William to Cape Wrath. It had been very wet and all that excess rain swelled the Falls into epic proportions. Not only did the raging torrent look impressive, but you could literally feel the thunder and power of it. The ground shook below my feet and the air was cooled by the draught from the icy, golden-brown waters. The sheer spectacle of power and energy was impressive, and even the most diminutive of streams had swollen so that every crossing was a nightmare. Some rivers were simply impassable. Leaving the awesome display, I had great difficulty in getting out from below the chasm when every side-stream had become a raging torrent. I eventually escaped with very wet feet and a new respect for fast-running water.

The Falls of Glomach route is well signposted from Inchnacroe. A footpath links with the old Forestry and Land Scotland car park at Dorusduain before heading north through the Dorusduain Wood to the confluence of the Allt Mam an Tuirc and the Allt an Leoid Ghaineamhaich. A bridge crosses the latter stream with a good footpath gradually winding its way up the hillside to the 1,700-foot/518-metre Bealach na Sroine. The path continues through the bealach and descends to the top of the Falls as the stream plunges into its narrow, dark chasm. You'll have to descend a narrow, often slippy, path to see the best of the cataract.

I couldn't leave the wonderful area of Glen Affric and Kintail without mentioning Duncan MacLennan. Duncan was born and raised at Fasnakyle, a 'dwelling in the woods', in 1914 and went on to become head stalker of the estate in 1942, a position he held until his retirement in 1989. I doubt if anyone knew Glen Affric, or Glen Affaric as he insisted on calling it, better than Duncan.

He was a good friend of Tom Weir's and I used Tom's name as an introduction when I visited Duncan in Cannich not long after he had retired. I was writing a feature about the glen and Tom had insisted I meet Duncan, 'who knows Glen Affric better than any man living'.

Over mugs of tea and buttered scones Duncan told me of his childhood in the glen. He had to travel three miles each way to school in all weathers and clearly remembered returning home from his last day at school and proudly presenting his father with his Higher Day School Certificate. After his father read it, he looked at young Duncan and said: 'That's very good. I hope it will help you get a good job in accountancy or something similar.' Duncan didn't contradict his father, but an old proverb went through his mind. 'It's better to hear the lark sing than the mouse squeak', meaning the outdoor life is far better than working in an office.

It was the outdoor life that saw him rise from the 'bottom rung of the sporting ladder' as a fishing ghillie, moving on to under-stalker and eventually head stalker. When sheep were put into the Glen Affric forest he became stalker manager. In this last managerial role he was more or less confined to the glen and he sorely missed the high tops. Curiously, he'd had a notion that this might be the case. 'I was seventy years of age and had enjoyed some magnificent views from the summits of the hills. But one day I had an odd feeling that was difficult to explain. I felt this might be the last time I would tread the heads of these majestic mountains and in case it would be, as a gesture of farewell, I put a large stone on each of the summit cairns. It was indeed the case and next day I was given an easier role in the running of the estate.'

Duncan MacLennan was a tough and hardy son of the hills, a true *bodach nam beinn*, and he loved his Glen Affaric with a passion. Like many of his ilk he had been brought up with the old stories of the glens and the hills, the folklore that was as widespread as the antlered deer or the voracious midge. He told me one story that stuck with me.

One cold winter's day a shepherd was searching a green corrie for sheep. He was very unhappy and depressed and was concerned for his future. A faery suddenly appeared on a knoll in front of him and asked him why he looked so unhappy. Would a wish brighten up his day? The shepherd said he had always wanted to sail the seas. 'You will have your wish,' said the faery. 'You will be given a large sailing ship with a crew. You can sail whenever you want and a fair wind will always blow at your back.'

The shepherd duly got his wish and sailed around the world, amassing a large fortune. Eventually he returned to Scotland and bought the finest deerstalking estate in the country. He also hired the most experienced deerstalker he could find. Day after day they stalked stags but for some reason could never get within shooting distance. Eventually the shepherd realised why. The fair wind was always blowing behind them, taking their scent to the hunted deer.

10

STRUMMING THE HEART STRINGS

He was Scotland's finest naturalist, a past chairman of the John Muir Trust and interim chair of the National Trust for Scotland. He was inspirational, down-to-earth, warm and hospitable. A friend to hillgoers, gamekeepers, landowners and royalty, regardless of background, colour or creed. He was my friend.

I met Dick Balharry in the mid-seventies when he was the local officer of the Nature Conservancy Council (NCC) in Aviemore and I was warden of Aviemore Youth Hostel. I was also a volunteer NCC warden at Craigellachie National Nature Reserve, a lovely area of crag, loch and birch trees that overlooked the hostel.

Gina and I had become friendly with Brian Lightfoot, the NCC warden at Craigellachie, who was in the habit of popping in for a cup of tea and a blether. On one occasion a van pulled up outside our kitchen window as he was enjoying his morning brew. 'Oh shit,' he said,' It's the boss, I'd better scarper.' Scarper he did, but not before I was introduced to the big, burly red-bearded man in the van.

In the years that followed I came to know Dick Balharry well. At one point he commissioned me to draw up a map of the burgeoning footpath network that was appearing on the Cairngorm Plateau, a great project that allowed me to get to know him better. Eventually we became neighbours in the

Badenoch village of Newtonmore. We made television and radio programmes together. I was his vice chairman when he chaired the local woodland community group and, for a short time, served as a trustee of the John Muir Trust after he talked me into helping him organise a national Wild Land Conference.

Vastly more important than any of that was the fact that Dick became not only a close friend but also something of a mentor and confidant. Whenever I needed advice on an issue, for example during the six years I chaired the Nevis Partnership, he was always my 'phone-a-friend'.

I want to tell you a wee bit about his background, because it was the foundation of what he ultimately became, one of the most influential naturalists that Scotland has produced. I would put him on a par with Seton Gordon and Frank Fraser Darling, but Dick lacked their privileged backgrounds and opportunities. He was brought up in Muirhead of Liff, a small village on the outskirts of Dundee, and as a boy was obsessed by natural history. He hand-reared several young wild animals, was an avid collector, hunter, and reputedly also an expert poacher before he even became a teenager. Like many poachers it wasn't long before he became a trainee gamekeeper. Poacher turned gamekeeper: a more common career move than most people know.

Dick's parents couldn't understand how nature conservation could become a career so they encouraged, nay, cajoled him into taking a course in engineering at the local technical college. He stuck it for a year before getting a job in a local factory, which he endured for less than an hour before packing his bags and running off to Argyll.

He managed to get a job as a kennel-boy and under-keeper on an estate near Tighnabruach which, like most keepers' jobs in those days, involved controlling predators and patrolling a river against salmon poachers. In effect he was charged with 'sterilising the environment of predators in order to maximise the number of birds and salmon available for guests to kill'.

Dick's own words. Sound familiar?

He also worked for the Red Deer Commission before, at the age of twenty-four, he became the warden of the UK's first National Nature Reserve at Beinn Eighe in Torridon.

He took great delight in telling me how excited he was to be interviewed in London for the job at the Nature Conservancy Council. Taking the sleeper to Euston, he walked through London resplendent in gamekeeper's tweeds and fiery red beard and hair. He must have made a formidable sight as he strode down Tottenham Court Road.

A colleague of his, J. Laughton Johnston, reckoned he was the perfect match for the job.

'Balharry arrived with all the enthusiasm of a young man given the opportunity to do just what he had always wanted. His background of gamekeeping and latterly as a stalker with the deer commission gave him just the experience he needed to slot into that side of the work, but he had not been in it so long that he could not view the management of deer with an open mind. He also enjoyed and made light of the hard work associated with the woodland programme. In addition he brought with him a love of wildlife and threw himself into observing and recording, visiting the eagle eyries, learning how to live-trap pine martens and for the first time recording encounters with wildcat on the Reserve. He wanted to share his delight in observing wildlife, however, and within a year he was to begin transforming both the thinking and the practice behind the development of facilities for the public on Beinn Eighe.'

It was here in Torridon that Dick really began his career in conservation, metamorphosing from gamekeeper and deerstalker to working conservationist. He was given responsibility for over 10,000 acres of mountain and Caledonian pinewood in addition to working with scientists. The job at Beinn Eighe also introduced him to what he always referred to as 'the establishment.' Let me quote him now.

'The establishment can be defined in many ways and it is fascinating, even today, to see how networks based on wealth, social status, formal qualifications and public school education influence decision-making and how they often override logic and evidence to protect their own interests.'

As a young warden, he wasn't considered part of this privileged network and it soon became clear that his dream job came with a very limited opportunity to influence decisions taken in Edinburgh and London. Tactful advocacy, persuasion, passion and promoting public support became the tools of his trade, and were to stand him in good stead throughout the rest of his life.

What I've just told you is crucial to understanding Dick's success. His passion for the natural world was evident and he spent his life enthusing others whether they were shepherds, stalkers, urban audiences, landowners, civil servants, politicians or even royalty. As outdoor campaigners, he and I worked in very different ways. I tended to shout things from the rooftops and use the media to get issues to the public, participating in radio interviews, appearing on television and writing articles for the Scottish newspapers. Too often I fell out with people who opposed my views, often to my side's detriment. Dick, on the other hand, was much less voluble. His technique, if I could call it that, was to enthuse and cajole all kinds of people into his way of thinking. He got alongside people to win their trust, and it worked. He once told me we worked well together as bad cop and good cop.

His two terms as chair of the John Muir Trust changed that organisation from a slightly shambolic, amateur group that wasn't quite sure if it was a conservation body or a landowner, into the professional, efficient campaigning NGO it is today, and his time as acting chair of the National Trust for Scotland saw massive and important changes to its deer-management attitudes. He was central to the conservation plans of several Scottish estates, including Corrour and Glen Feshie and the owner of the latter, Danish clothing tycoon Anders Holch Povlson, has recognised him as being instrumental to his hugely successful rewilding policies. Three days before Dick's death, Povlson hosted a gathering of conservationists to present him with the Patrick Geddes Award from the Royal Scottish Geographical Society, a richly deserved recognition of his conservation work.

While many sporting estates in Scotland are still maintaining 'artificially high' numbers of deer to make more profit from shooting them, others are erecting mile upon mile of deer fencing to protect native woodland from browsing animals. According to Dick Balharry, neither high numbers of deer nor deer fencing are acceptable in modern Scotland. He saw this as a major injustice, believing the land was being managed without regard to the wider public interest.

'High deer densities help maximise sporting opportunities for a few, but they also increase the numbers of deer that die in winter from lack of food and shelter,' he told me. 'Landowners tend to distance themselves from this responsibility, claiming that deer are wild animals for which they cannot be held entirely responsible.

'As it stands that is indeed the law, however, the decision to have high numbers of red deer on the hill and the decision not to provide native woodland for shelter remain unequivocally the management choice made by owners.

'To those who argue that fences are required to make sport shooting economically viable I would simply say that you are inviting society to question the legitimacy of your ownership model – one that places trophy stags higher than the long-term interest of the public and the planet.

'Traditional sporting estates can no longer take the moral high ground of estate ownership as they have tried to claim for over the last two-hundred years,' he said.

Now, it's one thing to have a vision, to have a dream, to suggest a theory, but something else to show that it can work, particularly on a large scale. Dick proved his vision of land management worked. At Creag Meagaidh, midway between Ben Nevis and Cairn Gorm, he was responsible for the success of the regeneration of the wonderful birch woods in Coire Ardair.

Just over twenty-five years ago, the future of these woods looked grim. Trees were dying without progeny due to overgrazing. The estate was sold to a private forestry group who wanted to coniferise the mountain's lower slopes, until a public outcry led to the purchase of the estate by the Nature Conservancy Council in 1985. The NCC's (followed by Scottish Natural Heritage's) subsequent management plan included two vital objectives: to allow ecosystems to evolve with minimum interference, and to encourage regeneration and extension of native forests and boreal scrub vegetation.

How on earth was the NCC to achieve these objectives without erecting fences to keep the browsing sheep and red deer away from the young plants?

Dick's answer was a simple one. Completely remove the sheep and drastically reduce the deer numbers. Under his supervision, a programme of deer- and sheep-removal began and the results were staggering. Juniper was recorded for the first time, and there has been tremendous regeneration of birch. There is also a plentiful growth of rowan, willow, alder and oak.

Over a quarter of a century later the rewards of those conservation objectives are obvious. In springtime and summer you find yourself walking through a green tunnel of new growth. Birch, alder, willow, rowan and oak, trees that have been allowed to grow without having their heads bitten off. There are even young rowans growing above 2,000 feet. There has been an increase in plant-eating invertebrates, and many species of plants have become abundantly visible. The remaining deer are bigger and healthier than their predecessors, and this has all been achieved without a single metre of deer fencing.

Dick maintained that deer fences to protect woodland and forest plantations are a tacit admission that traditional deer-culling methods have failed ... but why have they failed? Because there are not enough stalkers on the ground. Traditional deerstalking jobs should not be under threat. In many areas of Scotland we need more stalkers to keep deer numbers at a manageable level.

What Dick Balharry and his colleagues created forms a wonderfully encouraging start to a great mountain walk. Throughout the length of Coire Ardair there is visual evidence of hope, promise and luxuriant new life. At the head of the Coire, from the shores of Lochan a' Choire, gully-bitten cliffs rise to the sky, cliffs that have earned a reputation for being among the foremost winter climbing areas in Scotland.

Dick and I spent a day on Creag Meagaidh making a video many years ago. We had filmed near the Carsaig Arches on Mull, on Beinn Eighe in Torridon and then here on Creag Meagaidh. He regaled me with tales and stories all the way up the corrie, occasionally pointing out interesting plants and invertebrates, and when we arrived at the head, where Lochan a' Choire lies deep, we reflected on the huge array of vegetated cliffs that tower above it. Laid out for more than a mile and in places reaching higher than 1,500 feet above the dark waters, these cliffs are breached only by a high bealach, commonly known as The Window, a glaciated gap in the rock curtain which offers access to the higher plateau and summit slopes.

Sitting by the loch-side it was my turn to tell stories, mainly of the mountaineering history of the Creag Meagaidh crags. The climbers who have tackled these great buttresses and gullies make up a who's who of mountaineering. One of the first was Harold Raeburn, who first climbed the two gullies that lie on either side of Pinaccle Buttress: Easy Gully and Raeburn's Gully. Later Jimmy Bell and various partners climbed some of the steeper gullies, but the historical high-point arrived in the 1950s and 1960s with Jimmy Marshall and Robin Smith and, of course, the ubiquitous Dr Tom Patey.

Almost fifty years before Patey, a GP in Ullapool and one of Scotland's finest mountaineers, completed what he considered to be one of his finest expeditions. He called it Crab Crawl, and it was an awesome 8,000-foot/2,438-metre girdle traverse of the Coire Ardair face of Creag Meagaidh. Every time I make my way up the length of the corrie with that buttressed and gullied face drawing me towards it, the incredible achievement of his sideways climb impresses me more and more. Patey's interest was aroused by an article he had read, and he tried to tempt the well-known Lancastrian climber Don Whillans into accompanying him. 'I don't get much excited about girdles,' replied Whillans, 'especially 8,000-foot ones.'

'It's perfectly simple,' insisted Patey, 'you have two parties starting simultaneously from opposite ends, crossing over in the middle. The left-hand party is led by a right-handed leader and the right-hand party by a left-handed leader.'

'Look, mate,' Whillans interrupted, 'Do you know what you want to do? You want to team up with a crab. It's got claws, walks sideways and it's got a thick head. This isn't a climb, it's a bloody crab crawl.'

The route was named before an ice axe had been hammered into it. Perhaps Don Whillans guessed something about Patey's character, particularly his obsession with climbing solo and unroped. The doctor eventually managed to find companions and arrived in Coire Ardair with mountain photographer John Cleare, journalist Peter Gillman, and fellow climbers Jim MacArtney and Allen Fyffe. MacArtney's girlfriend, Mary Anne Hudson, came along too, on only her second winter route.

Some years after the event, Allen Fyffe, then an instructor at Glenmore Lodge, told me the story. It being pretty late in the day, and realising that Cleare was planning to take photographs, Patey decided to solo alongside the others. 'A rope of five with a leap-frogging snap-happy photographer is as mobile as a constipated caterpillar,' he later wrote, but Fyffe was convinced the climbers had been set up.

'He set us up as camera fodder,' he told me. 'That was his intention all along.'

By the time they reached the end of the first pitch Patey was disappearing into the mist. It was the last they saw of him, although he occasionally left encouraging arrows on the snow to show he hadn't forgotten it was a team effort.

Creag Meagaidh's array of cliffs are of most interest to climbers in winter, when the crags are protected from any warmth that's offered by the low sun. Above the cliffs, storms from the west blow snow across the rolling plateaux to topple down into the gullies and steep faces where shattered schist and frozen turf holds it in place, often when other crags are snow-free. The steep gullies are natural drains for the vast upland and, when those waters freeze, climbing conditions can be sensational. In summer conditions the cliffs are too grassy and wet for modern climbers.

While the cliffs of Coire Ardair attract winter climbers from all corners of the world, Creag Meagaidh has much to offer the hillwalker in all seasons of the year. I've lost count of how many times I've ascended by a variety of routes, and I've experienced its glories in all conditions, from the parched days of high summer to the Arctic cold of winter.

From our lunch stop it was a steep climb to The Window, first along a narrow, grassy moraine that gives way to loose scree and boulder slopes; but the climbing eases when you enter the narrow confines of The Window itself. A couple of hundred metres through the bealach the western views to the Loch Lochy hills beyond Glen Roy offer a few moments of respite before a faint zigzagging path leads to Mad Meg's Cairn, a huge mound of earth covered in stones, before a final climb to the summit at 3,701 feet/1,128 metres.

According to Dick, Mad Meg's Cairn, one that is often mistaken for the summit cairn on misty days, marks the grave of an eighteenth-century suicide who was denied burial in the local kirkyards. Her family apparently buried her up here, covering her grave with stones and sandy soil.

Significantly, the summit lies slap-bang on the mountain spine of Scotland, the ancient Druim Alban. You can clearly identify the watershed with the River Roy draining to the west, and Loch Spey (just hidden from the summit view by an intervening ridge) sourcing the infant Spey as it drains to the North Sea in the east. Great hills surround you: the Cairngorms, the Monadh Liath, the Loch Lochy and Glen Garry hills, Ben Nevis, the Grey Corries, the Treig twins and the Geal Charn/Carn Dearg ridge with Ben Alder's summit peeping above it. One of the best views in the country.

Not only does Creag Meagaidh form the watershed but more often than not she also forms a 'weathershed', with the hills and glens on one side blanketed by dark cloud while the other direction is bathed in sunshine. It's a phenomenon I've not experienced with such regularity on any other hill in Scotland, so don't be surprised to find the western hills cloaked in cloud while the hills to the east are clear.

If time permits, it's worth retracing your steps to the bealach above The Window and returning via the long undulating ridge between the Munro summits of Stob Poite

Coire Ardair and Carn Liath, the route followed by most Munro-baggers. However, if you can arrange transport at both ends, it's worth considering a full traverse of the mountain along the boundary of Lochaber and Badenoch.

Dick had suggested we do this, and had left his car near the foot of the Moy Burn for our return. Instead of returning to The Window, we descended by the two-and-a-half-mile ridge that curves seductively above the long and sinuous erosion corrie that has been formed by the Moy Burn. From the summit cairn we continued down a narrowing ridge with slopes falling into the Moy Corrie on our left and Coire an Laogh on the right, while a line of old fence posts led to a rather more permanent navigation aid.

Suddenly and without warning a drystone wall appeared, an incongruous sight in such wild and bare surroundings. This is no ordinary broken-down relic, such as you'd see throughout the Highlands, but a perfect example of the art of drystane dyking, delightful in its symmetry and form, that stretches down the spine of the curving ridge. Dick thought it may have been built to provide work for those who suffered from famine and clearance in the early part of the eighteenth century.

The earliest records for Creag Meagaidh date from the seventeenth and first half of the eighteenth centuries. It's thought there were perhaps four small settlements, 'ferm toons' as they were known, on and around Creag Meagaidh. Wood and peat would have been used for fuel, strips of land drained and cultivated, and hunting and grazing on the open hillside shared. Life was dominated through these years by a pastoral lifestyle interrupted by famine, disease and major rebellion.

In the mid-1700s Cluny Macpherson owned the land

at Aberarder as part of his territory in Brae Badenoch. However, Macpherson defied the government by supporting the Jacobite cause. After Culloden he fled to France, forfeiting his estates, which were then managed on behalf of the Crown by the Commissioners for Forfeited Estates, whose factor started legal proceedings to evict the tenants and organise the individual ferm touns into a single holding in 1770. The family estates were restored to Colonel Macpherson, grandson of Cluny, in 1784.

Beyond the end of the wall, steep slopes had to be negotiated down the slopes of Creag na Cailliche, and below the crags we had to pick our way over tricky ground, awkward because of the long grasses that hide rocks and boulders, and the tussocks that threaten to twist ankles. While cursing the long grass I couldn't resist pointing to the success of the Coire Ardair woodlands due to a reduction in browsing animals, those same beasts that would probably have kept the grasses short on these slopes that lead down to Moy. There are two sides to every conservation story.

As Dick struggled through the knee-deep tussocks I cruelly taunted him, suggesting this godawful terrain was his fault. He didn't argue.

Not that many years ago, during the debate on what became the access legislation within the Land Reform (Scotland) Act 2003, there was a tendency amongst hillgoers to be suspicious of conservationists. Some ecologists, encouraged by the attitude of Scottish Natural Heritage, suggested that areas of Scotland should become no-go zones, where wildlife could thrive with no human intrusion. Or at least, with little human intrusion. The conservationists didn't want to exclude themselves of course. They would still access the no-go areas to do bird counts or carry out experiments. The rest of us, Joe Public, would be banned.

Dick Balharry refused to become a member of that privileged group, and followed my own two three-year stints as president of Ramblers Scotland. He was hugely enthusiastic about introducing people to the countryside, and an evangelist in spreading the good news about the benefits of walking in our marvellous landscapes.

'How can we introduce young people to the wildlife of Scotland if they can't go out and see it?' he argued. Dick articulated his love of the outdoors in such a way that it touched others, enthused them and changed their lives.

I enjoyed many a good walk with him, and he was always challenging. He would suddenly stop and pick up an insect or point to a plant and say, 'Come on then, Cameron, let's see what you know. What's this?'

He didn't walk just for the sake of walking, but with purpose, and essentially that purpose was to re-connect with the biotic community all around us. The countryside, the great outdoors, the natural world, call it what you like. He believed implicitly in Scotland's access legislation because he sincerely believed we all need access to the green world to find renewal, peace, and natural beauty. The American writer Edward Abbey once said that we need a refuge even though we may never need to set foot in it: 'We need the possibility of escape as surely as we need hope. Without it the life of the cities would drive us all into crime or drugs or psychoanalysis.'

While we hear a lot nowadays about rewilding, we can't actually recreate that kind of poetic green land that Wordsworth and Byron and Ruskin wrote about. We can't turn the clock back but, given a modicum of political will, and with the wind blowing in the right direction for

1. Enjoying the peace of the pine woods in Rothiemurchus

2. Near the summit of Beinn Fhada, Kintail

3. On Sgurr nan Spainteach, Five Sisters, above Glen Shiel

4. The Falls of Glomach

5. The regeneration of the Caledonian pine forest, Glen Affric

6. The SYHA hostel at Alltbeithe, Glen Affric

7. Coming third in the Battle of the Beards to Dick Balharry
and Adam Watson

8. On Beinn Eighe, Torridon

9. Kay and John Ure of the Ozone Café, Cape Wrath

10. Duncan Chisholm,
one of Scotland's finest
traditional fiddlers

11. Marie Christine and John Ridgway with their
Lifetime Achievement awards

12. The gloriously atmospheric Sandwood Bay

13. A beehive shelter on Harris

14. A glorious beachside camp on Harris

15. The quiet glory of Hushinish

16. The atmospheric standing stones at Callanish, Isle of Lewis

17. A Shetland sunset from Eshaness

18. Muckle Flugga and Out Stack, Britain's most northerly islands

19. Lifting my beloved campervan onto the pier at North Ronaldsay

20. The tombolo connecting St Ninian's Isle to Shetland mainland

21. Approaching the summit of Ben Gulabin

22. Contemplating the Craigallion Memorial and all it means to me

23. The graveyard at Blackwater Dam

24. Paul Tattersall, first person to take a mountain bike over all the Munros

25. Fun is to be had in the hills, even when the years wear on

the various rewilding efforts that are now beginning, we can reinstate diversity. Given opportunities through better access, increased outdoor education and better outdoor evangelism, we can teach people that our wild places are worth preserving. It was the noted American ecologist Aldo Leopold who wrote: 'We abuse the land because we regard it as a commodity belonging to us. When we see the land as a community to which we belong, we may begin to use it with love and respect.' That statement lays the foundation for Leopold's Land Ethic.

Dick and I often discussed the need for a similar Land Ethic here in Scotland. There has to be a national mind change that turns the role of *Homo sapiens* from conqueror and owner to an ordinary member of the land community. Such a Land Ethic enlarges the boundaries of the community to include soils, waters, plants and animals ... or to put it collectively: the land.

A Land Ethic confirms the existence of an ecological conscience, and this in turn reflects a conviction of individual responsibility for the health of the land. Health being its capacity for self-renewal. Conservation is the sum of our efforts to understand and preserve this capacity. This is what Leopold wrote:

> It is inconceivable to me that an ethical relation to land can exist without love, respect, and admiration for land, and a high regard for its value. By value, I of course mean something far broader than mere economic value; I mean value in the philosophical sense. A thing is right when it tends to preserve the integrity, stability, and beauty of the biotic community. It is wrong when it tends otherwise.

Come By The Hills

Dick spent much of his working life in the Cairngorms where he was a senior manager with Scottish Natural Heritage, but if he was ever asked where his heart lay he would look north-west towards the mountain above the wood where he began his long and influential career. In the lexicon of any outdoor enthusiast some place names will strum the heart-strings more than others. Torridon is one such. For many, the area represents all that is good about Scottish hillwalking, the great steep-sided corrie-sculpted hills, skirts of native pinewoods and close proximity to the sea.

For Dick, Torridon also represented the official birth of nature conservation in Scotland, for it was here in 1951 that the government of the day formed the Nature Conservancy Council, purchased a site on the flanks of Beinn Eighe and declared it a National Nature Reserve.

Dick Balharry was its first warden.

This particular landscape is dominated by mountains, and Torridon's Munros are amongst the finest and most challenging in the country. The curvaceous shapes of Beinn Alligin contrast with the rugged drama of Liathach, while Beinn Eighe offers a bit of both, a mini-range of mountains and corries.

The legacy of mountain conservation continues here. Some of the area, including Liathach and Beinn Alligin, is now owned by the National Trust for Scotland while the Beinn Eighe National Nature Reserve is looked after by Scottish Natural Heritage and features wonderful mountain scenery with ancient pinewood fragments overlooking Loch Maree. The reserve is home to typical highland wildlife, including red deer, golden eagles and the elusive pine

208

marten. The woodland is rich in moisture-loving mosses and liverworts, and the bogs support an outstanding variety of dragonflies.

In a foreword to a book (*Beinn Eighe, The Mountain Above the Wood*) co-authored by Dick and Laughton Johnston, Chris Smith, (now Lord Smith of Finsbury) the only MP to have climbed all the Munros, said: '. . .in 1965 I climbed my first Munro: Beinn Liath Mhor, on the south side of Glen Torridon. I remember it was grey and wet and the cloud was low down and like many a mountain since I couldn't see a thing from the summit. But it was a place of wildness and freedom, and getting there was hard and exhilarating, and I thought then and there that this was something to be done again and again. And then the following day we climbed in the most glorious sunshine with half the western seaboard spread around us, and I knew that I was right. Twenty-four years later I completed all the Munros.'

More than anything else, the most fascinating aspect of Torridon is the antiquity of these mountains, the oldest in the world. Raised as a vast plateau thirty million years ago and carved into their present shape, it has been suggested that they are no older than the Alps, at least in their present form. What is really ancient is the rock of the original chain, now exposed as the grey quartzite caps, reckoned to be 600 million years old. The sandstone below them is even older and the platforms of gneiss on which they stand are believed to be in the region of 2,600 million years old. It's no small wonder they exude an air of primeval dominance. No small wonder that hillgoers, in turn, feel the insignificance of their flicker of lifespan.

If the enduring quality of these hills doesn't take your breath away, their visual impact certainly will. Take Beinn

Eighe for example. This isn't so much a single hill as a chain of hills, a complex mini-range whose terraced cliffs are cut at frequent intervals by long, vertical gullies that drop down into great fan-shaped stone chutes.

A hike over Beinn Eighe's seven peaks makes a long and serious expedition but a straightforward and scenic route traverses the two Munros, Ruadh-stac Mor and Spidean Coire nan Clach, and, as a bonus, visits one of Scotland's finest corries. Coire Mhic Fhearchair is one of the most impressive natural amphitheatres you'll find anywhere. Its shining lochan reflects the tiers of the spectacular Triple Buttress, an awesome structure of quartzite cliffs that rise from their sandstone plinth to fill the inner recesses of the corrie. It was one of the first walks I enjoyed in Torridon and I was 'guided' by Dick Balharry.

A place of 'wildness and freedom'. Chris Smith's description is one many of us will recognise but Dick also saw it as a place where people, plants and animals have struggled to survive, a place described by the naturalist Frank Fraser Darling as a 'largely devastated terrain'. Like Fraser Darling, Dick saw beyond the splendid beauty of the mountains and recognised an impoverished landscape. Much of that impoverishment was due to over-grazing, but he wasn't discouraged. He just wasn't that type of person. In the years since Beinn Eighe was designated as Britain's first National Nature Reserve things have changed remarkably. The pinewoods of Coille na Glas Leitir above Loch Maree have been protected and regeneration has been excellent. A fine complement of vegetation now exists from close to sea-level to above a thousand metres. One of Dick's favourite areas on Beinn Eighe lies on the north side of the mountain, a plateau that lies between the summit ridge and the lower slopes that fall away to Loch Maree.

'This area looks barren,' he told me, 'and plant cover is very sparse, with patches of ground-hugging shrubs such as heather, crowberry, alpine bearberry and the occasional mountain azalea with its tiny red and pink flowers. But extraordinarily, this high-level plateau is also home to one of the most extensive British populations of the sharp-leaved, prostrate juniper, as well as *Herbertus borealis*, a bright orange leafy liverwort, otherwise known in the world only from three sites in Norway.

'This is the country of our northern birds such as ptarmigan, dotterel and snow bunting, also of mountain hare and the summer home of red deer. Here, dragonflies hover over crystal-clear lochans and palmate newts lie doggo in the shallows. The terrain and its wildlife at this altitude mirror that of the arctic tundra more than 1,500 kilometres to the north.'

An excellent path offered us a fast highway through Coire Dubh Mhor between the eastern ramparts of Liathach and the steep slopes of A' Choinneach Mhor of Beinn Eighe. Beyond the watershed, and the combination of bog moss and scented bog myrtle, another path peels off around the skirts of Sail Mhor to climb past some sparkling waterfalls up a final, steeper rise and into Coire Mhic Fhearchair itself. This place is something special.

Many mountain commentators are of the opinion that Coire Mhic Fhearchair of Beinn Eighe is the finest corrie in Scotland, a claim that is difficult to contest. (Close contenders would be Toll an Lochain of An Teallach or perhaps the An Garbh Choire of Braeriach). Dominated by the great Triple Buttress of light grey quartzite which soars from an equally impressive plinth of red sandstone, the precipices loom over a rock-cradled lochan which spills out over the corrie lip in a series of fine waterfalls and cascades.

Unlike Beinn Eighe's other corries, Coire Mhic Fhearchair (the corrie of the son of Farquhar; try *corrie vic feracher*, with the *ch* harsh, as in *loch*) doesn't feel as though it's shut into the mountain and, despite its north-facing aspect, its open nature attracts a fair amount of sunlight, especially on a summer evening. More often than not highlighting the chocolate brown of the Torridonian sandstone and the glistening white speckles of quartz on the upper tiers of the cliffs. Bounded on the left by the scree-girt slopes of Beinn Eighe's highest summit, Ruadh-stac Mor, and on the right by the steep, broken cliffs of Sail Mhor, the lapping waters of the lochan reflect a scene of savage beauty, a ruffled image that has changed little in millions of years, the throne room of the Torridonian mountain king.

When Dick and I filmed on Beinn Eighe we gave ourselves time to sniff around Coire Mhic Fhearchair's inner recesses like dogs in a new kennel, searching out the resonances of the corrie's more recent history. Dick pointed out the remnants of the aircraft that crashed here in March 1951, the slivers of metal cold to the touch. A Lancaster bomber, which had been converted to maritime patrol duties, crashed here, killing all eight crew members. A twelve-year-old boy who lived in Torridon told his parents about a red glow in the sky near Beinn Eighe and a search mission began. Other aircraft from RAF Kinloss had been searching further north but now the search became concentrated. The missing Lancaster was eventually located just below the summit of Coinneach Mhor, directly above the Triple Buttress.

Dick outlined some of the routes he climbed in his youth with his regular climbing companion, the late Charlie Rose, an early leader of the Torridon Mountain Rescue Team. I eased up the lower moves of a rock-climb first completed over a hundred years earlier by Norman Collie, one of the founding fathers of Scottish mountaineering, who, with a lovely sense of exaggeration, described the last section as, 'not quite but very nearly AP.' The route most certainly steepens out, but isn't quite Absolutely Perpendicular as he suggests. I gazed along the line taken by Chris Bonington and the late Tom Patey in 1960 when they completed their Upper Girdle Traverse, a long horizontal route that followed the natural fault line between two layers of quartzite, and recalled with some nostalgia a rock-climb, The Gash (Severe, 200 feet/61 metres) I enjoyed many years ago with a friend now long gone.

We lingered for much of the afternoon, time slipping by without much notice. From somewhere close by we heard the raucous cry of a peregrine, but failed to actually see it. A flock of black-headed gulls floated on the loch, scavengers attracted by the crumbs left behind by hillwalkers, and a ptarmigan drew us away from its chattering brood by dragging her wings along the ground in mock injury. For most of the time we sat back against a pink-red rock that could be several thousand million years old, in silent wonder, trying to grasp some meaning behind such timescales. As usual, we failed completely, aware only of our own mortality.

I recalled our conversation about our fleeting mortality just a few years later. It was just before Christmas when Gina and I met Dick's wife Adeline in the bank in Kingussie. She looked troubled and then burst into tears. Dick had just been diagnosed with stage IV oesophageal cancer. It was a bolt from the blue and difficult to comprehend. How could this great man, a man with the constitution and strength of an ox, be terminally ill?

As far as I was concerned Dick Balharry was carved from the same rugged rock as his beloved Torridon. I just couldn't believe it. He fought the illness as hard as he could but by Easter was confined to a wheelchair when he was honoured by the Royal Scottish Geographical Society's Patrick Geddes Environment medal in recognition of his outstanding contribution to conservation. At his request, the honour was shared with Adeline.

I went along to the award ceremony in Glen Feshie with Margaret Wicks, one of my television producers who also happened to be a close neighbour of Dick and Adeline's. The great and good of the Scottish conservation world were in attendance when David Balharry read out a statement from his father calling for a more collaborative approach to wild deer management and how it should influence the Scottish Government's land reform programme. He was a campaigner to the very end.

Thomas Macdonnell of Kincraig played a lament on the pipes and three days later Dick passed away. In an obituary in The Guardian, his great friend and long-time colleague, the conservationist Des Thompson, recalled something Dick had written about his favourite creature, the golden eagle, a bird Dick reckoned was the very epitome of wild Scotland.

> . . .suspended motionless directly above us, her head dipped as if trying to penetrate the dark shadowy depths below. Then, suddenly and dramatically, she closed her wings and fell. She must have dropped over 2,000 feet before her wings eased open, with the resistance of the rushing air loudly adding to the drama we were witnessing.

11

Northness

'In the beginning,' say the Scottish mountain scriptures, 'God created the North-West, those magnificent landscapes that lie beyond Ullapool.'

Distinct from all other land forms in Scotland, Coigach, Assynt and Sutherland were sculpted by unusual forces to create spectacular mountain and coastal scenery with massive areas of exposed bedrock. It is as though some tremendous force has stripped everything away to reveal the bare bones of the earth. These bones are known as Lewisian gneiss, the oldest of rocks, with Torridon sandstone resting on this bedrock to form some of the most dramatic mountains in the land: Suilven, Cul Mor, Cul Beag and Quinag. Others are topped by paler Cambrian quartzite, while the larger part of the region is formed by the metamorphosed sandstones and schists of the Moine Thrust.

This faintly suggestive term describes a geological feature that was the discovery of Benjamin Peach and John Horne. Like Morecambe and Wise, or Ant and Dec, Peach and Horne are synonymous with each other, and worked closely together for over forty years. They first glimpsed the North-West Highlands, the scene of their most famous work, in 1883, having been sent north by Professor Archibald Geikie, at that time director of the British Geological Survey, to resolve a long-standing controversy about the geological structure of the area.

Geikie had long sided with the views of his predecessor, Roderick Murchison, who believed that the Cambro-Ordovician Durness Limestone (complete with fossils) reached upwards into the eastern schists of which a large part of the Northern Highlands are formed. However, some geologists, particularly Charles Lapworth and Charles Callaway, believed that the metamorphosed schists must be older than the limestones below them as the limestones were not metamorphosed, and that the junction was a steep fault. Since it can be observed that the junction is almost horizontal, Murchison's views were generally held to be correct. However, in 1883 Callaway and Lapworth suggested that the junction was a low-angle tectonic 'thrust', seriously interesting Geikie. It was during their first season of field mapping round Durness and Loch Eriboll that Peach and Horne recorded the true situation. Instead of the simple conformity that Murchison had suggested, they found gigantic structures of a kind never before encountered in Britain. The eastern (Moine) schists had been thrust westwards by a series of large-scale low-angled faults over the rocks of ancient Lewisian gneiss and their cover of Torridonian sandstone and limestone. During this process a series of smaller faults had been produced in the underlying rocks. The 'thrust zone' was eventually traced all the way from Loch Eriboll to Skye. These well-exposed structures are now easily recognised, but it was perhaps the most spectacular discovery in all of British geology. By 1884 Murchison's views had to be abandoned because of the rapidly accumulating evidence.

I've always regarded geology as one of the most fascinating yet complicated of all the sciences and, on various television jaunts to the North-West, found it difficult to explain to viewers how these incredible landscapes evolved. When we filmed one of our most successful programmes, *The Sutherland Trail*, a long walk between Lochinver and Tongue, I had to find someone who could explain the geological complexities better than I, so called on the help of an old friend, Donald Fisher from Scourie.

Donald worked as a geologist with Highland Council before heading south to work in South Wales. The pull of the Highlands proved too strong though, and he and his wife moved north again to the Sutherland coast, where he works as a part-time guide at the Scottish Natural Heritage interpretative centre at the Knockan Centre in Inverpollaidh.

Donald is one of the most engaging geologists you could hope to meet, and his enthusiasm is infectious. That's what makes him such a wonderful guide. I suggested that when you walk through an area like Assynt, that's been given international Geopark status, you can't help but wonder how it all began.

'Let's take the top of Suilven,' Donald explained. 'The landscape that you see is formed of raw, hard bedrock about 2,900 million years old. The rocks are so hard that they have determined the ways in which the land has developed.'

Geologists tend to bandy about massive timescales like 2,900 million years as though they were discussing what happened last year. I have to admit I can't get my head around such times, but can they?

'I'll let you into a secret,' said Donald, 'I can't either. I have a theory that no geologist really knows what a million years is like.'

I appreciated his honesty, but what is it that makes this area so special, and worthy of its international designation?

'We have here a special structure where rocks were sheared by compressional forces within the earth's crust. Older rocks, from far away, that is to the south-east near Inverness, were thrust, or pushed horizontally, toward, up and over, the younger rocks of Sutherland. This was known as the Moine Thrust.'

Simple.

Located on the north-west edge of Europe, the old county of Sutherland has historically been known as the 'Empty Lands' but, like many parts of the Highlands and Islands, it is reinventing itself. After years of depopulation, people are returning to the glens, not in great numbers perhaps but, as the tensions and economic uncertainties of urban Britain become increasingly intolerable, more and more folk are searching for an alternative. It's perhaps not surprising that this idiosyncratic landscape should become home to a couple who have shunned the normal concepts of civilisation, choosing to make their home on the stark edge of Europe, and whose whole lives have embodied the spirit of adventure.

In the aftermath of the Second World War some extraordinary things happened. Whether it was a new-found national optimism or an awareness that a new dawn was breaking, it appeared as though anything was possible. Roger Bannister ran the first four-minute mile, a British expedition under the leadership of John Hunt climbed Everest, and the Russian astronaut Yuri Alekseyevich Gagarin became the first man to be launched into space.

The next decade was no less progressive and, between headlines about Civil Rights movements, anti-war protests, and the pop culture of the Swinging Sixties, an event occurred that grabbed the attention of my fertile teenage imagination. I had just discovered the wonder and excite-ment of mountains, wild places and adventure, enthused and inspired by the writing of W. H. Murray, Eric Shipton, Tom Weir and Gavin Maxwell, when I heard that two men had rowed across the Atlantic. I couldn't believe it.

My own seagoing adventures had been limited to the likes of the Govan Ferry, or Sea Scout trips down the Firth of Clyde to Campbeltown. My father, originally a ship-yard worker but eventually a lecturer in ship joinery at a further education college in Glasgow, built a catamaran, a beautiful creation, but we only sailed it once. His joy had been in building boats, not sailing them. I had eagerly followed the voyages of Francis Chichester and Alec Rose, both well known yachtsmen who were often in the news, but sailing a fifty-odd-foot ketch is luxury compared to rowing a Cape Cod dory across the wild, inhospitable North Atlantic.

John Ridgway and Chay Blyth were soldiers in the Parachute Regiment, hardy, tough characters who were keen to make a name for themselves. No soft southern Atlantic crossing for them, they went for a North Atlantic crossing, taking ninety-two days to row their tiny boat 3,000 miles from Cape Cod to the Aran Islands off the west coast of Ireland, living in a cramped eight-foot-by-four-foot cockpit with no shelter and no bedding. They sat on hard wooden boards, ate dehydrated food and carried fresh water in old vinegar bladders and, remember, there was no GPS or digital radio in those days.

'Using 'O' level navigation, I took sights of the sun with my trusty sextant, from just four feet above the sea,' John later wrote. They carried a compass too, but *English Rose III* was battered by Hurricane Alma, by huge and almost overwhelming waves. Salt water gave them boils and got into the rations. Food became short.

> Basking sharks wider than the boat sheltered from the sun beneath the hull,' John recalled, 'and whales wider than the boat was long swept under us in the fog. On moonless nights, the luminous wake of speeding dolphins almost persuaded us they were sea serpents. At that stage in our lives, the intense solitude brought a new dimension to life, and the struggle to keep going and keep alive gave us a greater awareness of true values.

On a wild Saturday in September 1966, the rowers finally set eyes on the storm-lashed coast of the Aran Islands. John later described it as the single most dramatic day of his life. Chay Blyth's logbook records:

> The winds built up till it was gale force. We have been using the jets and props going to Shannon as a guide. We can't be far away now. All day we hear them. I was rowing at about 0900 hours; John was making breakfast. He stood up. "Land," he said. I wouldn't look. "I'll wait till we get closer," I said. The weather closed in then. We worked out it could only be the Aran Islands. The rain started to pour down. Both oars came out. We had approximately nine hours of daylight left. The seas were getting bigger all the time. About 1400 hours we could make out the cliffs. I started preparing the packs for an emergency landing. We were both singing now. I believed we hadn't come 3,000 miles to find death on a cliff.

John picks up the story:

> After months of glare off the sea, the memory of the vivid green grass will stay with me forever. With only the slightest difference in our landfall, wind and tide would have dashed us onto the rocks. I remember watching the spray flying upward in the storm, hundreds of feet up and over the tops of the cliffs.
>
> How can I express how plain lucky we were? There was no way we could stop the wind driving us at the islands; straining at all four oars we simply had to keep the bows pointing into the wind, trying to guide the boat into the narrow channel which led to safety. At dusk we landed at the little Irish village of Kilronan, on the island of Inishmore, after rowing across the Atlantic in a tiny boat only twenty feet long and five feet wide. We couldn't have made it by night: what a difference a few hours made in a ninety-two-day voyage.

Their dramatic arrival is still remembered on Inishmore. A few years ago I visited the Aran Islands as part of a cycling trip between Mizen Head and Malin Head, the most southerly and northerly points in Ireland. Hamish and I were keen to visit the Aran Islands and took our bikes by ferry from Doolin in County Clare to Inishmore, spending a day and a night there before returning to the mainland in Connemara.

Not far from our guest house in Kilronan we came across a small granite monument that celebrated the achievement of John and Chay. I had met John in the mid-nineties when I made a BBC television programme with his daughter,

Rebecca, the first woman to kayak around Cape Horn in South America, and had visited John and his wife, Marie Christine, at their remote home at Ardmore in Sutherland. Examining the monument, I realised it was almost half a century since the epic voyage. A fifty years celebration was surely on the cards?

Some time later I found myself walking along the same narrow, hilly and boggy footpath that John and Marie Christine had first taken some fifty years earlier. Newly married, and with all their worldly possessions in packs on their backs, they were heading for a white stone crofthouse that John had spied from an army parachute plane. On a rocky peninsula, fifteen miles south of Cape Wrath, the most north-westerly point on the Scottish mainland, Ardmore was a crofting township of four houses, only one of which was occupied, and here they hoped to begin their new life together, working as crofters.

The couple knew it would be tough. John told me what it was like in those early days: 'Ardmore, a place where nobody wanted to live any more. No vehicle access. An hour's hilly walk-in from the road-end or a mile up the sea loch. No electricity, only Tilley lamps, and no mains water. No shops. No pubs. It suited us just fine.'

Sadly it wasn't to be. They lived the hard lives of crofters for about five months but couldn't find a way of making a living, so John returned to the Parachute Regiment to think again. Two years later he rowed the Atlantic and life would never be the same.

'It was as if a page of small print had been obscuring my vision,' John told me. 'I could see a much bigger picture now. I hoped to live a life of adventure, not just on the sea but up mountains, through jungles, across deserts and down rivers as well. The whole world. I worked out my own simple code: self reliance, positive thinking, and leaving everybody and everything better than I found them.'

This became the philosophy of the John Ridgway School of Adventure the couple created in 1968. Today it's called Ridgway Adventure and is run by John and Marie Christine's eldest daughter, Rebecca, and her partner Mark. When I was first introduced to John and Marie Christine, John looked at me with distaste and proclaimed he didn't trust men who wore earrings. Not a good start. However, we discovered that he had been let down by a Channel 4 film crew who had claimed to be making a film about the School of Adventure but turned it into a full-scale critique of John, his staff and the teaching methods at Ardmore. He confided in me later that he feared the programme would put him out of business, hence his suspicion of, and aversion to, film crews.

Since then, Gina and I have become good friends with the Ridgways, visiting from time to time and occasionally meeting in Inverness for a meal. My admiration for the couple knows no bounds, although it is a major expedition to go and visit them.

Ardmore faces east, inland, and sits on the shore of Loch a' Chadh-Fi, an offshoot of Loch Laxford. The houses look across an uninhabited island towards the long ridge of Foinaven, the queen of Sutherland, while to the south-east the towering and unmistakable outline of Ben Stack dominates the skyline. From the croft houses the in-bye land runs steeply down green grassy slopes to the very edge of the sea. John calls this his 'magic carpet'.

'The magic carpet that has taken us to all corners of the

world. We have sailed our boat on the wind of a dream to just about jolly well everywhere and always back again to Ardmore, our sheet anchor.'

After his rowing adventure, John served for six months with the SAS before leaving the army for good. He planned to sail non-stop around the world as part of the 1968 Sunday Times Golden Globe Race.

'There were nine of us taking part in that race, but I don't think any of us were ready. Out of the nine, one got to the end, two committed suicide and the rest, including me, dropped out along the way. It really was pretty desperate.'

The next year John, Marie Christine and their two-year-old daughter Rebecca moved permanently to Ardmore, which has been the family base ever since. Running an adventure school in a location like Ardmore has its plus and minus points. On the plus side there can be few better locations for people learning to sail, kayak or climb hills, but on the deficit side absolutely everything has to be carried or brought in by boat. Marie Christine described their punishing regime for me.

'For me it was thirty-seven years of immense cooking each season, and on top of that I had to do all the office work, sending out brochures and letters, taking bookings – and remember we had no internet then. Indeed, we didn't even have electricity for eighteen years! Running kept me going, early morning runs round the loch. I would pass disgruntled male clients out on their early morning jog with comments like, "Got to get the porridge on . . . must rush." I think physical fitness was the key to those years of hard work. It was thirty-seven years, for seven months of the year, from six in the morning until we dropped into bed at night, totally exhausted.'

Every second winter John, Marie Christine and Rebecca would redecorate, refurbish, and do all the odd jobs that had to be done but, in the winters in between, they took off on a variety of extraordinary adventures that were often groundbreaking in their scope and intensity.

John sailed single-handed to Brazil; they traced the Amazon from its furthest source to the sea, crossed an unexplored ice-cap in Patagonia, sailed to the Spanish Sahara, participated in the Whitbread Round the World Race, took a climbing trip to Nepal, sailed to South America where Rebecca became the first woman to canoe round Cape Horn, and took part in numerous trips to Peru where John and Marie Christine adopted the orphaned daughter of an old friend who had died in a terrorist attack.

Somewhere between all this the couple twice ran the New York Marathon and John set a record for a non-stop double-handed circumnavigation of the world. When they both retired on John's sixty-fifth birthday, they set off to sail around the world again, John's third circumnavigation. This time they wanted to highlight the plight of that great seabird, the albatross, and completed by sailing up the Thames to present a petition at Westminster.

It's been an extraordinary life for John and Marie Christine Ridgway, and one that I'm delighted to say was recognised by the National Adventure Awards. I was given the job of travelling to Ardmore to present them with a Lifetime Achievement Award in recognition of their contribution to adventure and inspiring of others. We made a short film of the presentation, which was shown at the National Adventure Awards dinner in the Grand Central Hotel in Glasgow. The couple had been invited to attend but graciously declined. John told me they hadn't been south of the Great Glen for six years and took some pride in their new-found role as reclusive crofters.

Now in their eighties, the Ridgways have retired and are finally living the life they dreamed of when they set out together all those years ago, as crofters at Ardmore on the north-west seaboard of Scotland. Marie Christine sums up their retirement.

'We two have stepped back. We're home now. It's time to unpack after all the trips and look after the three crofts, our dream come true after lots of bumps along the way.'

The Ridgways may have retired but their adventurous lifestyle will remain an inspiration for years and years to come. In these days, when so much 'adventure' is simulated and virtual, I suspect we'll not see the likes of them again. I left Ardmore with John's final words ringing in my ears, and suspect he was throwing down a challenge, as he did to all the folk who survived his John Ridgway School of Adventure.

'It's about self reliance, in a place a long way from anywhere, and just being able to look after yourself to live. We've come this far, surely we can go a bit further? I want to do all of it, get at it, because you're only going to live a very short time. Life's short, I realise now how short it is. It soon goes by and you have to ask yourself, what did you do? What did you do with it?'

Just north of Ardmore, beyond the fishing port of Kinlochbervie, drive through the straggling croftships of Oldshoremore and Blairmore to arrive at the gate that heralds the rough four-mile track to Sandwood Bay. I don't think it's too much of an exaggeration to say that this track isn't the most exciting stretch of walking in the Highlands. It could even be described as dull, stretching over anonymous bog-splattered moorland, but such a walk-in only adds to the appreciation of arrival, when here is one of Scotland's finest and most extensive beaches and a sense of remoteness that is both stark and powerful. At the southern end, a hundred-metre-high sea stack, Am Buachaille (the Herdsman), stands guard on its sandstone plinth. Behind the beach and sequestered from it by a row of sand dunes covered in marram grass lies a freshwater loch, Sandwood Loch, and, sitting on the grassy hillside above it, the ruins of Sandwood Cottage, its gable walls forlorn and sad.

On the face of it, Sandwood Bay is little different from countless other bays and beaches that fringe the storm-lashed seaboard of Scotland, but there is another element at work, an atmosphere that is almost impossible to describe. I can effortlessly tell you about the impressive cliff scenery and the relentless pounding of the Atlantic surf, or the bare moor hinterland, and bird sounds that keep you company. Raucous gulls and cheeky seals and otters emerge from translucent green waters to play on rocky strands, and there are tales of mermaids and ghostly sailors and shipwrecks to go with them. I can write about all these things but still find it almost impossible to communicate the single, vital element that makes this tiny part of Scotland so indefinably special. Perhaps words cannot describe this spirit, and perhaps we need to find another way of expressing the soulful, almost spiritual feelings that Sandwood evokes. Can such an element of nature, of landscape, be best explained in music?

Duncan Chisholm had heard about its beauty, legends and inaccessibility, and wanted to experience Sandwood for himself. He is one of Scotland's finest fiddlers and several years ago recorded three albums of traditional music, the

Strathglass Trilogy, his first steps into writing and arranging music inspired by place.

'I spent seven years producing the *Strathglass Trilogy*, meaning Affric, Cannich and Farrar, and what I discovered was that I gained a lot from visual stimulus,' he told me at his home near Inverness.

'The trilogy was a big learning curve and I became fascinated by the fact that most of the indigenous music of the world is inspired by landscape. If you listen to the music of Norway or the north of Spain you realise how representative it is and how the human mind reacts to place. Thinking here of the dark long winter nights of the north of Norway and the music that represents that. I was lucky growing up with my teacher Donald Riddle. He was in his seventies and had a great amount of historical knowledge about the tunes. So I was getting a history lesson and a new tune at the same time. They came as a unit so it gave the melody a three-dimensional tone. Indeed, it gave the tune colour. As he told me the old stories it sparked a visual thought that has never left me. Instrumental traditional music gives people the opportunity to visualise, in the same way that classical music does.

'It's an interesting thought that what you see has a creative effect. We draw from what we see. If, for example, you observe a beautiful view then you have an experience you'll remember. Musicians and artists have the ability, through our skills, to reflect that in a certain way. I enjoyed the process with the *Strathglass Trilogy* so much I looked for a place that would inspire me in a similar way.'

Such was the background to the writing and recording of Duncan's brilliant album, *Sandwood*. The bay is certainly the kind of landscape that offers visual stimulus, but there's more than that. It's particularly atmospheric, with a wealth of legend and folk tales. There are those who claim this is the principal hauling-up place for mermaids in Scotland. You may smile, but a local shepherd, Sandy Gunn, was walking his dogs on the sand dunes a number of years ago when he saw the figure of a woman on a rocky strand which runs into the sea from the middle of the beach. He was convinced he was watching a mermaid.

There are many tales of hauntings, in particular that of a black-bearded sailor who haunts the marram dunes. Sailors at sea and fishermen claim to have seen him and believe that perhaps he was shipwrecked here. Seton Gordon writes of walking to Sandwood Bay early last century and how astonished he was at the number of wrecks littering the beach. They were, he believed, lost on this coast before the building of the Cape Wrath lighthouse a hundred years before. He even speculated that there might be Viking longboats buried in the sand. It was the Vikings who had named the place after all: *sand-vatn*, or sand-water. The ruins of Sandwood Cottage are also supposed to be haunted.

According to Marc Alexander in his book *Enchanted Britain*, two hillwalkers passing the night awoke to find the ruins shaking and the sound of a wild horse stamping above them. Could this have been the *each uisge*, or the water horse of ancient lore? I asked Duncan if he had experienced anything of this darker side of the bay?

'I've never felt frightened or scared in Sandwood Bay,' he replied. 'I've only ever felt very much at home. I felt I could have stayed there for days on end but I have a very good friend, a very wise and level-headed individual, who got totally spooked for no apparent reason. As soon as he came into sight of the place he became terrified and had to turn round and go home. He's never been back, and I've read about many people having similar experiences.

'It's worth remembering that the Celtic pagans used to refer to "thin places" and I'm sure such places are all around us. We're surrounded these days by all kinds of stimulus but we know that Sandwood has a dark history, a lot of ship-wrecks, the stories of ghost sailors and all of these things, but I think there are certain places where there could be a link to the past. I personally have a very scientific turn of mind but think there could be these thin places where we can become aware of an event or events that occurred in the past.'

At the beginning of his *Sandwood* album, Duncan records the following words: 'Out here there is no time, time is our imagination, past, present and future.' I asked him what he meant by that?

'The thing about Sandwood is that when you visit you're reminded about a sense of time and that's something I've thought a lot about. You've got the Lewisian gneiss rock, which has been there for billions of years. It's the place where the Picts first made their homes and the Vikings landed there. When you are in Sandwood you're very aware of that but you also feel as though you're somehow linked? Like time is not important? It's a timeless place. There's a definite sense that time is irrelevant.'

Understood, but how do you create a beautiful piece of music from such notions, particularly one that can define the landscape in a way that words cannot?

'The processes I go through include an imagined narrative – a journey if you like, picking up images on the way and trying to create a soundtrack to go with them. It's like trying to create a film in your head.

'Wanting to make the narrative a timeline I visited at different times of the year. The way I see it, the suite starts in March and goes through until October, November time.

'I went back and forth to Sandwood Bay about eight times, taking photographic stills and video and immersing myself as much as I could. I never tried to make music to the photos and the films but would look at them later as reference points. Working from memory is best when you're trying to put together a piece of music, and then it's about choosing parts of that narrative and what you feel you want to put into the track.

'It's like painting a picture, but your subject matter is the melody. Let's take one of the tracks, 'The Light of Tuscany', for example. That title was chosen before the music was written. It comes from a poem called 'The Altar' and the first few lines are a beautiful description of light and water.

> *When you plunged the light of Tuscany wavered*
> *and swum through the pool from top to bottom.*

'So that idea of azure light, the kind of light you find in Renaissance paintings, that colour is in there and it's beautiful, so the title came first.

'Then the melody is the sketch of what you see, so I imagined a pool of water like Sandwood Loch, and that particular colour. That's your focal point, the melody. Then when you work out the melody, the pace of it, how it will rise and fall, then the colour you put into the painting is the harmony and the instrumentation, and all the layers you put underneath it. The final element, the thing that makes it your own, is the performance. It's a fascinating process. The layers are so important, and I guess it's the same with classical music.

The more you listen to a piece of classical music the more you hear those layers. That's why I love the process in the studio, you hear this initial sketch come alive by adding different forms of instrumentation, the percussion, all of the different layers that make up the final recording.'

I first heard the music of *Sandwood* at the annual Celtic Connections festival in Glasgow when Duncan performed it live with a group of friends, all first-class musicians, both traditional and classical. It was a wonderful evening and I felt that he had tapped into the magical ether of that Sutherland landscape and had produced something quite exceptional, something that went beyond verbal description and story. With that work now firmly launched what was his next project? Was there another landscape in Scotland calling him?

'Not at the moment, but you never know. An analogy I always use about being involved in music is that you are on a railway journey, a train journey with no stations. The important things are that you stay on the train and that you have something to give. For me it's a life journey. I'd hate to be one of these people who had a huge amount of success in younger years and nothing to excite me anymore. Every time I think about a new project I get excited about it and I will never retire from what I do because I love it so much.

'I think retrospectively I've learned more about my own playing, and how I see music, over the last couple of years than I have done in my entire life. Just how I work as a musician, as an artist, where I see where I want to go and the realisation that you never really finish learning how to find your own voice. You're always learning new things and you're always inspired by other people and places, so I have to stay on the train all the way to the end.

Will that train journey always be in Scotland?

'I'm not sure. I'd love to delve into film music at some point because the music I've created so far is about films that are really in my own head, and when I've written music for documentaries I've found that it tends to write itself.

'I immerse myself in it and ideas spark off that. So I don't think my future work will inevitably be all in Scotland but there's so much here and it's on my doorstep. I can easily immerse myself in a place or a landscape here in the Highlands because there is accessibility although, granted, to get to Sandwood involves a three-hour journey from Inverness. So I guess if I lived in the swamps of Louisiana I could find something that inspired me or if I was out in the Middle East I could find something there.

'It's essentially about understanding the place and I have an understanding of the Highlands, I know the Highlands, the place is in my blood. I know the history and I love it so I guess at the moment it's the easiest canvas to work from.'

A few miles north of Sandwood Bay, along a wind-battered and ragged coastline, lies Cape Wrath and its lighthouse and I was becoming a little embarrassed by not being able to find it. With a BBC film crew I was walking the final section of our Scottish National Trail, a 470-mile route between Kirk Yetholm in the Borders and Scotland's most north-westerly point. We were within half a mile of the Cape Wrath lighthouse and the end of the route, but I couldn't see it. It was a misty morning, not an uncommon occurrence on the north-west edge of Scotland, and every time we walked to the top of a grassy rise there was another slope in front of us. A grey curtain of mist hid everything else. The Cape Wrath lighthouse is twenty metres tall and I should have seen it by now. It wasn't as if I was looking for a tiny orienteering flag half hidden in the ground. How do you miss a sixty-six-foot-tall lighthouse? I was about to check my map and compass again when the mist lifted a fraction and it appeared, a black turret atop a rather stumpy white tower.

For some reason I had always remembered this lighthouse as being dominant in the landscape, as lighthouses tend to be, but today the tower and its little collection of buildings were dwarfed by that same sprawling landscape and the vast spread of ocean that lay beyond it. To suggest there is a sense of spaciousness here would be a gross understatement. The whole of the Cape Wrath peninsula, or An Parph to give it its proper name, runs to almost 300 square kilometres of hill and moorland, rising to 1,591 feet/485 metres on the summit of its highest hill, Creag Riabhach. On two sides, the Parph is bounded by an open expanse of sea and on the third by the Kyle of Durness. Its remaining boundaries run out to the A838 Durness road and the minor road between Rhichonich and Kinlochbervie.

You couldn't technically describe the area as wilderness, but this northern extremity is as close to wilderness as you'll find in all of Scotland. In the early nineteenth century there were a number of small crofting communities here and as recently as the 1930s there were thirty to forty people living on the peninsula. Today there is just one permanent resident, John Ure, who runs the UK's most remote tearoom, the Ozone Café, in one of the renovated lighthouse buildings. Despite its isolation, this wild north-west corner is the focus of much tourism in the wider area. From April until October a tiny ferry operates from Keoldale, carrying passengers over the beautiful Kyle of Durness. Once ashore the passengers are taken twelve miles by minibus to Cape

Wrath where they can spend an hour looking around, or savouring one of John's excellent meals and home baking.

About three thousand people arrive at the Cape this way every year, as well as several hundred walkers who have enjoyed the rough hike from Sandwood Bay as part of the increasingly popular Cape Wrath Trail. Many of the visitors who have come specifically to visit Cape Wrath will stay locally at Durness, using the shops and restaurants there and at nearby Balnakeil. Remove the attraction that is Cape Wrath and the local economy would most certainly suffer. That's why there was so much concern when the Northern Lighthouse Board decided to sell the lighthouse to the Ministry of Defence, along with the associated buildings and fifty-eight acres of land. The MoD already owned the rest of the Parph, which it has long used as a bombing range. Now, for some reason, they wanted to buy the final parcel that would give them ownership of the entire area.

The MoD property in the Cape Wrath area is effectively closed to the public for about 130 days every year while bombing exercises are carried out. When a letter from the military was sent to the local MP, Lord Thurso, suggesting that sale of the lighthouse and adjacent land would likely mean a complete ban on public access, there was a huge outcry. A petition was organised and support was drummed up for the Durness Development Group, who had registered interest in a community buyout, under the Land Reform (Scotland) Act. Indeed, it wasn't until the Durness Group made enquiries about renewing their interest in a buyout that it became evident that the Northern Lighthouse Board was already in advanced negotiations.

For whatever reason, and many believe it may have been public pressure combined with the Scottish Government's decision to back the Durness Development Group's bid, the MoD withdrew its plans. The news was met with delight by the country's walking organisations and land reform groups, as well as the local community. Not least, the news was welcomed with a huge sense of relief by John Ure at the Ozone Café.

'I was delighted because, if the MoD had bought this land, the public would have been banned,' John told me. 'I was told that the rocket range in Benbecula was closing and there was a chance it could be moved here, to Cape Wrath.'

John and his wife, Kay, moved to the north-west of Scotland having worked in the fur trade in Canada. Sadly Kay passed away in 2016. John told me it was in Newfoundland that they discovered their love for living in wild places, a far cry from their native Milngavie.

'We were in Canada for about eight years and became used to wild weather. The Canadian winters knock the edges of the Scottish winter,' John told me. 'We regularly had eleven feet depth of snow with temperatures of minus 50. We don't get real winters in Scotland any more.'

The couple eventually became homesick and with their three children moved back to Glasgow where John made roller blinds for shops and Kaye renewed her work as a nurse. Inspired by their wild living in Newfoundland they began searching for remote properties that were at risk but that they could refurbish and live in. They registered with Historic Scotland, who kept them informed and, at one point, they became interested in the Ardnamurchan Lighthouse. Highland Region compulsorily purchased some of the buildings at Cape Wrath with the idea of turning them into a visitor centre and café. Council officials later decided that such a development wouldn't be viable over a short five-month season and abandoned their plans. Instead, officials contacted John and suggested they do a swap. Highland Region would take on Ardnamurchan if the Ures would have a go at Cape Wrath. They got the buildings for £25 on a twenty-five-year improvement lease.

'People often asked us how we filled our time here in the winter,' said John, 'but we were always busy. We did up a couple of the buildings, one to live in and the other as the café. We had to bring in coal to keep us warm, and water too. I captured rainwater as much as I could but we couldn't drink that, so we had to use it for the toilet and some washing. For everything else we brought in bottled water. In terms of hygiene standards we are exactly the same as The Dorchester, but it's a bit more difficult and time consuming. We had to keep the generator going, and that can be expensive, and work the radio off an old car battery. On top of all that we had five springer spaniels to exercise every day.'

It's the kind of lifestyle that many would aspire to but few could cope with, and the Ures' lifestyle was not without uncertainty. Some years ago John took Kay to their boat, which was moored in the Kyle of Durness. She was going to Durness to join a minibus of folk heading for a Christmas shopping excursion in Inverness. It was the 19th December. By the time she returned to Durness with her Christmas turkey, bad weather had made it impossible for John to drive the twelve miles to the Kyle.

'The road had disappeared under heavy snow and it all looked just like moorland. It was a total whiteout and had to be seen to be believed. It was minus 10 at one point.'

Meanwhile, Kay got use of a friend's caravan in Durness, where she stayed all through Christmas. The weather didn't abate enough for John to travel and pick her up until the third week in January. All this time John had to survive in one of the most isolated dwellings in Scotland. On top of everything else the café's generator broke down, so he lost his telly as well as lights and heating. His only company was his five spaniels, other than on Christmas Day when two hikers appeared, having walked five and a half hours cross-country. It would be another three weeks before he saw another soul. Christmas dinner was lamb curry.

'In thirty-five years together, Kay and I never spent Christmas or New Year apart,' he said. 'We'd speak each evening by phone and she kept me abreast of all the gossip in the village while I listened by candlelight. I distracted myself with odd jobs, cut firewood, took the dogs for walks and tried to keep warm. At one point Kay was offered the opportunity of coming home in a helicopter but she was terrified of flying and turned it down.'

In the third week of January, John made it back to the Kyle to see Kay on the other side, waving furiously. It had been thirty-one days since they'd seen each other. With the generator still broken the couple cooked the turkey in a gas-powered oven and carved it by candlelight. They opened presents and tried to convince themselves it was Christmas Day but, as John told me, 'It was now closer to Burns Night than Christmas Day.'

The big bonus was that the turkey had stayed frozen the entire time!

With the threat of a sell-out to the MoD behind them, the Ures began concentrating on the future. Most immediate amongst their plans was the creation of a ten-bed bunkhouse.

The thing they missed most was electricity and they hoped at some point to install solar power or a wind turbine although, ironically, the Cape Wrath winds could be too strong. The Lighthouse Board previously erected a turbine but the gales blew it down. It's easy to focus on the hardships of living in such an isolated place, but there were benefits as well.

'We didn't suffer from loneliness,' said John. 'We had each other, we had the dogs, and there was usually a walker or two about. In the summer the minibus kept us busy with tourists. I can sit here and watch fin whales and dolphins. Deer come at night to graze. I breathe what almost feels like pure oxygen and wouldn't go back to the city for anything.'

The name of the café? Where does that come from?

'We named it after the wafts of fresh ozone that drift down from Greenland from time to time. It smells a bit like newly mown grass.'

Several years ago, Kay became ill and couldn't live in the damp conditions of the old lighthouse buildings. For a while she helped John during the summer months, when the weather was warmer, but she sadly passed away in 2016, leaving John to run the café and bunkhouse. Their daughter comes north as often as possible to help.

Duncan Chisholm's deep sense of place and community helped him create a musical score to what is one of the most amazing landscapes in Europe, but it takes a special kind of person, with strong qualities of survival and perseverance, to actually live all year round on the edge of the North Atlantic. John Ure and the Ridgways have such qualities in abundance. People of the land and of the sea, and truly people of adventure.

12

BEYOND THE SHINING SEAS

When I was invited to speak at the Harris Mountain Festival in the Western Isles I didn't hesitate for a moment. Although offered accommodation in a Tarbert hotel I suggested to the organisers that, if they pay my ferry fare, I would sleep in my campervan. This wasn't just altruism on my part, the Outer Hebrides is one of the most welcoming places for campervans in the country and, because of the Scottish Government's Fuel Equivalent Tariff on Caledonian MacBrayne ferries, the fare wouldn't bankrupt my hosts. So, I may as well stop over for a few days to enjoy the island's wonderful hills, beaches and coastline.

My first real contact with the people of Harris and, in particular, the folk of the North Harris Trust, was in 2001 when I was invited to cross the Minch and officially open a new long-distance walking route, the twenty-six-mile-long Frith na Rathad na Hearadh, or the Harris Walkway. After enduring my efforts at the Gaelic language – 'Tha e a'cordadh rium gu mor a bhith an seo an diugh a-measg beanntan agus muinntir na Hearadh' – about fifty young-sters from the high school in Tarbert joined me on the first section.

The walk is filled with variety: through a bealach on the western slopes of An Clisham, down to what was once the most isolated village in Britain, Rhenigidale, and over the watershed via an ancient coffin route to the east coast and the end of the Walkway.

Apparently, the east of Harris is so rocky that people couldn't be buried there, so they were carried to the west coast and softer soil. Such coffin routes were common in the Highlands and Islands. The Scottish Rights of Way Society (Scotways) book, *Scottish Hill Tracks*, recalls the writings of Osgood Mackenzie, the botanist who planted Inverewe Gardens. When Lady Mackenzie died in 1830, five hundred men, taking turns, carried her coffin sixty miles from Gairloch to Beauly. When the bearers took a rest, everyone added a stone to a cairn on that spot, a custom that is responsible for many of the cairns which today mark some of these historical routes, including this Harris Walkway. Writing in 1906, the Reverend Thomas Sinton described a very similar funeral procession in my home area of Badenoch.

> In the absence of proper roads, bodies were always carried shoulder-high to their last resting place. They were often enclosed in cases of wicker-work or perhaps merely surrounded by long saplings placed side by side and withe-bound. Thus having been borne hither, young men and maidens in the bloom of youth, parents followed by their weeping children, infants taken from their mothers' arms, husbands and wives separated by death; soldiers, who had fought for their country in foreign lands; churchmen, who had dispensed the sacraments within that ruined shrine; chief men and peasants; bards, whose quips and cracks, and jests and jibes, were silenced forever; unknown strangers who had perished on the mountains. Huge companies of people from the Braes of Badenoch and the Braes of

Lochaber, who had journeyed to St Kenneth's, carrying thither their dead with the wail of pibroch and cry of coronach, and who thronged yonder burial ground in summer's sun and winter's blast, have themselves, long since, paid the last debt to nature and come to dust.

The Frith na Rathad na Hearadh was the first big walk I undertook in the Western Isles and, since then, Gina and I have made a point of heading across there at least once a year, sometimes to speak at the Harris Mountain Festival, sometimes to make television programmes with Richard Else, such as the BAFTA-award-winning live outside broadcast of climbers Dave MacLeod and Tim Emmett climbing a new route on the overhanging nose of Sron Ulladale, but our jaunts were mostly to enjoy the Hebridean ambience, explore the lonely hills and visit this wonderful archipelago.

The Western Isles offer sensational walking and many of the lay-bys on the island highways are ideal for stopovers in our wee red campervan, with polite little notices suggesting a donation for upkeep of the lay-by via a website address. There are only a couple of official campsites on Harris but there are waste facilities at the ferry port at Leverburgh. Much of this welcoming attitude is down to the actions of two community trusts, the North Harris and the West Harris Trusts. In the past few years the local people have bought the land where they live and work, and are keen to attract tourists. Interpretation boards inform, and a new distillery has been built in Tarbert. To my surprise and delight, a new shower block, public toilets and a camping area with electric hook-ups have been created at one of my favourite wild camping spots. For years I've been captivated by the magic of Hushinish on the west coast, with its cliffs and machairs lying close to the pulsing rhythms of the sea, and now I can spend the night and stay clean and fresh into the bargain.

Hushinish is a fine example of an environment formed by oceanic weather conditions. Machair abounds, and the bays boast superb sweeps of white shell sand. The word 'machair' is Gaelic, meaning an extensive, low-lying fertile plain, but has become a recognised scientific term for a specific coastal feature. Defined by some as a type of dune pasture (often calcareous) subject to local cultivation, it will have developed in wet and windy conditions. Such coastal strips generally run from the beach to where the sand encroaches on to peat. Among the rarest habitats in Europe, they are found only in the north and west of Scotland and Ireland.

The Scots-born environmentalist John Muir was never slow to publicise the special qualities of an area, believing that the more people who visit the more will be prepared to lobby for their protection. I wished he had been with me as I left the pier at Hushinish to climb the cliffs of Rubha Ruadh and Geodha Roaga. We could have climbed the grassy slopes to the summit of Cnoc Mor to survey the glorious scene, where I'm sure Long John would rhapsodise in typical Muir fashion, thrilled by the wheeling seabirds, the purple land and green ocean. Later, as we travelled inland below Husival Beag towards Loch na Cleavag, we would listen for the otherworldly call of the black-throated diver. Golden plover, wheatear, wren, rock pipit and stonechat are not uncommon and the golden eagle breeds here, a sure indication of the genuine wildness of the place.

Inland from Hushinish the area faces the unoccupied island of Scarp, at the mouth of Loch Resort, where a few years ago there were as many as fifty people living and the community had its own school. Today it's deserted, like so many of the islands that lie off the Hebrides.

An exception to that general rule is Scalpay, tucked away in the south-east corner of North Harris. The island was connected to North Harris by a bridge in 1997 and there is a real sense of prosperity here. There has been strong resistance to the traditional island problem of depopulation and numbers are holding steady, continuing to match those of a century ago. This is the home of Scalpay linens and the traditional Scalpay jersey, but I was more inspired by the machairs and moorlands in the south-east, near the lighthouse at Eilean Glas, one of the original Northern Lighthouses which dates back to 1789. Most of them were built by the Stevensons, the family of author Robert Louis Stevenson.

While Beinn Sgorabhaig is a mere 341 feet/104 metres above sea level its summit views are out of all proportion to its height, and I loved the views across the Minch to the Trotternish hills of Skye and west towards the glut and tumble that makes North Harris such a magnificent destination for the wilderness-seeking hillgoer. Some of the most underestimated hills in Scotland are located here: rugged, rocky mountains that attract surprisingly few walkers. If you delve into the byways that follow the glens you'll come across reminders of the spiritual history of these Outer Isles: Holy Wells, the ruins of ancient chapels and 'teampaills', and beehive shielings, curious small shelters that some believe predate Christ. Many of these beehive shelters, such as those close to the Harris/Lewis boundary, are suffering from the climate-change-induced storms of recent times. As a nation we should be doing much more to protect them and save them for future generations.

Brooding over this wild quarter of Harris is its Corbett, An Clisham, the highest hill in the Outer Hebrides at 2,621 feet/799 metres, which because of its height status will always be a magnet for walkers. It is best viewed from the south, by looking up into the impressively rocky Coire Dubh with its three summits of Mulla bho Dheas, An t-Isean and An Clisham itself.

The first time I climbed the hill, well over twenty years ago, I wandered up its south ridge from the old Whaling Station at Bunavoneadair, on the Hushinish road. The advantage of starting here is that you can traverse the three tops in a fine horseshoe route, descending the broad Tarsaval ridge. However, nowadays, most hillwalkers climb from the A859 Tarbert to Stornoway road, where a small car park has been built by the bridge over the Maaruig River. A footpath runs up the hill to the foot of Clisham's south ridge, where it becomes lost in a jumble of boulders and rock.

On our return visit we hoped to start at Bunavoneadair or, as the most up-to-date Ordnance Survey has it, Bun Abhainn Eadarra, but finding a place to park a campervan is not that simple. When we arrived, albeit late in the day, all the obvious parking spots were full, so we drove to the high point of the A859 and parked on the old road, which gave us a height advantage of a couple of hundred metres. Although keen to traverse the three tops that rise above Coire Dubh, after an hour or so Gina decided to call it a day. We had reached the interminable boulder fields that cover the south ridge of An Clisham and, for good reason, she doesn't like boulder fields. Having survived two ankle breaks, one at over 17,000 feet in the Himalaya, she was afraid she might not be so lucky a third time and wisely retreated to the campervan for a brew and a book. I battered on.

By this time, cloud had rolled in and progress for me had become a matter of getting the head down and negotiating the slippery boulders as best possible. The ridge narrows nicely as it approaches the summit with the trig point hidden inside a massive circular windbreak. A couple of walkers were enjoying their sandwiches in its shelter, so I didn't stop, lingering only to take a bearing for the bealach and An t-Isean. Care is required here in misty conditions. After a rocky descent to the grassy pass, another steep climb took me to An t-Isean. A shorter descent then led to the rocky slopes of Mull-fo-dheas and a scramble to the summit. For those not keen to use their hands, a path traverses the north side of the summit to eventually twist back to the twin cairns on top.

By now I was wondering what the best route back would be. A quick check of the map suggested descending Mulla-bho-Dheas's south ridge to where it flattens out over Mo Buidhe. From there I could drop down into Coire Dubh where an easy climb over Tarsaval would return me to my starting point. The route went well, and I enjoyed my sight of a golden eagle flying from the tiered rocks of Coire Dubh. Grassy underfoot, it didn't take me long to climb out of the corrie where, at last, I caught some views of West Loch Tarbert, the isle of Taransay and the Atlantic. Back at the campervan I was ready for a brew, knowing that we only had a few miles to drive back to Hushinish where, thanks to the vision and generosity of the North Harris Trust, we could enjoy the luxury of a hot shower.

While I am passionate about Harris I think my favourite Hebridean island is a sparkling jewel set between South Uist and Barra. While it shares many of the features of the other islands in the chain, like white cockleshell beaches, domed skies, small rugged hills and an air of tranquillity, Eriskay's claims to fame are out of all proportion to its size. I visited on one of our television jaunts and it remained in my memory as a bit different to the other islands, with a spirit of place that seemed less harsh, more welcoming and with a gentler environment than its close neighbours.

This time Gina and I spent some extra time on the island, learning more about it from the retired Roman Catholic priest, Father Calum MacLellan. I had met and interviewed Father Calum previously, but he had since become a television star. His contribution to life in the islands was huge. The native Gaelic-speaker was the first vice-convenor of Comhairle nan Eilean, the Western Isles Council, when the archipelago was unified under a single local authority in 1975, and he later had the Freedom of the Western Isles bestowed upon him for his contributions to island life. Many will recall him as a star of the BBC fly-on-the-wall series *An Island Parish*, which followed the lives of three Hebridean island priests, and some have dubbed him a real-life version of the Channel 4 comedy character Father Ted. In fact, Father Calum probably had more in common with an earlier Catholic priest from Eriskay, Father Allan Macdonald, who took over the parish of Daliburgh, which then included Eriskay, in 1884.

The people of the area, more than eighty per cent Roman Catholic, were very poor. Despite this and other difficulties, Father Allan encouraged the building of a hospital in Daliburgh that was only recently replaced by a modern facility in Balivanich on Benbecula, and the present church in Eriskay. Father Allan is also remembered as a Gaelic folklorist, responsible for one of the greatest collections of

Gaelic literature related to one locality. He died aged only forty-six in October 1905 after a bout of pneumonia.

Father Calum was a teenager of fifteen when the cargo ship the SS *Politician* grounded just off the shores of Eriskay and lost its cargo of 2,000 cases of whisky, many of which were 'liberated' by the local crofters, a tale that was humorously retold by Compton Mackenzie in his glorious tale of Hebridean cunning and wit, *Whisky Galore*. Father Calum recalled the police and customs officials searching the island for the hidden contraband. 'A number of crofters were charged with theft,' he told me, 'something that Compton Mackenzie didn't mention in his novel.'

Father Calum also explained to me how island life changed when the causeway to South Uist was built in 2001, making the tiny island part of a much larger, and more accessible, community. 'In the thirties there were over 400 people living on Eriskay, but by 2000 only about 130. Today that's risen to almost 150.'

Father Calum recently passed away at the age of eighty-six, a wonderful character who'll be remembered with great fondness by everyone on Eriskay.

Although Eriskay is nowadays attached by its stone umbilical cord to South Uist, the island still feels remote and unspoiled. It's a mere two-and-a-half miles by one-and-a-half, but much of that land is hilly with two prominent tops, Beinn Sciathan in the north and Beinn Stac in the south. Our ascent of Beinn Stac, 410 feet/125 metres, was straightforward, although climbing rough grassy slopes on a curving ridge from the tiny township of Acarseid we didn't see much. A thin veil of mist obscured everything but the most immediate of views, although we could just discern the southern islands of Eilean a' Gheoidh, Eilean Dubha and Eilean Leathan, rocky outcrops rising across the narrow strait of Caolas an Stac.

The walk was sufficiently short to return to Am Baile and the Am Politician pub in time for a bar meal. We were waiting for the mist to clear before we climbed the bigger of the island's two hills, Beinn Sciathan, but it was time put to good use. In the bar we were shown some of the whisky bottles that were rescued from the SS *Politician* on the fateful night, bottles that still contained whisky, although goodness only knows what it tastes like by now.

We combined our ascent of Sciathan with a wander through the island's main township, Am Baile, and along a superb cockleshell beach, the Coilleag a' Phrionnsa, the Prince's Strand, a name that commemorates the arrival of Charles Edward Stuart on July 23rd 1745. The prince arrived ashore on a small boat from the French ship *Du Teillay*. It was the first time he had set foot on Scottish soil and it began the second Jacobite Rebellion.

It was an inauspicious start to Charles' ambitions to win back the crown for his father. He was apparently met by Alexander Macdonald of Boisdale who, rather than welcome the Young Pretender with open arms, told him he would receive no support from the MacDonalds of Clanranald, the MacDonalds of Sleat in Skye, nor the MacLeods of Skye, and urged him to go home. 'I am come home sir,' retorted the Prince, before sailing with the Seven Men of Moidart to raise his standard at Glenfinnan. We all know the outcome of that adventure, but Charles left his mark on Eriskay.

As he removed his handkerchief from his pocket, he pulled out the seeds of a flower, the pink-and-white striped sea bindweed, or *calystegia soldanella*. With its fleshy stems and loudspeaker-shaped petals, this plant certainly isn't native to the Outer Hebrides; it is only recorded at one other site on the islands, although it's widespread on the Atlantic coast of Ireland. A commemorative cairn, erected on the 250th anniversary and built by local schoolchildren, lies beyond the marram.

From the south end of the beach, we took the ferry road to a junction where we turned right to follow the narrow road to Acarseid Mhor before taking another track past a small water-treatment building to the open hill where a small herd of white Eriskay ponies greeted us. One of them, braver than the others, sauntered forward shyly, but wasn't too keen on being stroked.

The Eriskay pony is the rarest breed in Europe and almost became extinct in the 1970s. The numbers are now increasing. These are not 'wild' ponies as such, each one has an owner, but they don't live in stables. Instead they run free on the island, and in parts of South Uist. Stocky beasts, and not particularly tall, their thick coats withstand the Hebridean chill. It's thought the Vikings took them from the Hebrides to Iceland, about a thousand years ago, and today, it appears, the Icelandic pony has very similar DNA characteristics.

We left the ponies munching tough deer grass to follow a series of marker posts towards a saucer of dark water cradled among some tumbled morraines. Loch Cracabhaig must be a good trout loch, and a lovely spot to spend an hour or two angling, but we had other fish to fry, so to speak. Beinn Sciathan rose in a series of craggy terraces and although it wasn't far to the top it would be a steep climb, and we would need to weave a safe line through the outcrops. The hills of Barra filled the horizon to the south-west and the sea between was splattered with small sunlit islands. By this time much of the cloud had dispersed and, to the west, the uninhabited island of Lingeigh looked like an upside-down pudding bowl floating in the water. Can there be anything finer in landscape terms than the combination of hill and shining sea?

Using our hands as well as our feet we clambered upwards, excited by the prospect of a clear view at the summit . . . and what a summit it was! The trig point stands on a rocky plinth offering expansive views across the Minch towards the Isle of Skye and south to the hills of Barra. To the north a jumble of lower hills lead the eye towards Beinn Mhor in South Uist while, below, Eriskay reveals itself as a sun-blessed, beach-fringed jewel, with most of its houses and buildings in the north end below the protective gaze of St Michael's church, built in 1903.

The weather was improving by the minute and, although there was drifting mist across the south-western shores of South Uist, a break in the cloud meant the sun illuminated the north-west corner, picking out each whitewashed building in a dazzling display. We lay against the summit rocks and sipped from our flasks, picking out the traces of old field margins and former cottages, the old homes from when Eriskay was relatively well populated.

When Colonel Gordon of Cluny purchased Eriskay, South Uist, Benbecula and Barra from the MacNeils of Barra, he immediately cleared most of the islands for sheep. Since it was thought Eriskay wasn't suitable for sheep farming he permitted many of the cleared crofters to establish them-selves there, swelling the population fivefold. Today, despite the initial success of the causeway in halting population decline, there is concern for the future, as there is generally in the Outer Isles. The primary school in Am Baile has closed and the children now go to school in South Uist. Some of the houses are holiday cottages, and tourism, with its very short Hebridean season, is the main industry. A ferry links Eriskay and Barra but, unlike the ferries from the mainland to Stornoway, Tarbert, Lochmaddy and Lochboisdale, inter-isles ferries don't benefit from the Fuel Equivalent Tariff, a Scottish Government subsidy, and are expensive.

With the sun now brightening the entire island and the blue-green sea glittering under evaporating mists, there was a temptation to suggest heavenly comparisons, a hint of paradise lost, a shining pearl in the Hebridean seas. My fundamental grasp of the English language doesn't do it justice, but I bet the Gaelic language does. The Gaelic scholar John Lorne Campbell of Canna recalls these words of Father Allan Macdonald:

> *Eilein bhòidhich, làn thu dh'éibhneas,*
> *Leug an domhain thu maduinn Chéitein,*
> *'N driùchd 'na chaorain geala sheudaibh,*
> *Boillsgeadh bristeach 'nad ghorm éideadh,*
> *Dealbh nan reul air cluain nan speuran.*

> *Beautiful island, thou art full of happiness,*
> *thou art the jewel of the world on a May morning,*
> *the dew shining like white diamonds,*
> *glittering brokenly on thy green clothing,*
> *the picture of the stars on the plain of the heavens.*

The stark reality is that these are islands on the edge; on the edge of Scotland, on the edge of Europe, and on the edge of an uncertain future, but at least that future is in the hands of those who live there. A sporting syndicate sold the assets of Benbecula, South Uist and Eriskay to a community-owned organization called Storas Uibhist in 2006 and a recent census recorded a population increase of seven-and-a-half per cent, compared with a Scottish islands' population increase of four per cent for the same period. There is hope and optimism for the future and I'm very glad of that.

Our descent was surprisingly steep, down grassy rakes and gullies between rocky crags, but in no time we were back on the lower slopes, following marker posts through common grazings back to the village, and another visit to the Politician, just in time for supper. We were well contented after our day on Eriskay, the loveliest and fairest of the Hebrides.

> *Bheir mi òro bhan o*
> *Bheir mi òro bhan i*
> *Bheir mi òru o ho*
> *'S mi tha brònach's tu'm dhith.*

'The Eriskay Love Lilt'

Once you leave the Harris hills behind, on the road north to Lewis, the whole feel of the landscape changes. Expansive peat moorlands predominate, but Lewis has more subtle attractions, and all day we had been struck by a real sense of the past. Ancient stone dykes line the in-by fields, and the ruins of old cots and black houses litter the otherwise empty landscape. Relentless toil against the vagaries of the Atlantic and the rough, rocky ground, which had to serve in the past, are obviously not for the modern Hebridean. There are over 3,000 crofts on the Isle of Lewis, but many are too small for economic viability. The current state of the agricultural industry obviously doesn't help. Apart from growing the year's supply of potatoes and raising a few hens, most modern crofters prefer to run the croft on a part-time basis, the main job in Stornoway or in the fishing or tweed industry offering a better return. As a result, the more exposed parts of this Hebridean coastline have been left to wheeling gulls and the ghosts of yesterday.

We stopped at the village of Callanish where, on a headland overlooking Loch Roag, stands the Callanish Stone Circle. The stone circle at Stonehenge may be bigger than its Hebridean counterpart, and its surroundings more manicured, but the Callanish circle is infinitely more atmospheric and romantic, positively exuding drama and mystery. I wanted to spend a night there, but Gina didn't fancy that at all. Local folk call the place 'Tursachan' which loosely translated means 'the place of pilgrimage', a name that throws little light on the reasons the stones are there.

The circle is believed to have been built some three-and-a-half thousand years ago: fifty-three massive slabs of Lewis gneiss, each positioned with mathematical accuracy, and no doubt immense physical labour. What made the people of the day take on such a task?

Equipped with a stove, some extra clothes and a bivvy bag, and with a forecast of clear skies and a good moon, I wanted to consider some of the theories that have been put forward as to Tursachan's origin, hoping that perhaps the circle's spirit of place would invoke in me some sense of purpose, a hint of its distant origins. I wasn't altogether hopeful. Some people were still wandering around the stones when I arrived so, not wishing them to know what I was up to, I wandered to the shore where the low moon cast a hint of silvery light across the loch, silhouetting a couple of small boats. The islanders have an affinity with the sea, and the ancient lore of the tides is as deep and mysterious as the stone circles, the dolmens and the brochs.

In the Outer Isles there was a belief that the soul of man leaves his body when the ocean tide is ebbing. Similarly, when the tide is in flood, life will be given. Ebb and flow, the cycles of nature, rhythmic, unceasing, timeless. But the tides are not all the same. The greater tides, the spring tides, arrive every fourteen days, at the times of the full moon and the new moon. For several days they sweep through the Minch but are succeeded by an equal period of lesser tides, the neap tides, when the ocean is quieter and the ebb and flow less impetuous.

Ancient man held the natural things of the world to be of great importance, hence the legends of the tides and of the rising moon, so it's not unrealistic to believe that these great stones were used to make astronomical observations. If that is the case, why is there a chambered cairn amongst the stones where, last century, archaeologists found the remains of charred human bones? Are human sacrifice, worship and astronomical observation linked together in ancient ritual? It seems likely.

Modern theorists have credited the Lewis builders with the ability to measure the major positions of the sun and moon in the same way as did their counterparts on Salisbury Plain. It's believed they could calculate a calendar with sufficient accuracy to predict solar and lunar eclipses, so could it be the stone circles were used as some form of ancient calculator, and also as a temple, a place of worship, learning and sacrifice? It's good to think of Callanish standing as a tribute to a people whose lives were so closely interwoven with the natural world.

Making my way back to the stones in the darkness, I stumbled more than once on the uneven turf. Only the ceaseless wash of the surf broke the silence and I found myself walking stealthily, feeling unsure and uncertain. The dark shadows were heavy with threat, and the chambered cairn looked distinctly intimidating. Earlier, in the confident clarity of daylight, I had planned to bivvy in the centre of the circle, to lie within the temple of the ancients and look up at the stars and moon as they must have done, to be receptive to the spirit of the place, and to allow the stones to teach me something of their purpose.

Now, on my own and in the darkness of the night I discovered I couldn't. I chickened out. Picking up my gear and vaguely embarrassed by the childhood bogies that were threatening to engulf me, I retired quietly to the shore feeling rather foolish, but where the life-pulse of the sea and the cry of the occasional sea-bird were soothingly tangible.

Next morning, with my ever-patient wife, and after a rudimentary breakfast, we wandered the clifftops in an aura of utter peace. The Atlantic gently pulsed against the cliffs. The calm, azure sea and warm sun were a constant temptation to stop and linger, but I wanted to reach Carloway and its broch, one of the best surviving examples of a circular, defensive tower of the Iron Age. I wasn't disappointed.

The drystone wall is almost perfectly circular, ten feet thick at the base and rising to a height of some thirty feet. Who were the people who built this fort, and why? Was it to offer protection from an enemy? Only a small, low doorway offers entry. The broch builders, and there are about five hundred brochs left in Scotland, were most likely to have been Picts, but did they create these structures as defensive forts, or offensives? Archaeologists cast little light on the matter.

If they were defensive structures, who was the enemy? The Iron Age in Scotland is reckoned to have been around 450 BC to AD 400, which would rule the Norsemen out; indeed there wasn't even an organised civilisation in Norway in such far-off days. Having said that, rock carvings of 1000 BC and earlier have been found in Norway and Sweden, carvings that depict longships. Is it possible that bands of Vikings sailed the northern seas in expeditions of plunder before the establishment of a kingdom in Scandinavia? The early Vikings were illiterate and kept no records, but history points the finger at those seafaring explorers as the enemy of the broch people of Lewis.

We elected to drive to our final destination at the Butt of Lewis, where the lighthouse stands 121 feet/37 metres high and was built between 1859 and 1862 by David and Thomas Stevenson. Unusually for a Scottish lighthouse, it is built from red brick.

Arriving at about lunchtime, we took various photographs, sat in the sun below the buildings and soaked it all up, feeling rather pleased with ourselves. So pleased, we treated ourselves to a marvellous lunch.

We had both read, and hugely enjoyed, Peter May's trilogy about the Hebrides. The first, *The Blackhouse*, was set hereabouts, so we toddled down to Port of Ness, home of the legendary guga hunters – the men of Ness who travel to the remote Sgula Sgeir every year to 'harvest' the gugas, the young gannets. In the village we discovered the excellent Café Sonas, where we tucked into superb steak mince enchiladas. Not very Hebridean I admit, but much preferable to guga.

13

ISLANDS ON THE EDGE

For about a dozen years I had the great privilege of being involved in two hour-long television programmes that were broadcast on BBC Scotland during Christmas week. I was seen by some as a kind of outdoor Reverend I. M. Jolly, comedian Ricky Fulton's alter-ego, who delivered his weary but hilarious sermon every Hogmanay. Like Ricky's show, our programmes became part of the seasonal holiday viewing for many thousands of Scots. When we stopped making them my inbox was inundated with messages from disappointed fans telling me Christmas wouldn't be the same again. The messages were very kind, and I appreciated people taking the trouble to write, but the fact of the matter was this: I wasn't getting any younger. For the first few years I was filmed hiking long-distance routes: the Sutherland Trail, the Skye Trail, Coast-to-Coast, Pilgrim's trails and a long length-of-the-country walk, from Kirk Yetholm in the Scottish Borders to Cape Wrath, that we called the Scottish National Trail. The format for these shows was simple enough: I would walk the route, sometimes with Gina and sometimes alone, and then I'd go back with a crew and film the interesting sections and interview various folk along the way.

Aware of the years creeping up, I was beginning to find these long routes more challenging, so decided to call it a day and retire from television. However, my producers, Richard

Else and Margaret Wicks, had other plans. For the best part of forty years I had used a campervan for a lot of my work. In some ways it was my mobile bothy, or 'tin tent', and I could enjoy a measure of comfort while collecting material and photographs for magazine articles and books. Richard and Meg suggested we change the format of our Christmas shows and use the campervan to take me on long road trips, stopping every so often to climb a hill or two, meet up with interviewees, ride my mountain bike or paddle my packraft.

Our executive editor at the BBC, David Harron, was enthusiastic about the change of format and thought it might bring a new audience to the show. He was right. Audience figures went through the roof and feedback suggested that, while the long walks had been great to watch, they were beyond the capabilities of most viewers. Breaking down the route into a series of shorter walks and bike rides appealed to many because they felt they could do it too. They also appeared to like the idea of leaving the beaten track. The route, as much as possible, should avoid main roads. It seemed to me that Robert Frost's poem 'The Road Not Taken' provided us with a workable theme and a title. Frost's mother had been a Scottish immigrant and much of his work was inspired by settings of rural life, using them as metaphors to examine more complex social and philosophical themes.

> *Two roads diverged in a wood, and I –*
> *I took the one less travelled by,*
> *And that has made all the difference*

Every January I would join Richard and Meg and over a few glasses of fine red wine would discuss and plan our route for that year's shows. It was usually a stimulating and even exciting meeting as we pored over maps and guidebooks and worked out which less-travelled routes we should follow, who we should invite as interviewees and which stories we should tell.

One of our programmes featured a journey between Dornoch Point in Sutherland and North Ronaldsay, the most remote island in the Orkney archipelago. Richard and Meg were excited by Orkney and while the route we selected looked to be fascinating, with plenty of interesting people, I was a little anxious that the programmes might lack the visual appeal of the glorious mountain landscapes of the west Highlands. While prevaricating, I asked myself an interesting question: were my concerns fuelled by my preconceptions of landscape appreciation? Such fears didn't really come to a head until we were well into our filming schedule in Orkney. We had landed on one of the islands, I think it was Sanday, when I suddenly became aware that the aspects of the Scottish landscape that I hold most dear, those elements that make Scotland one of the most beautiful countries in the world – hills and mountains, tumbling rivers and cascading waterfalls, pinewoods and forests – were all missing.

I might have felt bereft, but wasn't. Instead there was some strange emotion at work, a sentiment I battled with for the rest of the filming. Only later did I realise this was a mix of emotions, and landscape appreciation was only one. On- and off-camera I asked our various interviewees what it was about these northern places – the massive, silver beaches of Sutherland, the huge extent of the Flow Country peatlands, the flat, wind-scoured northern islands of Orkney – that appealed to them? It seems that in much the same way as hills and mountains thrill, inspire and refresh me, the folk I spoke to in Caithness and Orkney were sustained by the continual pulse of the seas, the enormity of wide, open skies and the magnificence of the raw, elemental powers that work in these places. Forces that can make you cry out in the same jaw-dropping awe and wonder experienced with a dramatic mountain view.

A sign near the railway station at Altnabreac warns that if you are heading off into the flat and bare emptiness of the Caithness Flow Country you should be fully prepared, 'just as you would going on a mountain expedition', but it wasn't until we reached the far-flung island of North Ronaldsay that I understood how these emotions are not only about elemental landscapes and how we appreciate them. There is a human element too.

The interior of North Ronaldsay is sectioned by ancient drystone walls. The Muckle Gairsty and Matches Dyke are treble dykes which divide the island into three parts: Northyard, Linklet and Southyard. Thought to be ancient, they probably date from before 1000 BC. Legend has it that three brothers shared the island. Today, less ancient drystone dykes separate the various crofts into a complex pattern of fields and, encircling the entire island, a six-foot-tall dyke runs for over thirteen miles. This is the Sheep Dyke and it's intended to keep the 3,000 unique seaweed-eating North Ronaldsay sheep out of the various crofts. The wall, which has cruelly suffered from winter storms, was constructed in 1831 to preserve the inland pastures for other domestic animals. The ancient breed of seaweed-eating sheep is allowed to come inland for lambing, but for the rest of the year they are banished beyond the wall where they thrive on algae. Their mutton is prized by top chefs and a 'mutton run', similar to the famous Beaujolais run, once took carcasses to Edinburgh and London restaurants. Sadly, mutton doesn't appear to be fashionable anymore, although the mutton I tasted on the island was superb. If you're a carnivore like me you can't beat this fresh meat with some lamb gravy, mashed tatties and peas. Wow!

Close to the north coast, near the automated lighthouse, a rosary of circular drystone walls bears testament to the island's continual fight against the elements.

These 'punds' or 'crues' date from the mid-fifteenth century and are essentially tiny shelters where the islanders grew cabbages, protected from grazing sheep and the raking northern winds. Built near the coast, they prevent frost damage. On this most northerly of the islands, battered by the North Atlantic, scoured bare by ever-present winds, the diminishing population of North Ronaldsay lives on the edge of sustainability. At the end of the nineteenth century there were five hundred people here. Today there are fewer than sixty, and only one child attends the primary school. Many of the island's houses are empty and in various stages of decay, the Rousay flagstone roofs sagging and on the verge of collapse, while newer houses huddle together for protection.

It's clear that the people of this northern island have struggled to coexist with a supremely challenging environment, but through it all the islanders cling to their way of life with optimism and fortitude. There is now a twice-a-week ferry from Kirkwall and several air flights a day to the Orkney Mainland. The excellent North Ronaldsay Bird Observatory, established in 1987, attracts ornithologists from all corners, primarily to study and record migrant birds. The island's pier doesn't have a slipway, so vehicles are lifted out of the ferry on a crane, an operation that can be rather disconcerting for drivers. 'Ach, they jist lift it oot on some auld fishin' nets,' I had been told in Kirkwall. No wonder I was nervous. Would my beloved campervan survive?

In fact, the operation is professional and slick, but it does deter tourists from bringing their cars, which may be no bad thing. It made good television though, the camera catching me fretting while the ferrymen lifted the van out of the boat and onto the pier. Scary stuff.

Despite the worrying offloading procedure, I took my campervan to North Ronaldsay as my accommodation, transport and television companion. This was the culmination of the televised journey that started at Dornoch Point. From there I journeyed north through some of the delightful little towns of Sutherland, the cathedral town of Dornoch, Brora, Golspie, Embo and Helmsdale before heading for the Flow Country. I had enjoyed the wide-open spaces and domed skies of Caithness before heading across the Pentland Firth for visits to South Ronaldsay, Rousay, Sanday and North Ronaldsay.

The whole journey was an eye-opener. Although I had visited Orkney before, when Gina and I cycle-toured between the main archaeological sites on Orkney's Mainland and the island of Hoy, I had never visited the more remote islands. I had been tempted north by the thought of lesser-known Neolithic sites and the opportunity to enjoy some birding on North Ronaldsay just as the autumn migration was about to begin. Would I catch a glimpse of rarities like the yellow-browed bunting, or a Pallas's grasshopper warbler? I didn't, but did see a wryneck and red-breasted flycatcher, as well as skuas, petrels and shearwaters and plenty of the more common species.

It didn't take long to appreciate that Orkney is extremely rich not only in wildlife but natural resources. The tides and flows in the Pentland Firth could generate enough power to fuel much of the North of Scotland, and that is just a start. On Rousay, retired farmer Bruce Mainland was extremely frustrated that, although his island community has erected wind turbines that are currently running at 107 per cent capacity, the islanders can't yet sell the extra to the grid. He pointed out the white-capped waves created by the powerful flow between Rousay and its neighbour, Egilsay, the tide race through the Rousay Sound. If that power could be harnessed, and the power of many similar tide races throughout this northern archipelago, Scotland would have no need to worry about future energy supplies, no need for concern about the dangers of nuclear power and no need to go cap in hand to foreign powers to beg for oil and gas price stability. Wave, tidal and wind are all clean, reliable and continual sources of energy, and everywhere I went on Orkney there were wind turbines. It was a superb example of what could happen in the rest of Scotland; small community-owned schemes using natural resources to create and supply power.

Wandering round North Ronaldsay's ragged coastline I became aware of another tugging emotion, an acute awareness of a wild environment that is less complex, less combative, less materialistic than that familiar to most of us, a place of peace and safety far removed from the frustrations, social divides and anger so prevalent in our towns and cities. I wish I could have bottled that emotion and brought it home, to be taken whenever the world becomes dark and bleak, a tangible spirit-of-place that is apparent in fewer and fewer locations in the world today.

Much as I enjoyed visiting the more northern isles of Orkney, the one island I'm desperate to return to is Hoy (Haey: Norse for high island). Gina and I went there as part of a cycle tour many years ago, when it was brought home to me that while you can occasionally take the man out of the mountains, you can't take the mountains out of the man. We spent a few days viewing some of the incredible ancient remains Orkney has to offer, but there are only so many standing stones and brochs you can take in before the mind blurs. Other than its incredible collection of prehistoric relics and wonderful coastlines, Orkney isn't dissimilar to most other agricultural landscapes, so I was glad when I glimpsed the hills of Hoy across the choppy waters of Scapa Flow. Hoy is the second largest of the islands, about ten miles long and five wide and roughly rectangular in shape. The tidal island of South Walls in the south-east is connected by a causeway.

Its hills are not high as Scottish hills go. Ward Hill, the highest, only reaches 1,570 feet/479 metres, but there is a wild and mystical feel here that is in keeping with Orkney's prehistoric past. The wildlife is superb too. We watched a short-eared owl quartering the fields in search of prey; heard the rasping sound of a corncrake, but couldn't see it; were half-heartedly dive-bombed by great skuas, the bonxies; and listened to a cacophony of cliff-sound from fulmars, guillemots, kittiwakes, razorbills and herring gulls. And Hoy isn't without its Neolithic remains.

An unusual rock-cut tomb, the Dwarfie Stane, lies in the Rackwick valley between Quoys and Rackwick itself, towards the north of the island. It is unique in Northern Europe, bearing a similarity to Neolithic or Bronze Age tombs around the Mediterranean. The tomb has a small rectangular entrance, hence its name, and it's believed that the big boulder outside was once used to seal the entrance. Could this be a similar tomb to that used in the Middle East in biblical times? It sounds very much like it, but how or why was such a tomb used here on an island at the very edge of the North Atlantic?

We know people travelled great distances two thousand years ago, and it's been suggested that Joseph of Arimathea, a wealthy tin trader whose family tomb was donated as the final resting place of Jesus, travelled to Scotland, possibly to the tin mines of Perthshire. It's even been suggested that the young Christ, between being presented to the Temple as a child and the evangelical journeys of his early thirties, may have travelled with him.

It's compelling stuff, and there is little doubt that the Dwarfie Stane was used as a tomb, but for whom? One local tale says it was once inhabited by a giant and his wife. Another giant, determined to become the head giant on Hoy, master of the island, imprisoned them inside, but they gnawed their way out and that is why there is a hole on top, a hole that curiously has been filled with concrete.

Mysteries of the past lie all around you on these Orkney islands. However, Gina and I hadn't come to explore more Neolithic remains, or even to view the wildlife. We had come to catch a glimpse of someone considerably older than any of the prehistoric relics: the Old Man of Hoy. Actually, the sea stack is not that ancient. It's thought to be only about four hundred years old, but its story began 400 million years ago, when a massive stretch of fresh water called Lake Orcadie stretched from the south coast of the Moray Firth to Shetland. Layers of sand were dumped onto volcanic rock at the bottom of the lake, building over the centuries. In time the lake vanished, leaving behind a base of dark basalt lava and alternating layers of soft, sandy, pebbly sandstone and harder flagstones of Upper Red Sandstone.

Over millennia the erosion of sea and wind created cracks and weaknesses and the Old Man, which was once a slight kink in the coastline, was progressively undercut and eroded until it stood proud of the cliffs behind it. Today the Old Man of Hoy stands at 449 feet/137 metres with its base only thirty metres wide. It looks as though a great gust of wind could blow it over, as it probably will one day.

To rock climbers, the Old Man of Hoy is iconic, and outdoor enthusiasts of my vintage fondly recall the BBC's outdoor spectacular of 1967 when a team of rock climbers negotiated a number of routes up its formidably vertical walls. It was first climbed the previous year by Rusty Baillie, Tom Patey and Chris Bonington, but then became the subject of what was then the BBC's most expensive outside broadcast when a team of climbers tackled the route for the television cameras. The climbing extravaganza attracted astonishing viewing figures of fifteen million. In comparison, *Strictly Come Dancing* averages about eight million. The sea stack is worth seeing as one of the natural wonders of Scotland.

If you're not into extreme rock climbing don't worry, the name Hoy comes from the Norse for 'high' and Hoy itself is not only the second-largest island in the Orkneys, but offers the best walking possibilities. A magnificent coastal trek follows the western cliffs of Hoy from St John's Head south to Rora Head, passing above the famous sea stack. The route offers a circular itinerary, and takes in the best of the coastal walking with a visit to the old (now virtually deserted) fishing community of Rackwick, and a look at what is the most northerly natural woodland in Britain.

A daily ferry runs between Stromness and Hoy. From the pier at Linksness a road, which gradually reduces into a track, straggles westwards towards Cuilags hill. You don't have to stay on the track for long and in springtime it's a delight to take to the moorland while it is still carpeted with wild flowers, principally sea pinks. These rough moors of western Hoy are dotted with small lochans, many of which provide sanctuary for a whole host of waders and ducks: red-throated and great northern divers, slavonian grebes, mergansers and pintail. Hen harriers swoop low on ghostly flights over the moors, as do short-eared owls, and the mournful call of the golden plover provides a constant dirge.

From the outflow of the largest of these moorland lochs, Sandy Loch, it's an easy ascent to the summit of Cuilags, at just over 1,509 feet/460 metres the second-highest hill on Hoy. From the grassy summit the going is fairly easy, and level, for just over a mile to St John's Head, a spectacular viewpoint above steep cliffs which fall into thunderous, crashing seas over a thousand feet below. The place is alive with the cries of whirling fulmars. The three-mile traverse of the clifftops south to Rora Head is the highlight of the day, a highly dramatic and breathtaking route that passes above the wide bay that's presided over by the Old Man himself. We sat on a grassy platform above the swirling tides and gazed in awe at this slim red-rock tower. Some climbers were getting to grips with the route, lost in their own vertical world as we were in our horizontal one. I had a strong tinge of envy.

Walking south towards Rora Head we kept looking back over our shoulders, beyond the dramatically named

Geo of the Light to that red tower. From Rora Head the route continues along the clifftop before descending to the stony beach at Rackwick. We camped there overnight and, I must warn you, we experienced a midge attack as never experienced before, waking in the morning to a curious low-pitched buzzing sound, the only time I've ever actually heard them. The insect netting that acted as a tent door was blackened by them, so we desperately packed everything we would need for breakfast, pulled our woolly hats as low over our eyes as we could, and made a run for the shelter of the bothy to breakfast in relative comfort.

A shorter and simpler hillwalk climbs the rather impressive and steep sided Ward Hill, the highest of all Hoy's hills. This route offers a very different experience to the Old Man walk, offering marvellous views across Scapa Flow. Almost a sea-loch, surrounded as it is by the Mainland of Orkney and the islands of Burray, South Ronaldsay, Flotta and Hoy, its best views are to the north, across the island of Graemsay to Stromness, George Mackay Brown's Hamnavoe, and up the west coast to the open ocean. Here, buffeted by the eternal North Atlantic winds, you realise how much of Orkney lies on the most extreme edge of the European continent. There isn't a higher hill between Ward Hill and Iceland!

Indeed, Ward Hill, as you see it when approaching Hoy on the Stromness ferry, is of distinct steep-sided Icelandic proportions. Its two-kilometre summit ridge taking a rough south–north line with three deep-cut corries biting into the sheer slopes. Heather and grass predominate with north-facing hints of cragginess above the Glen of Greor and around the curiously named Howes of Quoyawa, the big north-east-facing corrie. It's a steep climb however you tackle it, but a southerly route up the ridge beyond the Burn of Redglen is unrestricted by crags and gives access to the south end of the summit ridge.

From the summit trig point it's an easy enough descent round the edges of the Quoyawa corrie to the junction of the main road back to the pier at Moaness, and the road that runs between the hills, according to Orkney's own poet laureate George Mackay Brown, 'into utter desolation, a place of kestrels and peatbogs. One thinks of the psalmist and his vale of death...' It is the road that leads to lonely, and lovely, Rackwick Bay.

Once a thriving fishing community but now no more than a couple of crofts and a fish farm, and the bothy of course, there is an air of abandonment about the settlement. Empty, tumbled cottages scatter the hillsides, the doorways choked with nettles, but the place still smiles on you, bright in its south-facing setting.

As far as I'm concerned, Rackwick is one of the most beautiful spots in Orkney. We camped by the bothy at Burnmouth, where the Hoy Trust have renovated the old cottage and put in toilets and drinking water. Close to the pebble-and-sand beach below Rackwick's guardian cliffs, curiously named The Sneuk and The Too, this is as evocative a stretch of coastline as you'll find anywhere. Barefoot, we wandered the tideline, where the sea breeze kept the midgies at bay, and watched the sun go down beyond Rora Head. Later, sitting cross-legged at the door of our tent, a bottle of red wine couldn't have been enjoyed in better surroundings.

Visits to Orkney and its northern neighbour, Shetland, have always filled me with the emotion I like to refer to as 'northness', a sense of place defined by remoteness and natural wonders, and extremes. Awareness of this notion arrived years ago when I made a television programme about a dog-sledding trip across Baffin Island in Arctic Canada. Even in the modern town of Iqaluit there was a sense of frontier, close to the Arctic Circle. I never thought I'd experience such an emotion in Scotland, but that was before I visited Shetland.

> *North moves always out of reach, receding*
> *towards the polar night, which is equally the*
> *midnight dawn in the summer sky.*

So wrote the American writer Barry Lopez. I guess everyone carries their own idea of 'north' within them and, while Lopez's concept of northness is based on a harder Arctic environment, a place of dearth and wilderness, my own notion of northness is less hostile and remote.

In Shetland the spirit of northness lingers everywhere. You can sense it in the scattered timber houses and feel it on the bare peaty moorland hills of the islands' hinterland. You can see it in the raw, rugged, weather-scoured coastline. Shetland is different, and that difference is made more acute if you arrive after an overnight ferry journey. In one of NorthLink's comfortable cabins you go off to bed somewhere off the coast of rural Aberdeenshire and wake approaching the southern islands of this northern archipelago.

It's like arriving in a different country, and in so many ways Shetland is exactly that. The islands didn't become part of Scotland until 600 years ago. Until then the common language was Norn, the Norse language. You can still hear the echoes. Take a look at an Ordnance Survey map and read the names – Unst, Yell, Muckle Flugga, Fetlar, Papa Stour

– the wonderful vocabulary of a place that is so Scottish in many ways and yet so Scandinavian in others.

Sadly, our arrival coincided with a day that was to become a record-breaker. Never, since records began, had so much rain fallen in a single day. Lerwick was a ghost town. People had too much sense to wander the streets in a monsoon, so we tucked ourselves away in a lovely little marina-cum-campsite near Brae. I'm surprised we didn't float away with the boats, but the weather improved overnight and next day we began exploring properly. We were in Shetland to walk and walk we did, and for the next ten days travelled the length and breadth of the islands, marvelling at their natural beauty, our breath taken away by the rugged wildness of the coasts.

I've enjoyed coastal walking all over Scotland, but nothing compares with this torn and ragged edge. Bring together the elements that are born in the wide expanses of the North Atlantic, wind, tide and waves; now obstruct their gale-driven progress with an immovable object, like the cliff-girt coast of the Shetlands, and chaos will ensue. Geological chaos. Millions of years of constant pounding by the North Atlantic on the Middle Devonian volcanic rock of the Eshaness peninsula has created a coastline that is dramatically rugged, torn and wild. Wave-cut cliffs and massive sea stacks rise to 150 feet and blowholes erupt like geysers above the turbulent seas. It's as though the water is trying to claim the land as its own, breaking it down slowly and deliberately in an age-old war of attrition. But ... take a walk along the cliffs on a sunny day and it's as though a truce has been called, and their rugged beauty enhanced by the raw power of nature.

Parking the campervan at the Eshaness lighthouse we, purely coincidentally, bumped into a BBC *Adventure Show* film crew with one of my fellow presenters, Desiree Wilson, being filmed rock climbing on the great crags that fall to the sea below the lighthouse. Looking down the sheer rocks to the pounding surf she seemed understandably nervous. Leaving her to recce a route that would test her to the limits, Gina and I set off north along the coast but within a few minutes my dear wife became impatient with me taking photographs. The cliff scenery was astonishing and, although we were a little too far into the summer to enjoy the spectacle of nesting seabirds, there were still enough fulmars, kittiwakes, gannets and puffins to provide an ornithological spectacle. What fascinated me most were the names of the various rock features. This stretch of headland is called the Villians of Ure, and we passed Moo Stack, Blackhead of Breigeo, Grind of the Navir and Head of Stanshi as we made our way round The Burr towards the hamlet of Ure. This is the language of J. R. R. Tolkien, George R. R. Martin or Philip Pullman; we had walked into our own Scoto/Norse fantasy world.

With a ragged coastline of almost 1,700 miles it's not surprising that Shetland has more than its fair share of ship-wreck stories. A good example, and the subject of a good walk, is the White Wife of Otterswick, who commemorates a wreck on the eastern shores of Yell. No fantasy fiction here. In 1924, a German training ship called the Bohus set sail from Sweden for Chile, but her skipper made a navigational error and the ship foundered in fog and heavy seas. Strong winds blew it onto the rocks near the Ness of Queyon and four sailors were drowned. The ship's figurehead was later recovered near Otterswick and erected near the shore as a memorial. A fine coastal walk visits the site, before crossing a lovely, low headland where, on a summer's day, it is hard to visualise the conditions that could lead to such a disaster. The east coast of Yell is less wild and more low-lying than the west coast where the cliffs tend to be higher and the coastline more broken. Nevertheless, the headland of Ness of Queyon and Salt Wick is very rocky and gets the full brunt of the north-eastern swells. On a windy day it can be very dramatic.

St Ninian is credited with bringing Christianity to Scotland, even before St Columba, and he was, for a time, the Abbot of Lindisfarne. A lovely little island, just off the shore of Shetland's south Mainland, is named after him, although it's unlikely he travelled this far north. The ruins of a twelfth century church are here, but what makes the place so special is the double curve of cockleshell sand that links it to the mainland of Shetland, a shoreline feature known as a tombolo. Tides and currents sweep around the island and meet on either side of this golden strand, constantly washing sand up from the seabed, and this is the only tombolo in the British Isles formed by sand. Others are shingle or pebbles, although it's likely that St Ninian's has its origins in shingle.

A car park and picnic area below the hamlet of Bigton offer access to the 'sand road' and once through some marram dunes you can enjoy the walk to the island with the unusual aspect of waves lapping your feet on both sides. Arctic terns are very territorial and will swoop close, screeching and sniping. Once across the tombolo, a sandy path climbs onto the island. The remains of the old church lie to your right, but leave that exploration to the end of the walk. Instead, head south around St Ninian's Bay to enjoy the prospect of the ragged coast culminating in the cliff-girt islands of Inns Holm and Coar Holm.

Although the cliffs are sheer and rugged the sheltered

waters tend to be calmer and you may hear a raft of eider ducks crooning gently, or see seals basking on rocky ledges. Follow the coastline west, crossing a stile over a large wall, before turning north with views across a broad expanse of ocean and the distant outline of Foula. Pass Longa Berg and the seabird-haunted island of Hich Holm, before negotiating your way round the big cove of Selchie Geo.

Beyond a stone-built windbreak, follow the cliffs towards the long nose of The Neapack and its trig point. A narrow grassy ridge leads towards the bare rock of Loose Head. From here, views north take in the area of Walls and Papa Stour. To the west lies Foula and, away to the south, beyond the big lump of Fitful Head, lies distant Fair Isle, midway between Orkney and Shetland with, above everything, the continual, elemental cries of wheeling seabirds. Virtually every cliff has its own population of young fulmars; downy, fluffy lumps with two eyes and gaping, hungry beaks. Cooried doon, each on its own ledge, the chicks wait patiently, and sometimes not so patiently, for their parents to return and regurgitate their next meal.

Natural history tends to predominate on Shetland but there is human history here too, plenty of it. It's thought that man has used this island since the earliest mists of time. The ruins you come across as you make your way back towards the tombolo are the remains of a twelfth century church but it's believed the site was also used by Norse settlers and, before that, as a pre-Christian burial site dating to the third century. During excavations in the 1950s, a local schoolboy found a larch box containing twenty-eight items of Pictish silver ornaments. They are all on display in the Royal Museum in Edinburgh, a long way from their place of discovery.

How much better it would be if they were displayed to the public in a museum in Shetland.

My favourite walk on Shetland lies in the very north of the most northern island, or almost the most northerly. I immediately fell in love with Unst and the most northerly of all RSPB reserves, with their distinct atmosphere of northness. Here also lie the most northerly lumps of land in the British Isles, and here you'll find the most northerly brewery. The Valhalla Brewery and its White Wife pale ale are both wonderful. On a bright and windy afternoon, we risked attack by hundreds of bonxies as we made our way along the duckboards of the wonderfully named Burn of Winnaswarta Dale to the Hermaness coast. Sitting here we gazed through binoculars at thousands of beautiful, noisy gannets. Beyond, on its tiny rock island, stood the squat lighthouse buildings of Muckle Flugga and the tiny island of Out Stack, our most northerly stretch of land. We then climbed the most northerly hill in Britain, Hermaness Hill, only 656 feet/200 metres in height but with a disproportionate sense of spaciousness, the likes of which you'll never experience on any Munro summit.

I'm surprised how few hillwalkers I know have been to Shetland, and I would passionately urge them to go there. The coastal walking is phenomenal, the birdlife rich and varied, and everyone is welcoming. We took our campervan, and stayed in a few campsites, but had an equal number of wild camps in a variety of out-of-the-way niches, tucked away out of sight.

Best of all, though, is the opportunity to indulge yourself in northness: to enjoy the sharp clarity of the light, air free of the residues and dust that thicken the atmosphere at lower latitudes; to sit below a lonely headland, out of the wind, captivated by the comings and goings of otters; to envy the weightless flight of fulmars on the wind; to appreciate the handsome Concorde-like lines of a gannet in flight; to marvel at delicate Arctic terns diving into the shallows for prey; and, for a moment in your life, to take the opportunity of standing close to the edge of a high cliff and feeling winds that can be either gentle and caressing or wildly destructive, winds that continue to shape and evolve these northern islands, this place of extremes.

It's a great reminder, particularly to a hill bum like me, that you don't have to stand on a mountain-top to experience wildness in the raw.

14

A Place Apart

A spirit of place. I first came across this term in the writings of a dear friend of mine, the Welsh/English essayist Jim Perrin, who defined the phenomenon as a profound interplay of consciousness:

> On the coast of Llyn I know a set of steps cut once into the rock and smoothed by centuries of feet. They lead down to the wave margin and to a well. If you listen, the clamour of voices here, of wave-sound, tide race, the stilled pre-Cambrian magma – a drowned girl's scream, a pilgrim's prayer, slap of a launched coracle, the crack and hiss of cooling rock – are coexistent along the flicker of time. It happened here, and so much else besides. The distillation of these events is the spirit of the place.

The concept that past events might create an atmosphere we can tap into will be familiar to many who seek solitude in wild places. Some might suggest that what I'm really referring to is a 'sense of place', particularly when it has a distinct character and is cherished. As Jim correctly says, such places have echoes of people and past events, with occasionally an element of nostalgia thrown in. Others argue that 'spirit of place' means a deity or spirit inhabits them. *Genius loci* is

Latin for a spirit or guardian deity, while *anima loci* is the soul of a place. Our ancestors thought that certain sites, such as wells, springs and trees, have spiritual value and should be treated with respect. They also believed human consciousness and activity could have a strong effect on a specific area, making it a place apart. Perhaps that's why ruins, remains and relics can resonate with those few who are receptive. In my own experience, this *genius loci* could be interpreted as a location's distinct atmosphere, rather than a guardian spirit; an atmosphere created by personal circumstances like memory, nostalgia and deep longing. Blend such circumstances with external factors such as grandeur, beauty, music, or even a starlit sky, and you might experience a set of emotions that feel almost spiritual, mystic or even transcendental. Let me give you an example.

During Christmas week last year, I took a short afternoon stroll into the Northern Corries of the Cairngorms, a place I know well. Whenever I take the narrow path that climbs into the rocky clench of Coire an t-Sneachda, my mind fills with memories and a vivid sense of wistfulness, especially in winter. During the late seventies and early eighties this was my workplace, teaching cross-country skiing with Highland Guides and SYHA, running winter hillcraft courses while also running the activities at Craigower Lodge Outdoor Centre in Newtonmore, and also introducing the area to my sons.

It doesn't take long to reach the rocky basin of the corrie, immediately below the gleaming crescent of buttresses, gullies and ridges that form the headwall. Snuggling behind a pink granite boulder, after pouring hot tea from my flask, I visually traced the lines of various climbs enjoyed in the past with people like Jeff Faulkner, Brian Revill, Steve Spalding and my old friend John Lyall. I had been with John just two nights previously when he and mountaineer Sandy Allan came round for a beer and a blether. Sandy, a Newtonmore neighbour, was justifiably excited, just having completed a book on his bold traverse of the Mazeno Ridge on Nanga Parbat in Pakistan, a feat described by many as one of mountaineering's greatest achievements. I first met Sandy here in Coire an t-Sneachda many years ago.

As the gloaming closed in, the pale dimness temporarily brightened by snow flurries, I began down the slippery slope back to the car park and, almost by chance, stumbled across a couple of lads pitching their tent in the middle of the boulder field. They were struggling to tie it down in an increasingly blustery wind but, despite the prospect of a very cold night, I felt a pang of envy. What a beautiful place to spend a winter night, such a magnificent setting to awaken on a fresh, new morning.

The old day was dying as I crunched across snow slopes, searching for the path through the boulders. Below me, Loch Morlich was still visible, lying like a pool of molten lead, and pinpricks of light were beginning to appear in Glen More. How many times have I walked down this hillside at the end of a good hill-day? Dozens, or more like scores or even hundreds? Most likely the latter.

Just before the familiar bend that would bring the Cairn Gorm car park into view, I sat on a boulder to watch the first evening stars appear. There was no Christmas star to guide me home, only the comfort and familiarity of the evening sky in winter, shining on a place I feel passionate about. All day I had been troubled by thoughts of a dreadful accident that had taken place earlier in the week. An out-of-control bin lorry had killed six innocent men and women in George

Square in Glasgow while they were shopping or returning home from work. Folk going about their everyday lives. I know it's pointless asking why such things occur. Accidents happen, it's a fact of life, but that such a tragedy should occur at what is normally a festive time produced a profound sense of shock throughout the nation.

At times like this we ask ourselves 'why', a question that inevitably remains unanswered but, even with that terrible event in mind, I wandered out of Coire an t-Sneachda with a more peaceful, less agitated spirit than earlier, thankful for loved ones, friends, and all those precious moments that made me the person I am. Again feeling the insignificance of my own fleeting existence against the more lasting reality of the crags, distant hills and, most of all, the stars, for the moment at least, I was content to let the great mysteries of life be. Why tease at enigmas you will never understand? The spirit of place had woven its magic once again.

Some years ago, Gina and I were backpacking on the Southern Upland Way and had just crossed Penistone Rig to descend to St Mary's Loch beside the Selkirk to Moffat Road. She wanted to visit the historic Tibbie Shiel's Inn, formerly patronised by such worthies as James Hogg, the Ettrick Shepherd, and Sir Walter Scott, but I didn't want to stop. My mind was still at Riskinhope Hope, passed earlier in the morning, a lonely and deserted ruin with an indefinable air of melancholy.

It's an old farmhouse with only a few crumbling walls remaining, but drystone boundaries still mark out the in-by fields, tilting up steep slopes on both sides of the old steading, and nettles clustered around the crooked portals of the door are the only evidence of life. Hope, in this part of Scotland, means a valley with a meandering burn, and has nothing at all to do with expectation or optimism. Despite the dereliction, a spirit of the past was almost tangible, a little spot in the folds of the hills where people were born and died, laughed and cried, rejoiced and were saddened, worked and played. Could something of these human emotions remain in the ether of a place? I've experienced this same feeling in deserted Himalayan villages close to the Tibetan border, in ancient settlements in Jordan and Morocco, and in countless locations throughout the Highlands of Scotland. Might the strength and power of intense human emotions be bound forever into such ruins? Can this kind of presence pervade a place for years, for centuries? A spirit of place?

The Roman term, *genius loci*, tends to a belief in guardian angels, or faery folk, or even ghosts, while the Chinese *feng shui* celebrates something similar. Our own Celtic ancestors had a stronger sense of place than we do, and were more aware of its importance, so perhaps it's not beyond belief that such senses linger in our psyche, awaiting the right conditions to surprise us. It's an essential and welcome element in the whole outdoors experience, and brings us closer to the land and to those who inhabited these wild places before us. When we think of such folk, we tend to think of them as being settled, but the byways of the Highlands and Islands have always attracted those with more itinerant tendencies: soldiers, priests, vagabonds, drovers, tinkers and labourers. All have left traces, often in place names, song and story, but the navvies, especially, changed the face of the landscape, often dramatically.

One of the most poignant destinations of any route I've walked lies beyond Kinlochleven, on the edge of Rannoch Moor. Below the dramatically named Devil's Staircase, a water pipeline runs down to the town from the Blackwater

Reservoir, high above the birch-clad banks of the River Leven. It was springtime, there was a sheen of newly minted green on the trees and the sky was blue. Birdsong, especially that of the ebullient skylark, filled the air, and new life was all around. In the freshness and vitality of the season it was hard to imagine the desolation, strife and pathos of the industrial scene a hundred years before. In the distance a long, low wall ran across the horizon, the line of the Blackwater Dam, and as we approached it a dumpy, drumlin-like hillock took our attention. Fifty metres from the track a wooden fence straddled it, tracing the outline of the most unusual graveyard I've ever seen, much like the Boot Hill of a western movie.

Twenty-two headstones stood proud of the ground, concrete plinths, some with names etched on them, some without. Daffodils swayed in the breeze to offer a hint of softness in the harsh surroundings.

Here lie the remains of some of those who died in the creation of this great dam, and the reservoir that now lies behind it. Names are scratched on the stones: John MacKenzie, W. Smith, Darkey Cunningham, and, curiously, Mrs Reilly, the lone woman in this male-dominated environment. What stories lie behind these simple stones, gravestones not of marble or slate, but of the material with which these men worked, concrete? Another stone bears the word 'Unknown', a reminder that they were the misfits of the day, itinerant workers who knew no home or family. In its wild and remote setting, this is more than just a cemetery. It's a monument to those once described as 'the outcasts of a mighty industrial society'.

The Blackwater Reservoir project was the last of its kind, when men, largely using hand tools and without mechanical earthmoving machinery, gouged this great reservoir from the earth. It is thought to be the last major project of the traditional 'navvies', who made such a major contribution to the construction of Britain's canals and railways.

In 1906 the British Aluminium Company opened a plant in Kinlochleven, turning what had been a tiny settlement of two or three farmhouses and a shooting lodge into a 'model village' to house the hundreds of itinerants expected to work on the smelter project. To provide the power, the Blackwater Reservoir, four miles to the east, was slowly dug from the bowels of the mountains themselves. The dam at Blackwater was the product of the second major hydroelectric project undertaken in Scotland by the British Aluminium Company, which wanted to use hydroelectric power and knew there were suitable hills above the village. Hydroelectric power depends on height to generate a strong enough flow of water, but there was no suitable catchment nearby. The company had to create a new loch to hold sufficient quantities of water to generate the hydro power. Construction of the dam began in 1904 and employed over 3,000 workmen, many of them Irish. They were making one loch out of three, with a dam that was over 900 metres long, but didn't know what they were building. They referred to the construction simply as the 'waterworks'.

> If a man throws red muck over a wall today and throws it back again tomorrow, what the devil is it to him if he keeps throwing that same muck over the wall for the rest of his life, knowing not why or wherefore, provided he gets paid sixpence an hour for his labour. There were so many tons of earth to be lifted and thrown

somewhere else; we lifted them and threw them somewhere else: so many cubic yards of iron-hard rocks to be blasted and carried away; we blasted and carried them away, but never asking questions and never knew what results we were labouring to bring about.

The Blackwater Reservoir, seventy-five feet deep, nine miles in length, would eventually contain 24,000 million gallons of water. One of those itinerants, the author of the foregoing paragraph, was from Glenties in County Donegal, and he graphically described the terrible isolation and horrendous conditions they endured as they toiled. 'We were men despised when we were most useful, rejected when we were not needed, and forgotten when our troubles weighed upon us heavily,' he wrote.

Patrick MacGill's semi-autobiographical account of life as an itinerant worker in the early years of last century, *Children of the Dead End*, vividly portrays the horror of the work, and other contemporary accounts verify his descriptions. The nearby Moor of Rannoch is a silent witness to those who succumbed to its chilling wintry horror as they left the warm bar of the Kingshouse to make their way on foot to the site at Blackwater. Victims of hypothermia, they were still being discovered many years later. They had no one to report them missing. MacGill writes of one incident:

That night Maloney was handed his lying time and told to slide. He padded from Kinlochleven in the darkness, and I have never seen him since then. He must have died on the journey. No man could cross those mountains in the darkness of mid-winter and in the teeth of a snowstorm.

Some time afterwards the copy of a Glasgow newspaper, either the Evening Times or News (I now forget which), came into our shack wrapped around some provisions, and in the paper I read a paragraph concerned the discovery of a dead body on the mountains of Argyllshire. While looking after sheep a shepherd came on the corpse of a man that lay rotting in a thawing snowdrift . . . Nobody identified him, but the paper stated he was presumably a navvy who lost his way on a journey to or from the big waterworks of Kinlochleven. As for myself, I am quite certain that it was that of big Jim Maloney.

What of this young writer who became known as the 'navvy's laureate', whose words have informed several generations of the lives of individuals like Moleskin Joe, Carroty Dan, Norah Ryan, Gourock Ellen and Red Billy Davis. I'd love to see a statue of Patrick MacGill erected in Kinlochleven, to remind us of the lives that were lost and the terrible conditions thousands of men endured to earn their meagre pay.

By all accounts he was an extraordinary young man. Arriving in Scotland at the age of fourteen after 'escaping' the County Tyrone farmer who had 'bought' him at a hiring fair in Strabane at the age of twelve, he worked in Ayrshire as a tattie-howker during the potato picking season and as a navvy the rest of the year. Reading in any spare time he had, he aimed at a future life as a journalist and author, joining a number of circulating libraries, consuming the works of Thomas Carlyle, Victor Hugo, Rudyard Kipling, Bret Harte and Montaigne. It's also said that he read to take his mind off the horrors that life was throwing at him, intolerable conditions that allowed young boys and girls to be lodged alongside drunkards, gamblers and prostitutes.

Whether he was writing of life on the open road as a tramp, or that of a gang labourer or navvy, digging and toiling in the most horrendous conditions that a Scottish winter can throw down, he achieved something extraordinary in transforming the experience into poetry and prose, often with more than a dash of humour.

His first published works appeared when he was only twenty. Not surprisingly they were poems of emigration, including *To Erin*, *The Exile of Erin* and *A Tale of the Bogland*. He was working on a repair gang, plate-laying on the Glasgow to Greenock Caledonian railway. His poetry, much of it based on experiences, reflected his growing preoccupation with the poor and the downtrodden and those who, like himself, while toiling in the dirt to build a civilisation, lived outside of society.

By this time MacGill had published several volumes of poetry, which he sold from door to door in Greenock, where he was living at the time. The relative success of these books, together with articles in the *Daily Express*, led to him being offered a job by that newspaper. Bound for London, his life would change overnight.

Here was a young man who had never worn a collar or tie, or learned how to use a knife and fork, who had never mixed in the kind of society that now engulfed him. He didn't take readily to London, or to journalism, but it was here that he wrote his first major success, an autobiographical novel called *Children of the Dead End*.

In the space of a very short time the twenty-three-year-old Irish navvy became a journalist in Fleet Street with an acclaimed literary success under his belt. His journalistic career didn't last long. He was taken to Windsor Castle by the eccentric but influential Canon Sir John Dalton, who had been chaplain to Queen Victoria and tutor to the Princes Edward and George, and was now in of charge of administration of the Castle buildings including the magnificent St George's Chapel. MacGill was appointed King's Librarian to George V and worked in the Chapter Library at Windsor Castle translating old manuscripts. His socialist ideals did not wane, and he still gave the occasional radical lecture, but the clouds of World War One were closing in. His years of fighting on the front line provided more raw material and further opportunity to write from experience. He published five books about the war and, as in his earlier works, his main theme was humanity and humour prevailing through suffering and adversity.

He later emigrated to America where he continued to write with some success, but with the 1930s came changing tastes and styles and the Great Depression. MacGill's final years were spent in poverty and ill-health. He contracted multiple sclerosis and continued to write, but with little further success. He died in 1963 and is buried alongside his wife in Fall River, Massachusetts. In *Children of the Dead End*, he described the mountains that look down on Kinlochleven, recognising, perhaps prophetically, a cruel irony in their timelessness.

> Above and overall, the mystery of the night and the desert places hovered inscrutable and implacable. All round the ancient mountains sat like brooding witches, dreaming on their own story of which they knew neither the beginning nor the end. Naked to the four winds of heaven and all the rains of the world, they

had stood there for countless ages in all their sinister strength, undefiled and unconquered, until man, with puny hands and little tools of labour, came to break the spirit of their ancient mightiness.

That 'spirit of ancient mightiness' remains. Instead, it's the smelter that's been run down while the hills stand undefiled and unconquered. Once again, the workforce 'has been rejected when not needed' but, paradoxically, there is a ray of optimism shining on the area. Tucked away at the head of fjord-like Loch Leven, Kinlochleven nestles at the foot of the Mamore Forest, completely dominated by high peaks and soaring ridges, the same mountains that offer hope for a 'green' economy. The highly popular West Highland Way, the ninety-six-mile trail that runs from Milngavie to Fort William, passes through, bringing revenue and jobs, and a bunkhouse and campsite have been established. An indoor climbing wall with a permanent ice climbing facility, the Ice Factor, attracts climbers at all times of the year, and the hill slopes around the village boast a remarkable network of stalkers' paths which attract mountain bikers and hill-walkers keen to access the clutch of Mamores Munros.

Kinlochleven has reinvented itself, just as Patrick MacGill did all those years ago.

Personal reinvention was something of a trait for working-class men in the middle years of the twentieth century. My father followed his own father into the Glasgow shipyards, Fairfields and Harland and Wolff – and if fate hadn't lent a hand I would probably have ended up there too – but, like Patrick MacGill and a host of others, and urged on by an ambitious wife, he spent much of his spare time at evening classes, or night-school as it was called then. He achieved some educational qualifications and went to Jordanhill College to train as a teacher.

The aspirations of working-class men and women from Glasgow and nearby Clydebank was a subject shared repeatedly around a great fire that burned in a hollow just outside Milngavie. Since time immemorial mankind has taken comfort from the warmth and light of a flickering fire. The glow of flames not only offered cheer but also protection against wild animals and, in more recent times, particularly since we no longer fear the predations of sabre-toothed tigers, a fire has often become the central point of many social gatherings in the outdoors, where like-minded souls share mesmerising visions in the flames, and companionship creates bonds of friendship through shared experience. The aromatic whiff of woodsmoke can send many walkers off in a dwam of sentimentality, recalling old friends and events of long ago.

In modern times, camping stoves that burn methylated spirits, butane or propane gas, by-products of the oil and petrochemical industry, have turned the open fire into something of an indulgence. Our ancient and deeply rooted instincts, that once equated fire and flame with warmth, comfort and cooked food, are now more satisfied by the social construct of the barbeque, and open fires tend to be frowned on because few have the knowledge or skill to control them.

Yet, within living memory the tang of woodsmoke on the wind was commonplace, the skills of fire lighting and maintenance were parts of our hillcraft and the gathering of like-minded souls around an open fire was considered to be fine and worthy. During the troubled years of the

1930s, Depression fires were seen as beacons of hope, and focal points. In the Peak District, the Yorkshire Dales, Northumbria, the Lake District and throughout Scotland, the open fire was emblematic of a new community of working-class outdoors folk. Until the early years of the last century, the moorlands, hills and mountains of Britain were the preserve of privileged, moneyed men and women attracted to wild places by the Romantics: Wordsworth, Coleridge, Ruskin, Byron and Scott. But even before the Great War the first working-class outdoor clubs were being formed. It didn't take long for ordinary men and women to realise that wild places offered something to them too, an escape from the deprivation of the cities to hope, renewal and healthy living amongst the rocks and heather of our uplands.

An old, now departed, friend of mine, Peter Ferguson (known to everyone as Peter the Plumber, for that was his trade. Sir Alex Ferguson is his nephew) had been a member of the Creagh Dhu mountaineering club from Clydebank, just outside Glasgow, and told me about a great fire that burned through the 1920s until it had to be extinguished because of blackout regulations during World War Two. Later, Tom Weir described it to me as 'a kind of university of knowledge on the great outdoors.'

The Craigallian Fire was created by the circumstances of the time, unemployment in the twenties and Depression in the thirties, and quickly became a focal point for a dynamic and diverse community. Freed from the divisions of social class the fire attracted an eclectic mix of minds: idealists, intellectuals, academics and political activists, bound by a love of Scotland's outdoors. In his excellent biography of the climber and outdoorsman Jock Nimlin, one of Scotland's most successful pre-war climbers, author Iain Thomson records Nimlin's thoughts on the Craigallian Fire:

> The firelight played on a ring of faces; a gallon-size community tea can bubbled between the logs. Someone threw a handful of tea into the can and pointedly remarked at the newcomers that the can had been a Rodine (rat poison) container. We were not impressed . . . Established some time earlier, the Fire had become a magnet for all the outdoor types escaping from the smoke and grime of the Clyde basin. Already it had a mystique, a glow which drew the cauldrife (those who felt the cold) into the community, and the other fires which were soon to glow in the woods and howffs of the Highlands were projections of this parent; shrines of the heat-worshippers. There was a popular fire-chant based on the old hymn, Rock of Ages:
>
> > *Long may old Craigallian woods*
> > *Send forth abundance of their goods;*
> > *May the fire be always lit*
> > *So that we may come and sit.*

The Craigallian Fire burned in a secluded tree-fringed hollow near Craigallian Loch, within a few metres of what is now the West Highland Way, only a few miles from its start in Milngavie. Most Friday and Saturday nights would see a gathering of like-minded souls swapping yarns, making plans, re-telling adventures. It was a fellowship of outdoor enthusiasts, intellectuals, socialists and working-class lads and lassies, and politics was a common conversation theme.

It's fair to say that most of the fire visitors would be left-of-centre in their views. Tom's climbing pal of the time, Matt Forrester, was a regular visitor:

'At all seasons it was a howff for walkers and climbers. Coming along the track of a winter's evening the glow of light and the merry shouts of laughter brought joy to the heart ... Craigallian Fire was a grand fire, a symbol of something great and fine.'

I recently made a television programme for BBC Scotland about the history of recreational walking in Scotland, walking with and interviewing the two sons of one of those 'heat worshippers' or 'weekenders'. These individuals were fortunate to have jobs and could only be free on Saturday and Sunday (although Jock Nimlin worked until 9pm on a Saturday and Tom Weir had to work until lunchtime on a Saturday before he was free). Professor Sir Robert Grieve, who was born in a tenement in Glasgow's Maryhill, became a civil engineer and town planner and was first chairman of the Highlands and Islands Development Board in 1965.

Bob was a man of wide literary interests, particularly poetry, and became president of the Scottish Mountaineering Club, the Mountaineering Council of Scotland, the Scottish Countryside Rangers Association, the Scottish Rights of Way Society, Friends of Loch Lomond and many other organisations dedicated to the intelligent expansion and preservation of Scotland's countryside. His two sons, Iain and Willie Grieve, listened to their father's tales of the Craigallian Fire since childhood and were aware of just how important and influential this place had been to him.

'I remember my father reminiscing about the Fire,' Willie said. 'It had clearly been deeply significant for him, and was part of a tapestry of stories about his early life in the outdoors, which throughout his life formed such an important, indeed indispensable part of who he was.'

'There was a vividness and a sense of something unrecapturable in his stories – a sadness, perhaps – which I can now understand better as a man myself in my sixties,' said Iain. 'A clear memory I have is of him describing the first time he tramped to Loch Lomond in his youth, presumably via the Fire, arriving in late evening and trying to sleep under bushes wrapped in a thin blanket. Waking early with the cold, he stood shivering on the pier at Rowardennan, gazing transfixed at the transcendental beauty of the loch in early morning as it emerged from darkness and mist. This was a different world – magical, mythic and of profound beauty.'

Along with a friend, David Campbell, Willie and Iain began a project to create a Craigallian Fire Memorial. The Friends of the Craigallian Fire raised the money and artist Tim Chalk designed the memorial, which echoes the 'ring' and 'standing stone' art of the ancient Celts. It stands close to the West Highland Way on the banks of Craigallian Loch, although some folk suggest the actual site of the Craigallian Fire was slightly further north and west, where the Auldmurroch Burn passes under the Carbeth Road. The truth is there were a number of different fires burning regularly in those far-off days, but the selected site, on the West Highland Way, means that more people will see it, and be reminded of the early stalwarts of the Scottish outdoor movement who once gathered there.

I went back recently on my own, walking south past the Carbeth Huts, wooden holiday huts that came into existence about the same time as the Fire. There were strong links between the 'hutters' and the 'fire sitters', forged by the same desire for freedom and adventure. My return to the site of the Fire was something of a pilgrimage for I've long had a fascination for these early days in the history of Scottish hiking and climbing, and a strong appreciation of the hardy nature of those pioneers.

I was also aware that the memorial site has a strong sense of place. The usual playgrounds for the pioneers were the Campsie and Kilpatrick Fells, Ben Lomond, the Trossachs and the Arrochar Alps. On a good day of hitch-hiking they might reach Glen Coe. Their common bonds were love of the open air and the enduring struggle by Scottish people for freedom to access the land and mountains they loved. This long political battle eventually bore fruit in the Land Reform (Scotland) Act 2003, legislation that provided some of the finest access arrangements in the world. We should never forget those doughty fighters of yesteryear who longed and campaigned for freedom to roam and camp in the wild places of Scotland.

I believe the Craigallian Fire was unique. By its flickering light early working-class mountaineering clubs were formed, such as the Creagh Dhu and the Ptarmigan clubs, and the Lomond Mountaineering Club, of which I was a member in my early days. Those of us who wander the hills and mountains share a common bond in our love for these places, but we are produced from varying lineages and social backgrounds. Your lineage may be drawn directly from the Kinder Trespass, or the great influx of hikers and climbers who took to the fells of Cumbria, or the mountains of Snowdonia, in the fifties and sixties, or from the streets of Belfast to the wonderful Mournes. When I began going to the hills as a teenager I could, through the writings of Tom Weir and Jock Nimlin, trace direct links to the early pioneers who drank tea from a tin can that once contained rat poison.

In my teenage years their whispers could still be heard in the traditions of those I hiked with. As a working-class Glaswegian I'm proud of those traditions, proud of what was achieved and that we have such a wonderful memorial to remind us of the men and women who created them.

The flames of the Craigallian Fire may have been doused seventy-odd years ago but the ghosts of those who shared its light whisper in every corrie and glen to this day. You might, if you listen carefully, hear the echoed refrain of the old hiking songs, words and tunes handed down, a stream of musical consciousness that was matched by that of another strand of society, the travelling folk.

A recent television series examined the use of the Gaelic language in our landscape and reinforced my long-standing conviction that we have a wonderful cultural heritage in the hill and mountain names of Scotland. Take Ben Gulabin for example. This fairly innocuous Corbett overlooks the Spittal of Glenshee in Highland Perthshire. Wandering up its heather slopes years ago, when first climbing the Corbetts, I had little knowledge of its significance in terms of Celtic or Scots culture, but when later delving into the folklore and myth associated with many hills and glens I discovered two things of interest: (1) some accounts associate Ben Gulabin with the heroes of the Celtic tale of Diarmid and Grainne, and (2) the legendary folklorist and poet Hamish Henderson spent the early years of his life in a cottage in its shadow. Recognising the influence of those early years on his life he requested that his ashes be scattered near the mountain's summit.

Hamish was born in Blairgowrie but lived with his mother in a cottage at the Spittal of Glenshee until he was of school age. Gaelic was spoken in the glen and this had a deep influence on the young Henderson. He later wrote:

Spring quickens. In the Shee Water I'm fishing.
High on whaup's mountain time heaps stone on stone.
The speech and silence of Christ's world is Gaelic,
And youth on age, the tree climbs from the bone.

Gina and I could be described as folkies of many years' standing and, although I never had the good fortune to meet Hamish, we have known several of his colleagues at the School of Scottish Studies including Dr Margaret Bennett. I first met Margaret in the early eighties when we were both involved with the Badenoch Folk Club in Newtonmore. She was living in Kingussie, raising her son Martyn, who became one of the most original and exciting musicians in the country. Tragically, Martyn died from cancer in his early thirties.

It was Margaret who introduced me to Ian MacGregor, son of the traveller/singer Sheila Stewart, and I interviewed both Margaret and Ian about travelling people, berry picking at Blairgowrie, pearl fishing and the legacy of Hamish Henderson for one of our *Roads Less Travelled* programmes on BBC Scotland. His connection with travelling people is legendary, and in his early years at the School of Scottish Studies in Edinburgh he regularly visited travellers in and around Blairgrowrie and Rattray in Perthshire, recording songs and pipe music for the School's archives. In doing so he fashioned traditional music's own royalty, especially a woman by the name of Jeannie Robertson of Aberdeen, a singer who was often described as the 'Queen Amang the Heather'.

To sum up the respectability that Hamish gave the travelling folk I can do no better than quote Sheila Stewart: 'All the Stewarts loved Hamish,' she said, 'and he loved us. In the old days we were treated like scum. He changed our lives. Now we are, almost, treated like ordinary people.'

Through Hamish's recordings many of the travellers' songs carried into the mainstream of Scotland's musical tradition, a carrying stream that flourished during the late fifties and sixties in what is now referred to as the Folk Revival. Songs like the 'Berry Fields O' Blair' and 'Bonnie Glenshee' have become classics, as is Hamish's best-known composition, 'Freedom Come-All-Ye'. This wonderful song was written in 1960 but it is easy to imagine it as an anthem sung around Craigallian Fire in the thirties, with its socialist echoes and mention of the great John Maclean. Many people regard the song as Scotland's unofficial National Anthem because of its overtones of anti-imperialism, justice and winds of change, but apparently Hamish disliked the idea. He felt the song's strength was that it was 'alternative', and didn't fancy it being in any way considered 'official' or establishment. Understandable, when you remember it was written for the peace marchers at the Holy Loch nuclear base near Glasgow.

Given my admiration for this Scottish poet, songwriter, communist, soldier and intellectual, a wee pilgrimage to Blairgowrie, where he was born, and to Ben Gulabin, where his ashes were scattered, seemed in order. If any place is worthy of the title 'spirit of place' it is surely here but, first, a few words about the ceremony on the summit of the hill.

In the second volume of Dr Timothy Neat's biography of Hamish Henderson, *Poetry Becomes People*, the author describes how he and a small group of friends, poet George Gunn, Hamish's son-in-law Charlie Marshall, and the literary critic Angus Calder, carried the urn containing his ashes to the 2,644-foot/806-metre-high summit. George searched for, and eventually found, the ideal spot, a tumble of boulders overlooking Glenshee Water, the hump-backed bridge at the Spittal of Glenshee, and the cottage where he lived as a youngster. After a celebratory dram, George began to pour the ashes from the urn into a cavity amongst some rocks, 'the hollow of the granite tomb.'

'As he did so, through fissures in the rocks, plumes of white ash shot up all around us in the heather – as though a family of dragons had woken,' Neat later wrote.

Once the group had descended to the Spittal: 'the sun was shafting a marvellous orange light on to the hills to the east. We scanned the sky and, above the ridge opposite, an eagle appeared. As we watched it closed its wings and began a stoop that it sustained for almost a mile, then opened its wings and alighted on the crags of Ben Gulabin, where we had left Hamish just an hour before.'

How wonderful, although Gulabin has never really been associated with golden eagles. It's been translated as the hill of the whimbrel, or hill of the beak. Hamish liked to refer to it as his 'whaup mountain'. It's also likely that one of the first folk tales that Hamish Henderson heard was the Laoidh Dhiarmaid, or the Lay of Diarmid.

The Fingalian warrior Diarmid O'Duine sealed his fate when he ran off with the beautiful Grainne, lover of the Fingalian leader, Fionn MacCumhail. Knowing that he couldn't kill Diarmid in one-to-one combat (Diarmid was invincible in battle but had, like Achilles, a weak spot in his left heel), the wily MacCumhail organised a hunt in search of a magical boar whose flanks were covered in poisonous bristles. Diarmid eventually slew the great beast and Fingal invited him to measure its length by pacing along its carcass, knowing that should one of the bristles pierce Diarmid's heel, revenge would be taken. MacCumhail's scheme went according to plan, and Diarmid died on the spot.

Years ago, I searched for, and found, an ancient standing stone in the Forest of Knapdale in Argyll that purports to mark Diarmid's grave. Since then, I've been to various hills that make the same claim. Ben Gulabin in Glenshee is only one of many. Indeed, Ben Bulben in the west of Ireland, which frowns over the last resting place of W. B. Yeats, is a more likely setting, but these old stories are spread across the Celtic nations, no doubt carried by early travellers and wandering monks. The Lay of Diarmid associates Glenshee with the Fingalian legends and near the Spittal is a stone circle which local tradition claims is his grave.

> *This glen beside me is Glenshee,*
> *Where blackbirds and other birds sing sweetly;*
> *Often would the Fiann run along this glen behind*
> *their hounds.*
> *This glen below green Beann Ghilbainn,*
> *Whose knolls are the fairst under the sun,*
> *Not frequently were its streams red after hunts had*
> *been held by Fionn of the Fiana.*

Peter Drummond points out in his excellent book *Scottish Hill Names*, that there is often a feature named after boars (torc in Gaelic) close to those areas associated with Diarmid and Grainne. In confirmation, just over the Cairnwell from

Ben Gulabin, and beyond the sprawling mass of Glas Maol, lies the Munro of Carn an Tuirc, the hill of the boar.

All these thoughts flitted through my mind as I tramped up the track from the A93 to the broad bealach between Ben Gulabin's northern slopes and its neighbour Creagan Bheithe. The wide strath of Gleann Beag rose in front of me, its final slopes below the once infamous Cairnwell and the modern road that straightened out the bends, curves and twists of the old Devil's Elbow. My path was less than ruler-straight but it made easy work of Ben Gulabin's steep and heathery flanks and I was soon high above the glen, its silvery, sinuous river brimming with snowmelt. On the south-east edge of one of Scotland's wildest regions, icy snow still pockmarked the slopes and it was easy work kicking steps towards the ridge that connects the main summit with the lower peak over Spittal of Glenshee.

I've often questioned the motives behind my long-term addiction to hills and mountains but here the rationale became obvious. If there is an antithesis of claustrophobia, this is it. The span and spaciousness of the outlook is breathtaking, and for the next thirty or forty minutes I lay by the cairn and revelled in it, tracing distant horizons beyond rolling, snow-patched, tundra-like hills and ridges: the Glenshee hills, the hills of Mar and the high tops of the Cairngorms beyond them. To the west lay the snow-capped Atholl tops and beyond them the hills of Feshie, an area often claimed to be the wildest in Scotland.

Only in the south was there any hint of softness. The wooded, tumbled scenery of highland Perthshire appeared less harsh: man-managed, farmed and pretty, rather than wildly impressive. Appropriately, it was to the south I went after paying homage to Hamish at the summit cairn, across to the hill's minor top and down the steep, knee-jarring heather slopes to the Spittal, once a hospice that welcomed weary travellers, like those who brought the colour and romance of the Celtic tales to these shores, or knee-wrecked hill bashers like me, down from the high tops and badly in need of a brew.

Resting for a moment or two at the foot of the hill, something made me look to the sky where, just as it had appeared to Hamish's pals, there was the soaring outline of a golden eagle, wings held in a shallow 'V' with the tips extended like widespread fingers. It was a moment of surprising elation and, as the great bird soared beyond Hamish's 'whaup mountain', I returned to my car singing aloud in considerable delight and triumph.

Freedom Come All Ye!

15

THERE'S ALWAYS THE BIKE

I climbed my first mountain at the age of fourteen, unknowing that mountains and wild places would become not only my long-term passion, but also my long-term career. In my mid-twenties I began writing, and for thirty years, between the ages of thirty and sixty, I edited climbing and hillwalking magazines for a living. Mountains and wild places dominated my life. I moved to the Scottish Highlands to be close to mountains, family holidays were spent on or near them and, as well as editing magazines, I wrote over twenty books about them, as well as leading treks to some of the most remote mountain areas of the world. More . . . I made television programmes for the BBC about climbing them. Such a fortunate man.

How many people can say they had a long and varied career doing the things they most cherished? There's an old saying that people on their deathbed very rarely say: 'I wish I had spent more time in the office', but do you know something, I would say that. My office being the mountains and wild places of the world. In essence, I lived the dream, and thought it would last forever. I was wrong.

The first indications of vulnerability crept up just before my sixtieth birthday when, leading a trek in the deserts of Jordan, I began to have problems with my feet. I thought it might have something to do with the heat and the condition would pass, but it didn't. Later that year, while walking coast to coast across Scotland, the problem appeared again.

Over the next few months the pain became worse. My GP reckoned years of bashing up and down hills with heavy packs had had a detrimental effect on my feet, knees and joints, and advised painkillers. They helped, but over the next few years the problem worsened further, and the pain seemed to be exacerbated by walking. Climbing presented no great difficulty, but descents became a living hell. On reaching the bottom I was virtually on my knees, and very painful knees at that, and soon became cruelly aware that I could lose almost everything that made me the person I am. I have been given two lifetime achievement awards for my work, written award-winning books and have a large television following, and my friends are all mountain-going people, but suddenly I was operating outside the stockade, no longer part of that community. I felt like a fraud.

Still writing about mountaineering, backpacking and hill-walking, I was now struggling to participate, and envious of those who climbed with ease. I avoided going out with friends because I didn't want them to see how geriatric I had become, and turned into a loner, reclusive with my sorrow and loss. I use those terms advisedly. Being unable to walk the hills felt like bereavement, having lost what had driven me for over fifty years, my sense of belonging among mountains and wild places. I could still hobble about the hills but became painfully aware that age can rob us of so much, and the sense of loss was profound. Speaking with others of a similar age, who had also had their mountain careers shortened by injury or age, I learned of some who couldn't cope and had even become suicidal.

I never fell to those depths, because I love my family and

grandchildren with a passion, and have other interests. I love music and books, but wasn't prepared to sit back and accept the consequences of growing old. It wasn't that I feared old age, but being unable to stay physically fit. I was terrified of becoming disabled and housebound. Other than sore feet and occasional twinges in my knees, I was strong and healthy but what to do if I couldn't walk any distance without pain?

Then someone suggested I buy a bicycle.

Doubtful as heck, I feared I wouldn't get the same outdoors thrill on a bike. No far-flung horizons, no buzz of adrenaline at the summit, no wind on my upturned face, no multi-day trips in wild and remote places. I was a climber, not a cyclist, and life could never be the same. I had tried cycling years before. My old friend and colleague Peter Lumley gave me a mountain bike when he was editor of *Cycling World*. A Specialized Stumpjumper, it was one of the new-fangled so-called mountain bikes. I didn't know that similar machines were being used on gravel tracks and serious down-hill courses in California. I took the name at face value, and genuinely thought these bikes were for climbing mountains.

Colin Smith, a friend from Aviemore who was working in the outdoor industry, had also got hold of a mountain bike and we thought we'd try a wee expedition to the summit of Ben Macdui. To make things easier and quicker we persuaded the staff at the Cairngorm Ski Centre to let us use the chairlift to get close to the top. They were, to put it mildly, sceptical about our chances. To cut a long story short we struggled badly and carried the bikes most of the way while, from time to time, being overtaken by groups of elderly ramblers. We persevered, struggling, but eventually stood beside the giant cairn, wondering how we were going to descend. In fact, we slithered and bumped our way down the summit slopes but managed to ride across the plateau. Eventually reaching Point 1141, at the top of the Fiacaill a' Choire Chais, we were utterly spent, and the thought of carrying the bikes down the rocky ridge was almost too horrendous to contemplate. It was then I had an idea.

Just below our feet lay the great snow wreath known as the Cuidhe Crom, a vast, hanging swathe of snow that fills the upper slopes of Choire Chais until well into spring. My thinking was that we could cycle down this. If we slipped we could use the handlebars or pedals like an ice axe to arrest the fall. It sounded fine in theory, but Colin was deeply sceptical, suggesting the heat of the day had affected my brain. However, after considering carrying the heavy bikes down a thousand feet of rocky ridge he agreed to give it a go.

Cautiously at first, I wheeled my bike onto the snow, threw my leg over and hovered over the saddle as the wheels slipped from underneath and the bike and I parted company. Careering downwards like something on the Cresta Run I suffered horrific visions of giant boulders at the foot, but got lucky. Instead of giant boulders there was an area of fine black granite scree and I hit it, on my backside, at about 200 miles an hour.

Thankfully nothing was broken, but my arse looked like a pound of raw mince. Colin was wise enough to descend slowly and carefully before coming to my aid and it was a sorry me who limped back to a car park full of ski-lift attendants waiting for the bus.

'Did you get to Macdui?' one of them shouted. I gave him a thumbs up sign, desperately trying not to turn my back to him, but he had already spotted the fiery, bloody mess of my backside. 'But ye've fair skint your arse,' he cried, as the whole queue burst into laughter. Later that evening I stood under the shower at home while Gina attacked the grit in my nether regions with a small scrubbing brush. I couldn't sit for a week and swore I'd never throw my leg over a bike again.

Finally accepting that my days of multi-day or multi-week backpacking were over because of pain in my feet, I forgot that bad cycling experience, took advice and bought a bike and lycra clothing. It didn't take long before I was really enjoying my cycling and my distances became longer and longer. At the age of sixty-two, with Hamish Telfer, who was suffering similar age concerns, I cycled from Land's End to John O'Groats. The following year we cycled between the Channel and the Mediterranean through France, and followed that by cycling the length of Ireland, from Mizen Head to Malin Head. The next year we enjoyed a long and hilly tour of the Picos de Europa in northern Spain.

Between the long trips I cycled more or less daily, and it became my way of keeping fit, a daily habit, a daily fix. At one time I had seven bikes in my garage and amongst them was a mountain bike. Not into fast single-track descents, I adapted it to carry all my camping gear and spent occasional nights out in places like Rothiemurchus Forest, upper Glen Feshie, the shores of Loch Ossian and other delectable spots. When I put on my lycra gear and went off on my bike I felt like a twenty-one-year-old again. The bike was my salvation.

Now, in my eighth decade, I appreciate the importance of being adaptable. I've consulted an army of doctors, podiatrists and healers and, with a variety of cortisone injections, orthotics and painkillers, can still enjoy the occasional wander in the mountains, but the bicycle has become my drug of choice. It's my release from day-to-day concerns and pressures, my exercise machine, and it keeps the worst of the inevitable aging processes at bay. I suspect it's the variety that keeps me sane. I can go out on a daily short or long ride depending on the weather or on how the mood takes me. I can cycle on roads or take to the byways of the forest or moorland trails. I can load up panniers and take my camping gear for the cycling equivalent of backpacking or load up my touring bike and enjoy a two-week tour at home or abroad and, now, have come as close to the hillwalking experience as I can get on a bike.

A generous company loaned me an electric mountain bike for a couple of weeks. At first, I was doubtful. I cycle mainly to keep fit so why rely on an e-bike? Very quickly, the benefits became apparent. With a little help from the battery I could cycle some of the mountain tracks that were too remote or too steep for me before. I could experience the thrill of the far-flung view again, the mountain breezes on my face and, best of all, the descent, so painful on foot, became exciting, even thrilling. I am now the proud owner of a Trek Powerfly 5 e-Mountain Bike and, while I still grieve for what I used to do in the hills, the grieving has been tempered by new plans, new objectives, and a different way of getting into and around wild and lonely places. I've also recently learned that the loss of youthful fitness and vitality isn't necessarily confined to oldies.

When a number of personalities took on a pilgrimage between the St Bernard's Pass in Switzerland and Rome (for a television series), one of the celebrities, the Olympic and European long jump champion Greg Rutherford, admitted that he felt at a bit of a loss. Recently retired from track and field he didn't know what he would do with the rest of his life. From the age of fifteen he had trained as a long jumper, from that age his world had revolved around the sport, and suddenly it was over. He lacked purpose and direction, and was worried about it. I knew exactly how he felt and discussed the situation at some length with Hamish, who is a respected track and field coach and sports academic and has previously worked with top athletes whose careers came to a sudden end because of injury. Many of them had required help from mental health counsellors. Indeed, some even became suicidal. It was as though their world had come to an end in their late twenties or early thirties.

It made me realize how fortunate I was. I've enjoyed a wonderful life and career, travelled the world, climbed some of the most wonderful mountains you could imagine, and met many inspiring people. I've had great writing and television careers to boot and now, in my early seventies, can sit back and relish wonderful memories ... but it's not yet time for pipe and slippers by the fire. I don't want to give up. Perhaps I can't do some of the things I enjoyed throughout my life, but I still enjoy and appreciate the great outdoors, still travel to exotic places and see incredible sights, and enjoy the company of like-minded people. I still meet inspiring people, and still write magazine articles and books. The only difference is that I now spend much of my time perched on the saddle of a bike. It's all about adapting, and I hope I still have a good few more years of pedal-pushing before I have to think of doing something else.

For almost thirty years I made occasional television programmes, but I was always at the sharp end of the camera and the mystery of using a video camera, and the ensuing editing, remained just that, a mystery. Then I began to think that I could perhaps make my own videos, without necessarily learning a host of new skills, having been deeply impressed by a film of two young cyclists on the Tour Divide, a long-distance bike race in the US. Lee Craigie from Glasgow and her friend Rickie Cotter from Wales filmed their trip on nothing more than an iPhone and a tiny Go-Pro camera. It was wonderful, and won a major award at the Banff Mountain Film Festival, one of the most prestigious adventure festivals in the world.

Like me, Lee is an adventurer in the broadest sense of the word but, while I have shared my adventures of mountain-going exploits through print and broadcast, she shares in a slightly different way and to a slightly different audience. She shares with those less privileged, with the aim of encouraging them to dream big and follow their dreams. I was intrigued to discover a Scottish-based charity that moti-vates young folk to get on their bikes and fulfil their desires. Even more intrigued to learn that the founder of this charity was none other than the star of the Tour Divide film, Lee Craigie.

The charity, the Adventure Syndicate, is a collective of female endurance cyclists who aim to increase levels of self-belief and confidence in others (especially in women and girls) by telling inspiring stories, creating an encour-aging community and delivering enabling workshops and training. They do this because they love the way adventuring by bike makes them feel, and passionately believe we are all capable of more than we think we are.

Now, that's all very well, but you can't tell the tales or motivate others unless you have experienced adventures for yourself, been there and done that and worn the t-shirt, and Lee, one of the directors, has, more than most, experienced the ups and down, highs and lows of adventuring. Her name had been popping up on my radar for some time as a mountain bike racer, bikepacker extraordinaire and fellow outdoor enthusiast and I met her, very briefly, when she gave a talk at the Fort William Mountain Film Festival. Later I listened, with delight, to a six-week BBC Scotland radio show, *Life Cycle*, that she presented.

As a long-in-the-tooth backpacker I'd newly enjoyed the cycling equivalent of going on a multi-day trip with everything I need – tent, sleeping bag, stove and food – carried on the bike, but I was keen to discover what had turned a highly successful Commonwealth Games and Team GB mountain biker into the cycling equivalent of a wilderness backpacker. So, I arranged to meet her in the friendly biking atmosphere of the Velocity Café in Inverness, where you can enjoy good coffee and cake dressed from head to foot in lycra and no-one bats an eyelid. I should point out that Lee and I were more formally attired, or as formally dressed as outdoor geeks can be. Although living in Inverness, she is originally from Lenzie, just outside Glasgow, and comes from a sporting family that includes international squash and rugby players.

'My family is full of PE teachers,' she told me, almost apologetically, 'so I was always going to be doing something physical, and I didn't want to be in school, or to be governed by a bell. I was always looking out the window at the Campsie Fells and wishing I was out there. The Campsies were perfectly framed in my French class window and I'd often skip lessons to ride my bike over the Tak-ma-doon road and along the Carron Valley.

'I've always been a keen cyclist. As a little girl, I used a wee red BMX to get about and have a bit of independence, but I left cycling for a while when I got into climbing, walking and kayaking, particularly when I became an outdoor instructor.'

Such a sport-focused schooling led to a degree in Outdoor Education, and Lee taught and participated in climbing, kayaking, hillwalking, mountain biking and other outdoor activities both at home and abroad. After working and travelling as a technical mountain guide in America and Australia, she returned to work with young people, but with more focus on personal and social development rather than hard skill acquisition. This led to her move north and retraining as a Child and Adolescent Psychotherapist. This training was to prove valuable later, but about this time she became attracted to mountain biking and realised, very quickly, that she had a talent.

'The personal improvements I made were addictive and in 2009 I became the fastest female cross-country racer in Scotland, winning both the Scottish Series and the title of Scottish Champion,' she told me.

She continued to improve and was selected to race in the European and World Championships in Slovakia and Champery for Team GB. She later won the British National Championships on the proposed Commonwealth Games course in Glasgow.

'I represented Scotland in those Games and was part of the Great Britain squad for a couple of years, but I realised that in international terms I was a small fish in a very big pond. Competing on the world stage I'd be lucky to finish in the top forty.

'That disappointed me at the time, which is curious because I look back now and think, "Hey Lee, you made the top forty in the world", but then I felt rubbish in comparison, and while you're in that bubble it's difficult to look out. Now, retrospectively, and with maturity I think, it's easier to put it into perspective.

'It's about reality. I can't think of any great pleasure I took from my competitive performances. When you encourage a youngster, and see the light shine in their eyes, that's real. Enjoying the feeling of being out on my bike in the hills, that's real too. What's not real is a performance that means you squashed your personality; you shat on other people; you had to adhere to an arduous training programme rather than just enjoy riding your bike; you may have been tempted by performance-enhancing drugs; you may have had to make all sorts of sacrifices to get there. Then on the day you might not do all that well.

'The former Scotland football team manager, Craig Brown, summed it up when he said so many people strive to "get there" but when you actually get "there", you discover there is no "there". No such place. I think that's pretty profound, and summed up how I felt about my competitive career. We strive for success, but don't really know what success is. It's so difficult to define.'

Few competitive mountain bikers in this country have been as successful, in the broadest sense of the word, as Lee Craigie, so what was it that made her give it up and go off adventuring on her bike instead?

'Well, I came from there, that's the difference,' she told me. 'I was returning to my roots if you like. I raced competitively for ten years. It was my full-time profession. I thought of nothing else, but it came from an internal place of adventure cycling . . . that fourteen-year-old who really enjoyed the pleasure of riding a bike and being able to explore and be free. So, that was always there. Even when I was competing, there was this challenge between two different parts of my personality, and that's probably what kept me motivated for so long. When I was too busy looking at my heart rate or too hung up on a race goal, I'd ask myself a simple question: Why am I doing this?

'I had to remind myself that I was doing it because I love riding a bike and being physical out on the hills. So, I'd go off for a bit and do that, whereas my colleagues were on treadmills or turbo trainers, or indoors doing skills sessions. I would go off for days at a time, totally different from everybody else. More often than not a race is more about your mental state than your physiological state, and you've just got to be in love with your sport. There's got to be a reason for doing it.'

Combining her cycling skills and her training in psycho-therapy, Lee founded Cycletherapy, securing a Scottish Government grant to deliver services to socially excluded young people in the Highlands of Scotland. Using a combi-nation of mountain bikes, coaching and bike maintenance skills, Cycletherapy proved to be successful at engaging and promoting the self-esteem of children who could not cope with mainstream education. Understanding how riding a bike in the Scottish countryside could actually change lives for the better, Lee, along with her associates, was keen to build on the success of Cycletherapy.

'The Adventure Syndicate came about because a group of female friends, who loved to do full-on things in the outdoors, decided there weren't enough female role models out there, not just for girls but for anybody. There is this general assumption that women who ride bikes just ride around the corner, wear pink lycra and eat cake, but there's a whole bunch of other women who like to get dirty and go out for days at a time and, if we're talking about competition, they can be better than a lot of men, especially in endurance events.

'We just wanted to say to youngsters, "Look, you can be anything you want to be. Don't get sucked down this one route, there are lots of different routes open to you". We decided to keep doing the stuff we do, but also tell our stories so that more girls could see women who do all sorts of different things.

'We considered ourselves to be bike adventurers, but we're really storytellers. We make films and podcasts, write features and articles, any way we can engage with anybody at all, to get people out both to challenge themselves physically and just be outside. It helps you to hit 'reset', no matter who you are and what your background may be. Everyone can benefit by being outside and doing something physical.

'We go about it in different ways. We got funding to work with schools, to take teenage girls into the hills and teach them bikepacking. We approached some schools and offered them the opportunity. Because of our online presence, individuals get in touch and we invite them on training courses. Quite often much of it is just online support, creating little communities of people who can go off and have their own adventures.'

There is little doubt as to the ongoing success of the Adventure Syndicate. Girls and women of all backgrounds have come through the courses and are now enjoying full-on adventurous things like racing the Transcontinental, a two thousand plus-miles off-road route in the USA, even winning it. That's at one end of the scale, but there are also individuals who arrived unable to ride a bike but are now going out overnight in the hills and returning home next morning in time for work.

'Just as important as winning the Transcon!' Lee claims. 'It's been brilliant, and we initially had no idea it was going to work like this. Women are doing some great things. A girl called Jenny Graham came on board with us two years ago and recently rode her bike around the world, with no backup, faster than any woman had done before. Earlier this year she cycled between Land's End and John O'Groats in four days. That's wonderful, and a real measure of our success.

'There are four of us involved in the Adventure Syndicate, who go on adventures and tell stories, with two other directors and a whole raft of people below that, a whole community that shares our aims, and we want it to grow like that.'

Having been a 'successful' mountain bike racer, an adventurer who has biked across the Alps, off-road, following the route of the GR5 between Geneva and Nice as well as cycling, again off-road, between Canada and Mexico, and a host of other adventures besides, I asked Lee about her remaining personal ambitions? Is her BBC Radio Scotland cycling show the way of things to come?

'I love the storytelling, and think that's what it has to be about. It's easy to go off and have your own adventures but I think unless you're communicating and sharing, encouraging and connecting, it can feel a bit empty. So, I want to continue with that, and to simply keep riding my bike. I want to keep adventuring, exploring and meeting people and keeping that balance.'

What advice would she offer someone who feels they are at a dead end and needs a bit of encouragement and motivation to peer over new horizons?

'My advice would be to follow your heart and your gut

in any career path. If you remain motivated by love, you'll do well and be successful. If you lose your way and focus on money or status you'll never be truly happy, but that pure unadulterated love of moving through the hills is the most primal motivation you'll ever have.

'Don't get dragged unthinkingly down the standard pathways and be an outdoor instructor who loses the will to run, bike or climb themselves. Working with others is hard work but rewarding if you do so with an open heart. The outdoors can offer creativity as well as physical and emotional well-being. Take some risks, find your own path and, even if things don't work out the way you plan them, at least you'll have learned something.'

Lee's advice would be recognisable to a number of folk I know, particularly a man who was attempting to take a mountain bike to the summit of all (277 in those days) Scotland's Munros. I thought he must be completely naive ... or stark raving mad!

I never did hear if he succeeded until one evening when I was sharing Barrisdale Bothy in Knoydart with a good pal, a Wester Ross-based climbing instructor by the name of Paul Tattersall. The subject of mountain biking came up and Paul, somewhat self-consciously, admitted to being the Munro-bagging mountain biker. Astonishingly, he had succeeded.

'To be honest,' he admitted, 'there were very few hills that I managed to actually cycle up. In almost every case I had to carry the bike, but I do remember some great descents. Perhaps the most memorable was trundling down the tourist path on Ben Nevis without a saddle, just the seat post. That was uncomfortable. I'd snapped the saddle post on the hill and had to have it replaced later.

Fortunately, I didn't have an accident, which could have ruined my manhood!'

Paul's Munro-biking adventure took place in 1989, before the days of the Internet, outdoor forums and blogs where, nowadays, news of such exploits becomes widespread overnight. Other than a brief report in a climbing magazine, and a short piece in *The Scotsman*, Paul's achievement attracted very little publicity and the reason for that has much to do with the man's own modesty.

'I didn't set out to break any records,' he told me, 'it was purely a personal trip and I didn't even know if there was a record for climbing the Munros. I don't even know if anyone else has climbed them with a bike since. I've no idea. It doesn't really matter.'

For the record Paul took eighty-one days to climb all 277 Munros (as of the 2009 revision of the tables, published by the Scottish Mountaineering Club, there are now 282 Munros over 3,000 feet/914 metres). Fourteen of those days were spent resting or travelling between mountain areas. Hamish Brown, the first person to climb all the Munros in one continuous round, took 112 days in 1974. Last year fell runner Stephen Pyke completed all 283 summits in forty days.

Paul Tattersall is a self-effacing individual who lives in a small isolated cottage in Wester Ross with his wife Angela and daughter Amy. He is a freelance mountaineering instructor who fills his time between instructing by studying for an Open University degree in mathematics. He looks back on his expedition of 1989 with some fondness and admits it was, in many ways, a hare-brained scheme. If he had known what some of Scotland's mountains had been like he wouldn't even have started.

'I had been a climbing bum in Australia, New Zealand and Asia for nearly three years after finishing a geology degree at Sheffield University,' he said. 'When I returned to the UK in 1988, I went to Edinburgh to visit people I had met in Australia. I'd got hold of a mountain bike in New Zealand, but they were in their infancy and there weren't all that many there. I had enjoyed a fair bit of bushwhacking in New Zealand so when I came home to the UK I bought another.

'I didn't know much about Scotland. I'd been over the Border once, to Arran on a university field trip, but didn't know the rest of the country, thought I'd do a bit of cycle touring with this mountain bike and ended up in the Cairngorms. Two weeks later, after I had made my way back to Edinburgh, my friends and I we were chatting about some of the hills I had climbed with my mountain bike. It appeared I had climbed a number of Munros, but I had no idea what a Munro was. Never heard of the term! I was a rock climber, not a hillwalker. My pal Henry told me there were, at that time, 277 mountains over the height of three thousand feet in Scotland, and that comment planted the seed. I decided to come back the following summer and do them all, with my bike. I thought it would be a nice way to spend the summer, and I'd be travelling through a country I didn't know. The promise of exploration was the main catalyst for the expedition.

'Of course, I was being completely and utterly naive. I'd only seen the nice rounded Cairngorms, and some of those are perfectly rideable, especially the southern Cairngorms. If I had known what the Skye Cuillin was like, or the Torridons or the peaks of Glen Shiel, I would never have set out. 'Course not, I really hadn't a clue. It's not that I had a

319

false impression of what these hills were like. I didn't have any impression at all! Or any idea what the west coast hills were like or understood the logistics of getting in and out of a place like Knoydart. I couldn't even navigate.'

Paul had been a self-confessed climbing bum for years, and a first-class rock climber at that. He had a string of first ascents to his credit and the noted mountaineer Andy Kirkpatrick counts him as one of his all-time climbing heroes and mentors. Paul had no aspirations to a normal career. He worked on building sites and in bars and restaurants to raise money to fund his climbing trips so, after his visit to Edinburgh, he returned to his native Lancashire and worked on a building site all winter to earn enough to finance the trip.

'I'd always lived like that, with just enough money in my pocket to see me through. I didn't own anything, didn't have anything, so I had nothing to lose. It was just me and my mountain bike!'

The bike was a Ridgeback 602, and it wasn't adapted in any way, just a straight-off-the-production-line bike. It had a heavy steel frame, bog-standard gears and brakes and it weighed eighteen to twenty kilograms.

'I wrapped the frame with the closed cell foam stuff that you insulate pipes with, to make it a little more comfortable to carry, popped it over my shoulder and wandered up. What I soon realized was that I couldn't just wander from camp to camp in backpacking style carrying everything over each hill, so everything was planned as day trips, from a number of base camps. A few folks helped me out. My mum brought me up to Scotland initially and stayed around for a few days. Other friends gave me a lift from time to time, but I'd call it minimal support. Nothing was really organized. I used youth hostels on a couple of occasions, bothies where I could, and on the few occasions I walked from hill to hill with all my gear it nearly killed me. It was hard, hard work. These long days, moving from one area to another, were supposed to be rest days but they ended up being some of the hardest of the whole trip. It was awfully slow.'

Adventure has been described as a journey in which the outcome is always in doubt, but Paul had little doubt about eventual success. If he stuck with his plan what could go wrong?

'I didn't expect things to go awry and I'm not sure whether that was arrogance or simple naivety. As far as I was concerned, I just had to get up every morning and move on. Pack my things and cycle a bit more. What could be hard about that?' But things did get hard.

After a good start on the Southern Highland Munros he could hardly get out of his tent on the morning of day three. Next morning, he climbed the Crianlarich giants of Ben More and Stobinian, then added Cruach Ardrain and Beinn Tulaichean in the afternoon, all in low cloud and driving rain. It was his first epic day, but more were to come. He climbed the notorious Buachaille Etive Mor by its sheer north face, up the climbers' route called Curved Ridge, because the walkers' route was covered in snow and he didn't have an ice axe or crampons. A few days earlier he had endured a massive day on the hills of the Blackmount Deer Forest north-west of Bridge of Orchy. After climbing seven Munros he still had a long journey back to camp.

'I'd broken the derailleur on the bike so couldn't ride, and remember sitting on the summit of Beinn nan Aighenan watching the sunset and realizing I was miles from anywhere with still a long way to go while carrying the bike.' He reached his campsite at two in the morning and after a short sleep spent ten more hours traversing the Munros east of Bridge of Orchy.

Paul's biggest challenge was still to come: the traverse of the Cuillin Ridge of Skye. The nemesis of many an aspiring Munro-bagger, the eleven Munros of the Cuillin Ridge are unlike anything else in the country, a steep-sided roller-coaster of a route where your hands are often used as much as your feet. Paul had heard so much about the tough nature of a Cuillin traverse that he decided on a different approach. Rather than simply sling the bike over his back he took the wheels off and strapped the frame to his rucksack. While the bike wasn't exactly rideable, it still went with him.

'My attitude to the Cuillin was fairly innocent. I was a good rock climber, and the Cuillin involves a fair bit of climbing, so even with a bike on my back, I was sure I could scramble along it. That weekend worked out perfectly. I arrived on Skye but the weather was awful. Friends from Edinburgh arrived to go climbing. By Sunday things were looking better and one of them, Rachel, said she'd come with me until she ran out of time and had to go back to Edinburgh. We started early and she carried a rope, just in case. If I'd been on my own, I wouldn't have bothered and would probably have got away with it, but it was handy for getting off the Inaccessible Pinnacle, the isolated finger of rock that is the high point of Sgurr Dearg. My original plan was to simply down-climb it.

'The In Pinn was interesting. It was hoaching with people, a bit like Blackpool promenade, and I had to slot in. I came across this guy all roped up and perched on the crux. He was shouting to his mate that he was stuck, couldn't find the route, and he had a real note of panic in his voice. Just then I appeared over his shoulder, with a bike strapped to my pack. He looked at me and said, 'Oh my God'. I said to him, 'Don't move, I'll climb round you', and climbed over him and off I went.

'I did the whole ridge in one go, and what a day that was. I hadn't realised there was no water up there so was completely dehydrated, the worst I've ever been. I thought we were doing all right to reach the In Pinn by mid-afternoon, but that was only halfway. Rachel dropped off Beinn Dearg to head back to Edinburgh, and I wandered on, relishing the steepness and the views. It just went on and on and on . . . and I got thirstier and thirstier, and really groggy with the heat and dehydration. Fortunately, I could see where I was going. If it had been misty, I would have got lost. At Sgurr nan Gillean, the sun was down and I was exhausted. I met a guy on the summit who had run up the hill after work at the Sligachan Hotel but didn't have any food or water with him. I stumbled down the hill after him, and when I reached the first stream just sat beside it for ages, drinking as much as I physically could get down. I don't think I got off the hill till midnight.'

After eighty days on the go, Paul carried his bike to the summits of Ben Klibreck and Ben Hope, the most northerly of the Munros, and his odyssey was over. Back in Edinburgh, his long and uncomfortable relationship with his trusty bike came to an abrupt and dramatic end.

'I ended up back in Edinburgh just odd-jobbing and using the bike to get around the jobs, but someone pinched it and I never saw it again. It wasn't that the bike meant that much to me, after travelling in Asia and places like that and learning from Buddhists you develop a different attitude to possessions. It was a shame, losing the bike like that, but a bike's just a bike and I didn't particularly mourn the loss.'

While Paul had lost his bike, his trusty Munro steed, he had gained something else: a deep love of Scotland's glorious landscapes that became an ongoing affair. Within a few years he met his partner Angela and together they found a new home in Wester Ross.

'By far the greatest thing about the Munro trip was the pleasure of seeing these magnificent places for the first time, and not knowing what was around the corner, what was over the horizon. It was an education. Sure, I'd travelled a lot abroad, all over the place, but mostly what I saw was climbing crags and a few climbers' backsides. This was totally different, an ongoing revelation. I kept thinking it couldn't get any better, but it did, day after day!'

Paul Tattersall earns a living by teaching climbing from his Wester Ross base, and occasionally rides a fat-bike with massive tractor-like tyres over the fields, foothills and coastlines around Gairloch. Like Lee Craigie and many others, his love of Scotland has been increased by widening his outdoor skills, and horizons, to see beyond the crags and summits, and appreciate the more secretive aspects, and the spirit, of Scotland's great outdoors.

For me that is one of the gifts old age has given. Summits and hill-lists are no longer my prime reason for climbing. I don't have to prove anything to myself or others. These activities are great and I've loved being involved, but, now I can no longer do these things with any great satisfaction, I've learned that the hills and wild places still have much to offer, and they excite me, motivate me and provide more great memories to add to those a lifetime in the outdoors has already given.

The cares of tomorrow can still wait 'til this day is done, as I discover a whole new world not only of mountain ridges and summits but also of islands, forests, history, folklore, legend and, most of all, people. Those who have made their home here in the magnificent landscapes of the finest 'wee' nation in the world: Scotland.

Whether it's on my battered feet, or on my bike, or with Gina in our little red campervan, or in the company of our two beautiful granddaughters, there's still a lifetime of exploration to be enjoyed in the land where legend remains. Scotland has blessed me abundantly throughout my life, and continues to be the glorious gift that keeps giving.

INDEX

Index